W9-BKX-856

STUDY SKILLS IN THE CONTENT AREAS

Study Skills in the Content Areas

Eunice N. Askov
Pennsylvania State University

Karlyn Kamm
Learning Multi-Systems, Inc.

Allyn and Bacon, Inc.
Boston London Sydney Toronto

Library of Congress Cataloging in Publication Data

Askov, Eunice Nicholson.
Study skills in the content areas.

Includes bibliographical references and index.
1. Study, Method of. I. Kamm, Karlyn, 1944-
II. Title
LB2395.A77 371.3'028'12 81-17583
ISBN 0-205-07743-9 AACR2

Printed in the United States of America.

10 9 8 7 6 5 4 3 2 1 86 85 84 83 82

To David and Karen, Kari and Ross

Contents

Preface

In writing this book our assumption is that we cannot teach what we ourselves do not know. We can imagine talented art teachers who though perhaps are not great artists themselves can bring out artistic talents in others. When we think of reading, however, it is hard to imagine a successful teacher who does not know how to read! Likewise, a teacher who does not know how to read a map, table, or graph will probably not be able to teach these study skills.

Study Skills in the Content Areas can be used by both elementary and secondary teachers. Its purpose is to "fill in the gaps," to help teachers master the skills that they plan to teach. Of equal importance is learning *how to teach* study skills as part of content area subject matter. The pedagogical aspect of study skills is also addressed in the text, thereby distinguishing it from one that might be used in a reading improvement class.

Subscribing to the philosophy that we all learn best in a "hands on" situation, we have designed this text for use as a workbook. Space is provided so that you can write your answers as you work through the material. The best way to learn study skills is to practice them.

This text is suitable for teachers of academic content area subjects, such as science, math, and social studies, and nonacademic subjects, such as industrial arts and home economics. Its focus is skills that should be taught and applied in grades 3–12. Because study skills are necessary for mastery of any content area subject matter, we feel they should be taught *along* with that subject matter. We have, therefore, drawn heavily on samples from content area textbooks to demonstrate how to teach study skills realistically as part of the content areas.

Both preservice and inservice teachers will find this book useful. Preservice teachers in an elementary or secondary reading methods course can use this text as a supplementary workbook on study skills. Despite the importance of study skills, they are often slighted in favor of word recognition and comprehension skills in reading methods textbooks.

This book may be used as the main text in a reading/study skills course for either undergraduate or beginning graduate students. Inservice teachers will also find the book useful for either self-study or organized inservice workshops. Teachers can work through the various parts of the book together, led by the reading supervisor, curriculum coordinator, or building principal.

ORGANIZATION OF THE BOOK

The book opens with an introduction to study skills emphasizing their importance in school and lifelong learning. Part 2 provides a diagnostic-prescriptive framework for teaching study skills. If diagnostic-prescriptive strategies are presented in another textbook in a reading methods course, this part may be assigned for optional or supplementary reading only.

Parts 3-6 are concerned with the general skill areas within study skills. Each of these parts employs the same format: An overview of the skill area (such as maps) followed by an indepth discussion of each component of that skill area (such as map location skills). For each skill-area component, a section entitled *Developmental Perspective* shows the fundamental, background skills and understandings that should be learned in the primary grades. These then serve as prerequisites for the study skills that are presented in detail in this book.

Development Activities further subdivide a skill area into component skills. These activities are presented in workbook format—the "learn by doing" part of the book. (The answers to the activities are provided in the back of the book.) Following these activities are illustrations that provide examples of how the skills may be integrated into content area subjects. *Practice Exercises* give the reader a chance to design instructional activities for teaching specific study skills, given particular content area settings. Each part concludes with a section on pedagogy—teaching study skills in the content areas.

The final section of the book (Part 7) contains suggestions for implementing study skills instruction systematically throughout the school.

OTHER USES FOR THIS BOOK

In addition to helping teachers master study skills and incorporate instruction in study skills in content studies, this book can make teachers more aware of the quality and quantity of study skill instruction found in curriculum materials. Many elementary- and secondary-level textbooks are inadequate in their development of skills needed even to read the textbooks; for example, maps found in social studies textbooks.[1] Knowledge of study skills can heighten teachers awareness of the strengths and weaknesses of content textbooks and provide guidelines for the selection of new textbooks.

This book should be useful not only to those content teachers who use a textbook but also to those who no longer use a single textbook but prefer teacher-made materials or materials from multiple sources. When students are working with a variety of materials written at various levels of difficulty, it is important that teachers have study skills related to the content area well in mind. Systematic skill instruction ensures that essential skills are not overlooked.

Teachers who perceive the need to individualize content area instruction should also find this book a handy reference, especially the section on the consideration of individual differences in skill instruction and attainment found in Part 2. A diagnostic-prescriptive approach in the content areas facilitates individualized instruction in spite of large, changing content classes. The suggestions and techniques presented are realistic even for the busy content teacher, with five to seven classes per day of upper elementary through high school students.

In summary, the reader is urged to read this book actively, with a pencil in hand. Some skills may seem more elementary in orientation while others seem more appropriate for the secondary level. We have avoided labeling the skills by levels since our intent is to help teachers individualize skill instruction. We hope that teachers will provide instruction in those skills needed by students in studying content materials and preparing for lifelong learning whatever the age of the students. A secondary student, for example, who has not mastered alphabetical order or use of book parts must begin there before more complex skills can be learned. Conversely, advanced elementary students should not be deprived of the study skills that enable them to pursue challenging independent learning tasks. Our hope is that the reader will first consider the needs of the student and then provide study skills instruction accordingly.

ACKNOWLEDGMENTS

We gratefully acknowledge the following people for their authorship and assistance with authorship of specific portions of this book:

Michaeleen Peck, University of Wisconsin, Green Bay—Overviews for Location of Information in Books and in the Library, Reading for Information in the Content Areas, Graphic Skills: Graphs, Tables, Charts, and Graphic Skills: Maps.

Anne Mallery, Millersville (PA) State College—Overview and other sections pertaining to Test Taking Skills.

We also appreciate the insights of our reviewers who have suggested directions that our book might take.

Our typist, Bonnie Schaedel, must be acknowledged not only for her excellent typing but also for her enthusiasm and rapid delivery.

Finally, we must acknowledge both of our families for their patience and understanding throughout the process of writing this book.

REFERENCES

1. Askov, E. N., and K. Kamm, "Map Skills Instruction in the Elementary School: A Developmental Framework," *The Elementary School Journal,* 1974, *75* (2), 112-121.

Introduction 1

Preservice and inservice teachers readily see the need for teaching word recognition and comprehension skills. It is obvious that students must learn to identify words and gain meaning from words, sentences, and larger units of meaning, but what are the study skills? Why are they particularly important today? Study skills are basic learning tools that, when developed and applied, can enable a learner to acquire knowledge efficiently and independently. Learning on one's own is particularly important today since the wealth of media sources makes vast quantities of information easily accessible. In order for students not to become overwhelmed by these sophisticated, fast-paced communications systems, they must acquire the basic tools that will allow them to keep up with the increased demands.

Taking these issues into account, the need for students to learn study skills is greater than ever before. No longer is it enough to learn dates and facts about a content area. With the amount of knowledge about our world increasing every day, one can learn and remember only a few important facts. Think back to a history class in high school. Can you recall now a date or fact learned then? You are more likely to remember concepts and ideas that were taught as part of the class.

Perhaps you also remember learning the skills that make retrieval of dates and facts possible. Today's modern public libraries no longer rely on a card catalog, for example. To locate a particular book, we can now quickly consult a microfiche reader to find out the call numbers on the book. When we want to research a particular topic we can use a computer search to locate information related to the topic. The ERIC (Educational Resources Information Center) system, for example, has indexed published and nonpublished articles, paper presentations, symposia, and reports by descriptors that enable us to call these sources up, providing bibliographic information as well as abstracts.

With the modern technology available to our students, instruction in the skills of locating and using information from all sources becomes increasingly important. Unfortunately, in the past content area instruction has often focused on memorization of facts, which are quickly forgotten after the final exam. Even today too little attention is being given to instruction in the skills that enable students to retrieve information when it is needed. These skills, *study skills,* are the focus of this book.

COMMENTS ON STUDY SKILLS MASTERY AND INSTRUCTION

Until recently few attempts have been made to investigate the teaching and learning of study skills in the classroom. With the increased focus on objective-based reading instruction during the last decade—instruction geared to specific skills and objectives—more attention has been given to examining appropriate learning sequences of all skills including study skills. Most of the study skills research, however, has been connected with the development of one of the skills management systems, the *Wisconsin Design for Reading Skill Development* (9). Efforts have been made to investigate whether students and teachers have acquired the study skills, whether the skills were being taught in the classroom, and if so, how they were being taught and what results were produced.

Teachers' and Students' Mastery

One study shows that elementary teachers have not attained mastery of selected study skills, as indicated by low scores on tests measuring knowledge of the skills (1). It is also reported that students who have not been taught study skills do not pick them up on their own throughout their elementary and secondary school careers (2). If teachers are not familiar with the skills, either they do not teach them or else they do a poor job of teaching them (8).

Regarding the teachability of the skills, students appear to learn the skills with appropriate instruction. In the results of one case study, students' scores on standardized reading tests (comparing students to a norming group) and criterion-referenced tests (measuring attainment of specific objectives) greatly increased after only one year of implementation of the study skills program (6). In another five-year study done in Jefferson County, Colorado, similar gains are reported (4, 7).

These findings seem to point to the need for teachers to acquaint themselves first with the broad range of study skills and then to begin a systematic instructional approach by incorporating into their daily curriculum the development and application of the skills.

Development Phase

Study skills instruction can best be described as having two phases: development and application. During the *development* phase, the teacher usually introduces a skill that he or she has determined the students do not know and then familiarizes them with different aspects of it. For example, the teacher may have observed that the students have difficulty with the map skill of using latitude and longitude. After an introductory lesson the teacher may have the students practice describing locations using just latitude (30° south) first; then the teacher may follow up with activities in describing locations using only longitude (145° west). After learning these two aspects separately, students may use the whole skill by, perhaps, telling where a city is in terms of both the latitudinal and longitudinal dimensions.

In the development phase of instruction, typically most of the lessons are based on worksheets, games, and commercial learning kits. The instructional materials may present contrived situations rather then realistic application of a skill. A sample task in learning the latitude-longitude skill may be for students to examine a hypothetical map and respond that point A is located 20° north latitude and 30° west longitude. The activities are mainly teacher directed and do not require students to use the skills on their own.

In the skill development phase, it is also important to focus on only one skill—or even one aspect of a skill—at a time. By focus on one skill we mean teach one skill independently of other skills. In the latitude-longitude example, students learn to use each separately before they must apply the complete skill in a realistic situation.

If a skill cannot be conveniently divided into parts for instructional purposes, then the activities for teaching that skill should be carefully sequenced by the teacher. That is, the easiest use of the skill should be taught first, followed by more sophisticated uses. For example, in the map skill, to determine intermediate directions, the first activities may involve locating a point on a simple map where North is in the conventional position (that is, near the top of the map), say, northwest of point X. Later activities may involve locating points on detailed maps using *all* the intermediate directions where North is not necessarily in the conventional position (for example, as on a polar projection).

There are several advantages to focusing development instruction on one skill or on one aspect of a skill and sequencing the teaching activities according to their difficulty. Students learn a skill more easily than if it were introduced in conjunction with other skills. The students can concentrate on one task and work on related activities. Students also learn a skill thoroughly and, therefore, they retain it and are ready to apply it when the opportunity to use it is provided in real-life situations. And, students are less apt to become overwhelmed and frustrated at the start of development instruction. Early success can have a very positive effect on students' attitudes about learning additional study skills.

Being sure that students learn a skill thoroughly—even to the point of reviewing the prerequisite skills—aids their retention and helps them in applying the skill and integrating it with others later on. Partially learned skills are difficult for students to use independently.

Application Phase

In the *application* phase of instruction—which follows the development phase—the main emphasis is on students' independent use of the study skills they have developed. Students use the skills with a variety of materials and in diverse situations so that they can acquire confidence in using them and experience the real-life application of the skills. As the students improve their abilities, use of the skills should become automatic when they are interpreting graphic material, searching for information, or recording information from written sources.

Application activities can be as diverse as a teacher's imagination. For example, to use the latitude-longitude skill in a social studies class a teacher may require students to compare the customs of peoples living at 30° north and 30° south latitudes. Or, in a science class students may compare climates based on their locations described in terms of latitude and longitude. In another class, students may have to describe the location of their city.

Application activities may incorporate the use of two or more skills students have learned. For example, to practice map and library skills students may locate an atlas in the school library and find a map that would answer a particular question such as the latitude and longitude of a particular city.

Students who go through only the development phase of becoming familiar with a skill are not likely to see the relevance of the skill to real-life situations, and, therefore, may not remember it over a period of time. Without the experience in applying a skill in varied contexts they may not gain confidence in using the skill independently and, therefore, may not use it when seeking information.

Because of the importance of applying skills some investigators have interviewed and observed a number of teachers instructing in study skills to find out whether or not application activities were used and why or why not. The main finding was that most of the teachers' efforts appear to be concentrated on the development phase of instruction and very little attention is given to skill application (6,8).

The teachers involved in these interviews volunteered several reasons for their lack of emphasis on providing students with opportunities to use study skills. Many elementary and secondary teachers said they are unaware of the importance and need for skill application. Secondary teachers felt that instruction should have covered those skills at the elementary level, thus making further instruction unnecessary. They also said that their instructional materials do not emphasize it and they are required by their administrators to follow their materials.

Other teachers strive to provide skill application activities following development but often teachers have difficulty finding the time for them. Many teachers contended they thought students had mastered a skill after development instruction, but given a chance to apply the skill the student was unable to do so. (In such a situation the student has mastered the development aspect of the skill. Because she or he has not had an opportunity to apply it in a real-life situation, the skill learning is quickly forgotten as an isolated exercise.)

Another set of problems in providing for skill application concerns class schedules. Even in elementary schools, teachers have difficulty arranging schedules so that the same groups of students and teachers are together for not only initial development of a skill, but also for later follow-up work in a content area as well. In secondary schools, where individual departments establish the academic curriculum, teachers have been hesitant to give too much attention to "reading skills" that seemingly take away from their "content" time. Even in situations where department heads have recognized that particular study skills are relevant to their materials (for example, teaching latitude and longitude as part of social studies), the teachers have had difficulty agreeing on which skills should be taught: that is, which ones are critical to the students' learning of the content, how much time should be given to the skills, and whether or not the students should be tested on them.

Taken together, these various problems present good reasons why teachers give so little emphasis to study skills application and why most instruction that does occur focuses on the development phase. The intent of this book, then, is to encourage teachers to provide both skill development and application opportunities for their students. We provide examples of each to encourage both phases of study skills instruction.

To summarize our discussion, we have found that many teachers are not familiar with the study skills themselves, and so tend not to teach them. Some assume that skills taught once, usually at the elementary level, do not need to be taught or even reviewed at higher levels using more difficult instructional materials and more abstract content. Teachers who do teach the skills tend to focus on the development phase of instruction for a variety of reasons ranging from a lack of awareness of the importance of application to not being able to easily locate suitable activities. The focus of this book is on familiarizing teachers with study skills and with development and application activities so that they may gain confidence in their ability to build skill application into their total curriculum and then to carry out skill application as an integral part of teaching every content subject.

OUTLINE OF THE STUDY SKILLS

Our first step in proposing activities and guidelines for instruction was to identify the specific study skills we considered most important and fundamental. After surveying a number of skill lists, we chose those in the Study Skills element of the *Wisconsin Design for Reading Skill Development* (3). The *Design* identifies three areas of study skills with accompanying behavioral objectives that are representative of the broad range of skills that exist. These skills frequently appear in curriculum guides and standardized tests. In addition, the Study Skills element has been implemented widely, and data are available to support the teachability of the skills and the general acceptance of the skills by elementary and secondary educators (5, 10). The parts of this book are organized around the skills selected and adapted from the *Wisconsin Design;* a few other skills have been added to make the list more complete.

The skills areas presented in this book are as follows:

(Part 3): Location of information in books and in the library
- Book skills
- Library location skills
- Library resources

(Part 4): Reading for information in the content areas
- Notetaking and outlining
- Test taking
- Rate and flexibility

(Part 5): Graphic skills: Graphs, tables, and charts
- Determining differences
- Determining purpose and summarizing
- Making projections and relating information
- Solving problems

(Part 6): Graphic skills: Maps
- Representation
- Location
- Measurement

STUDY SKILLS AND THE READING PROCESS

A final consideration is how study skills relate to reading skills. When we think of reading we usually think of two aspects: recognizing the words and understanding the meaning. A child's early experiences in reading primarily involve these two aspects of reading, but when a child is ready to use reading as a tool by which to gain information, other skills become important. These are the study skills that help the student locate sources of information and interpret the information in usable ways. When one thinks of reading needs beyond schooling, one often thinks of study skills ranging from locating a book on a a favorite hobby in a library to taking notes in preparation for presenting a talk to a local organization.

When reading is broadly defined, therefore, study skills must be considered an aspect of reading. We are concerned in this book with the broader definition of reading that is applicable when the child moves from "learning how to read" to "reading in order to learn." This transition is not a sudden one, however, and, for the average reader, usually is made some time during the primary grades. When the child begins to use written sources in order to learn in a content area, then study skills become important. Hence, this book is directed toward Grades 3-12, those years when study skills should be taught and applied through realistic learning tasks.

Content area teachers, of course, are primarily concerned with teaching their content subject. But without study skills the student cannot learn efficiently and effectively from written sources of information. Since most content area teachers use textbooks as the vehicle for conveying content information, teachers must teach the study skills that students need in order to learn from their textbooks. And, if library work is needed, students must also learn to locate and use library resources.

Whether they are called "reading skills" or "study skills," many content teachers now see the need for teaching these skills to their students. We have written this book with a sincere desire to help teachers with this task.

REFERENCES

1. Askov, E. N., Kamm, K., and Klumb, R. "Study skill mastery among elementary school teachers." *The Reading Teacher,* 1977, *30,* 484-488.
2. Askov, E. N., Kamm, K., Klumb, R., & Barnette, J. J. "Study skill mastery: Comparisons between teachers and students on selected skills." In *Perspectives in Reading Research and Instruction; Twenty-ninth Yearbook of the National Reading Conference,* edited by M. L. Kamil and A. J. Moe, pp. 207-212. Washington, D.C.: The National Reading Conference, 1980.
3. Chester, R. D., Askov, E. N., & Otto, W. *Wisconsin design for reading skill development: Teacher's planning guide—Study skills.* Minneapolis: National Computer Systems, 1973.
4. Division of Assessment and Evaluation. *Are we on target? Basic skills program—Sixth annual report.* Denver: Jefferson County Public Schools, August, 1976.
5. Kamm, K. *A bibliography of materials related to the Wisconsin design for reading skill development.* Reading Project Document. Madison, Wis.: Wisconsin Research and Development Center for Cognitive Learning, 1977.
6. Kamm, K. *The Wisconsin design study skills element: A one year case study.* Working Paper No. 203. Madison, Wis.: Wisconsin Research and Development Center for Cognitive Learning, 1977.
7. Kamm, K. "A five-year study of the effects of a skill-centered approach to the teaching of reading." *Journal of Educational Research,* 1978, *72,* 104-112.
8. Kamm, K., White, S., & Morrison, B. *A report of the procedures used in the implementation of an objective-based reading program in 15 schools.* Working Paper 246. Madison, Wis.: Wisconsin Research and Development Center for Cognitive Learning, 1977.
9. Otto, W., & Askov, E. *The Wisconsin design for reading skill development: Rationale and guidelines.* Minneapolis: National Computer Systems, 1972.
10. Otto, W., Kamm, K., & Weible, E. *Wisconsin design for reading skill development: Rationale and objectives for the study skills element.* Working Paper 84. Madison, Wis.: Wisconsin Research and Development Center for Cognitive Learning, 1972.

Diagnostic-Prescriptive Instruction in Study Skills 2

In this book we provide a continuum of study skills which begins in the primary grades and extends through the high school and college years. Activities are also included so that readers can master skills rather than be superficially acquainted with them. Once teachers have in mind a scope and sequence of study skills and master the skills themselves, it is important for them to consider next which skills are necessary for grasping a particular content area at a particular level. An English teacher, naturally, may select skills different from those selected by a mathematics teacher. When the study skills useful in a particular content area have been identified, it is appropriate next to consider the various proficiency levels of the students.

A diagnostic-prescriptive framework for instruction can be used to individualize instruction in study skills. By *individualization* we mean instruction that is appropriate for each student's needs, not instruction on a one-to-one basis. When students with similar needs are grouped together, interaction processes within the group can help make instruction efficient and often more effective.

One may ask how a content teacher who teaches in a departmentalized situation with possibly five classes of thirty students each can take time to group students and provide differential instruction. This is a legitimate question which will be analyzed in this part through the presentation of various techniques for individualization in reading/study skills. Indeed, the busy content teacher cannot afford to *not* group students and provide differential instruction if the teacher is to be effective.

Mainstreaming, the concept of integrating physically and mentally handicapped children into the regular classroom for part or all of the day, has only accentuated the differences that already exist among members of a typical, hetereogeneously-grouped classroom. In all content areas—whether social studies, science, home economics, or music—there is a need to individualize instruction. Differences in ability to handle content demands are obvious, just as is the range in abilities in handling the reading requirements of content study.

Diagnosis of abilities, both in relation to the content requirements and reading demands, is a necessary, preliminary step before instruction. Diagnosis of abilities in specific content areas (such as computational skills of mathematics students) is not treated here. Instead, the focus is on the reading/study skills requirements made in most content area studies.

DIAGNOSIS OF READING ABILITY

The diagnosis of reading ability is two-fold. First, a diagnosis of general reading abilities must be carried out to determine whether students can use content curriculum materials. It is not at all unusual in a seventh grade social studies classroom, for instance, for some students to function in reading ability (as measured by standardized reading tests) at, say, a third grade level while others are functioning at upper high school levels.

Second, the diagnosis must also be concerned with the mastery of study skills. Proficiency in specific study skills may vary widely depending on past experiences (map reading on family trips), prior instruction (a prior social studies unit that incorporated data collection and tabular presentation), and general ability level. Although proficiency in specific study skills is certainly related to general reading ability, it is possible for poor readers to have achieved mastery of some study skills through opportunities in the classroom or through nonschool activities such as scouting.

Sources of Diagnostic Information

Information about students' reading abilities is available from a variety of sources. Previous teachers may pass on information about particular students' reading abilities. The librarian may also be able to provide information about students' use of library resources, if library use is required in the content study. A questionnaire may be given to the students themselves to determine their assessments of their own reading abilities.

Students' cumulative record folders usually contain reports of testing in reading done throughout their school career. These scores represent the results of the survey level of testing which is conducted primarily for the purpose of screening. Norms are provided so that individual and group scores may be compared to those obtained by students of the same grade placement. General reading scores, or even separate scores for vocabulary and comprehension, however, do not provide diagnostic information about the student's strengths and weaknesses in reading. While these scores do indicate a general level of functioning, they often represent a frustration rather than an instructional level of performance. Standardized tests, therefore, are of limited use to the teacher for instructional planning.

Additional information that is more useful in planning instruction may be obtained from the diagnostic level of testing. Although a few formal group diagnostic tests are available, most do not measure the student's reading abilities in relation to specific content areas. Therefore, informal measures created by the content teacher may be more useful in guiding instructional planning.

Considerations in Using Informal Tests

Teachers must, however, be aware of the limitations of informal tests. While not diagnostic in nature, standardized, norm-referenced (survey) tests do have the virtues of usually being valid and reliable. That is, they measure what they purport to measure (validity), and similar results are obtained if the test is readministered under the same conditions (reliability). Items are typically reviewed by content experts to be sure that they adequately sample the material. Most tests have also been field tested with large numbers of students to ensure the results are reproducible. With informal, teacher-made tests, however, one does not know whether students miss an item because they have not grasped what is being measured or whether it is a poorly written item. Likewise, the test may not emphasize what is covered in instruction (therefore, it is not valid), or the results may not be reproducible (therefore, the test is unreliable).

Several steps may be taken to overcome the shortcomings of informal, teacher-made tests. First, teachers may systematically review their objectives for instruction and write items to measure attainment of those objectives. In other words, they may create a criterion-referenced test which measures whether or not students have mastered a particular objective which is stated in behavioral terms. Mastery level (say, 80% correct) should be determined by deciding what level of performance can be expected realistically. One hundred percent is usually not recommended due to inevitable test error.

Next, the items should be reviewed for their appropriateness in measuring the objective. This can be done by other teachers of the same content area. Sometimes one aspect of an objective is inadvertently given disproportionate weight, or perhaps the wording of distractor choices for given items may be confusing. Colleagues can often identify these problems when they are looking at the items objectively.

After the test has been used with a group of students, the responses to particular items should be studied closely. Special note should be given to the items missed by students who achieve high total scores. If the same items are difficult for the high scorers, the wording may be ambiguous or the choices may be confusing. Local norms can be created by collecting data over a period of time. In other words, a student's performance may be compared to those who have taken the same teacher-made test in previous years.

Finally, the accuracy of the test as a predictor of success in reading content materials should be considered. At the end of the school year the results of the informal teacher-made test, perhaps given at the beginning of the school year, may be compared to each student's final course grade and to the teacher's assessment of the student's ability to handle the content reading materials. If high test scores were obtained by students who proved to be successful in the course, test validity has been demonstrated. If the test indicated deficiencies in an otherwise strong student, and these deficiencies were overcome through instruction, then the test's diagnostic value has been established.

In spite of the limitations of informal assessments, they probably provide the best indications of strengths and weaknesses in study skills as applied in particular content areas. Therefore, teachers usually rely on them to supplement information from standardized achievement tests. In the next section we describe specific informal diagnostic instruments that are related to study skills.

Assessing Reading Ability Through Informal Measures

The content teacher needs to assess both the general reading ability in content materials and the student's ability to apply specific study skills. Although our focus in this book is on study skills, we will briefly describe one technique for informally assessing reading ability because it also yields information about study skills. The criterion-referenced group reading inventory (2) is an adaptation of the informal reading inventory which is an individual assessment used extensively by elementary teachers and reading specialists. The criterion-referenced group reading inventory may be administered at one time to a classroom of students. Instead of reading orally a series of paragraphs graded in difficulty, students are asked to read silently a selection from the content textbook to determine their reading ability in relation to the textbook itself. If several textbooks of varying difficulty are available, then a selection should be taken from each to determine which is most appropriate for each student.

Some general guidelines for constructing a criterion-referenced group reading inventory are provided here. More detailed information may be found elsewhere (2). In constructing a group reading inventory, first the teacher selects a representative complete section of the textbook 4-6 pages in length. This section forms the basis for diagnosis of comprehension skills and reading rate. The teacher creates approximately 10-12 questions that assess various comprehension skills at the literal level, such as identifying the main idea, the significant supporting details, and the sequence of events or ideas. The teacher should create approximately the same number of inferential comprehension questions that ask students to draw conclusions or make predictions and comparisons, as well as questions about the meanings of important vocabulary words. Reading rate is assessed by noting the time each student takes to read the selection. The number of words in the selection is divided by the student's time to determine the number of words per minute read by the student.

As part of the criterion-referenced group reading inventory teachers should also assess students' abilities to apply certain study skills in relation to the content textbook. The teacher may also go beyond the textbook and include assessment of study skills as they are related to the use of the library or standard reference materials. The important first step is for the teacher to determine which study skills are necessary in order for students to use content materials effectively. Some common skills, regardless of content area, may include book skills such as use of the table of contents, index, and glossary.

Content teachers should consider graphic skills that may be unique to their content areas. For example, social studies teachers may include the assessment of map reading skills while science teachers may assess the interpretation of tables and graphs; home economics teachers may wish to focus on the students' abilities to read charts and diagrams.

After administration to the classroom group, the teacher can create a chart that summarizes test results. Shown in Figure 2-1 are the results from the study skills portion of the assessment. The students' names are entered in the left column with columns on the right side designated for the skills assessed. For each student the number of correct items in each skill assessed can be entered in the chart. For example, if John answered eleven out of twelve book skills questions correctly, the number eleven (or 92%) would be written in the Book Skills column beside his name. The teacher may then circle the scores on the chart that are below the mastery level (which may be 80% correct). Thus it becomes readily apparent which skills have not been mastered by individuals or by the group as a whole.

The teacher may group together those students who need help with a particular skill. Based on our example, John, Polly, and Michelle need instruction in map skills

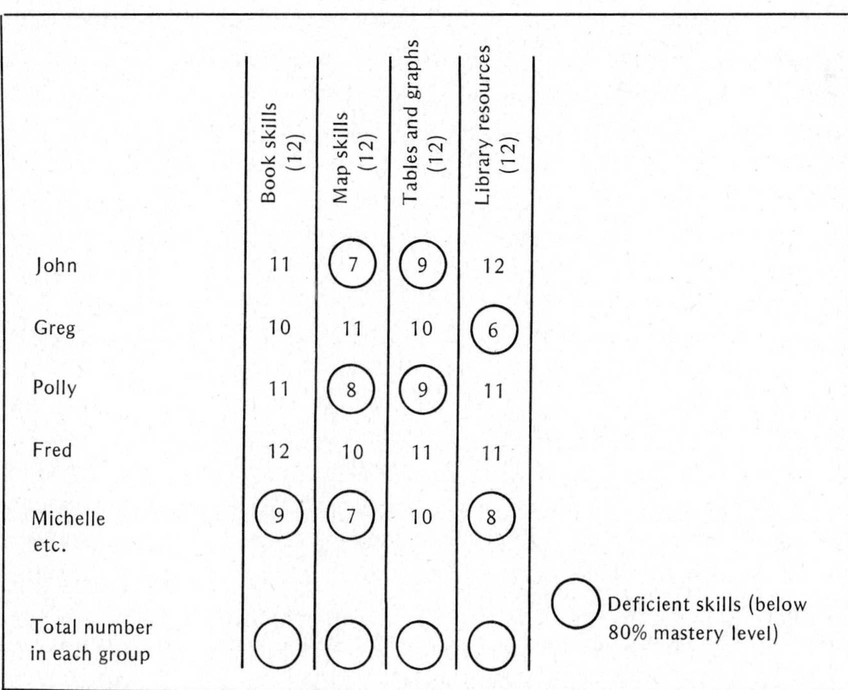

	Book skills (12)	Map skills (12)	Tables and graphs (12)	Library resources (12)
John	11	(7)	(9)	12
Greg	10	11	10	(6)
Polly	11	(8)	(9)	11
Fred	12	10	11	11
Michelle etc.	(9)	(7)	10	(8)
Total number in each group	◯	◯	◯	◯

◯ Deficient skills (below 80% mastery level)

FIGURE 2-1
Class results from administering the study skills portion of a criterion-referenced group reading inventory

before they can be asked to apply map skills in their assignments. If only one or two students need a particular set of skills, as in the case of Book Skills, the teacher may offer instruction through a set of independent learning materials. The teacher can readily see which students are generally weak in study skills such as Michelle, and which are strong overall like Fred.

In addition to determining the level of proficiency in each skill both for individuals and the group, the teacher may also draw conclusions about the suitability of the textbook for individual students. Some authorities (2,3) advise that scores above 90% correct indicate that the reading material may be too easy, while scores between 70-90% correct indicate an appropriate instructional range, and scores below 65% correct indicate that the reading material is at the frustration level, that is, too difficult for use in instruction.

Therefore, if independent readers (those scoring above 90%) are to use the textbook, they should also be given supplementary reading material to provide greater coverage of a topic or perhaps different points of view. Material that is at the instructional level for students is appropriate if the teacher provides introductory help on new vocabulary and concepts as well as questions after the reading to ensure comprehension. In other words, the directed reading activity procedures, ensuring teacher guidance in vocabulary and comprehension, should be applied to content materials for those at the instructional level. Students who score at the frustration level ideally should be given reading material at their instructional level. If alternative reading materials are not available, with the teacher's guidance they can read headings, introductory and summary paragraphs, and graphic material. Also, audiovisual material may be used to supplement the textbook. In addition, students may dictate the main ideas gained from limited use of the textbook and audiovisual materials to the teacher who can write them on chart paper or on ditto masters. Thus the students create their own "textbook" using the language experience technique (1).

Further Assessment of Study Skills

Rather than attempt to assess students with a battery of standardized tests for study skills at the beginning of the school year, teachers more realistically may assess levels of skill attainment through the criterion-referenced group reading inventory described above, or as the initial step in the instructional process. Having the specific study skills in mind for the particular content area, first the teacher must decide what level of skill attainment is realistic and necessary for grasping the content study. Understandably, fourth and eighth grade English teachers will have different expectations about their students' use of library resources. Similarly, within the same classroom a teacher may set higher expectations for the more able students than for those who have generally lower levels of skill attainment.

Next, the students' abilities to perform the skills necessary for content study should be checked. For example, a science teacher may choose table and graph skills and certain locating and reading for information skills as necessary for content study. In preparation for having students make line graphs showing the differential growth of plants exposed to the sun and those kept in a darkened room, the science teacher assesses students' ability to read and interpret multiple line graphs. An activity such as one found in Part 5 of this book could be used diagnostically to determine whether instruction in the study skill is necessary. The activity should focus on the study skill in question using familiar content and concepts. At this point, the purpose is to determine whether or not students have mastered a particular study skill, not whether they have grasped the content. Those students who do not demonstrate the ability to use the study skill successfully in the activity should be given instruction before having to apply it in content study. For those who appear to have grasped the skill, a quick review stressing how the skill can be used in the content materials may be sufficient.

PRESCRIPTIVE TEACHING STRATEGIES

In planning prescriptive teaching strategies an initial consideration to keep in mind is how closely does skills instruction relate to the content instruction. That instruction in study skills must be integrated with content study is a theme stressed throughout this book. If the skills are taught in isolation, if they are not related to content study, or if they are not applied in content study, then instruction is not meaningful and retention of skill mastery is difficult. Therefore, the interaction between content study and skill development is an important consideration. This interaction may be helped or hindered by the timing of the study skills instruction and application. The advantages and disadvantages of each time sequence are presented below.

When Should Study Skills Be Taught?

Study skills instruction before content study

After the teacher has identified the skills necessary in the particular content area, and after the capabilities and deficiencies of the students have been determined, the teacher may wish to provide instruction in those study skills *before* the content instruction is undertaken.

To take an example, if a social studies teacher determines that nonpictorial symbols are necessary in reading a particular map in the textbook or unit materials and that some students have not mastered this skill, the teacher may choose to instruct the students in the skill before the map is presented. Instructional materials should pertain to the content area but actually may not involve the use of a map in the textbook or other instructional materials. This instruction may occur at the beginning of the school year and be reinforced each time the skill is applied in content study. This approach provides students with opportunities for independent skill application in content study when the skill must be applied in a reading assignment. The drawback, however, is that students may not sense the relevancy of the initial skill instruction and not retain skill mastery, particularly if a period of time elapses between skill instruction and content application.

Study skills instruction during content study

Another option is to delay instruction in necessary, unmastered study skills until the point when they are needed to understand the instructional materials. Using the example above, under this method the social studies teacher would provide instruction in nonpictorial symbols when students are required to read and interpret a map containing those symbols. Instruction in the skill would include reading that map as one of the major teaching activities. Other activities and materials could be used, of course, but the map in the textbook or other instructional material would be the basis for instruction. The obvious advantage of this approach is that skill instruction is highly meaningful since it helps the student solve an immediate problem in studying content material. The teacher, however, must build in further opportunities for skill application to maintain skill mastery.

Actual study skill instruction may occur in various settings. Teachers may provide direct instruction themselves, or they may structure students' independent learning. Regardless of which approach or combination of approaches is chosen, skill development materials and activities should relate to the content study. Exercises found in this book may be used if they are adapted to the particular area of content study. We will consider the advantages and disadvantages of each prescriptive teaching strategy next.

How Should Study Skills Be Taught?

Study skills instruction through direct teaching

The teacher may teach study skills in a small group setting to those students who have been identified as deficient in particular skills. If an industrial arts teacher identifies that certain measurement skills are necessary for the next instructional unit and that certain students lack mastery of these skills, then the teacher may teach these skills to those students as a group while other students, who have already mastered the skills, pursue independent work.

An advantage of this approach is that the teacher may quickly offer instruction in the skill and then assign follow-up activities for practice and reinforcement. A disadvantage is that provisions must be made for the rest of the class while small group instruction is occurring. A further disadvantage is that time for each aspect of the curriculum is limited; it may be difficult if time must first be devoted to direct instruction on study skills to those students deficient in the skills.

Study skills instruction through contracting

Teachers may contract with students individually or as a group (if all group members are deficient in the same particular skill) for skill instruction work to be done independently. The teacher, of course, first must have identified appropriate materials for students' independent use in skill learning. Worksheets or learning activities are designed by the teacher for students' independent learning. Pupils may also be given choices in specifying the means by which they are to attain skill mastery.

Perhaps the greatest advantage of contracting is that the teacher can tailor each contract to the ability, learning style, interests, and needs of individuals. Because two or more students are working on the same skill through contracting, it does not necessarily follow that they will use the same materials and activities or require the same amount of time to achieve mastery of the skill. The amount of teacher time required to prepare instructional materials for independent use is an obvious disadvantage to this strategy.

Study skills instruction through learning centers

Instead of direct teacher instruction another option is to establish learning centers for independent pupil work. Learning centers can consist of one or more stations or areas in the classroom which may be blocked off with bookcases or shelves. They should contain a series of activities that are graduated in difficulty until skill mastery is attained. Assessment of skill mastery may take place as part of the learning center or afterwards in a quiz given by the teacher. Pupils may work at the learning centers individually or in groups. This approach may be combined with contracting whereby students contract with the teacher to work through a learning center or centers in a specified amount of time.

Most of the teacher's efforts in using this approach are in identifying or making materials that may be used independently at learning centers. Again, the teacher's preparation of materials may be time-consuming. However, after the materials for a given center have been devised, they can be kept together—perhaps in a labeled box—for use with other students in the future.

Some teachers claim that they do not have enough space in their classrooms to put up several learning centers. Learning centers do not have to take up a lot of room; they may be placed on window ledges, radiators, in corners, and so forth. Secondary teachers who change classrooms may have a more difficult time. Learning centers, however, do not have to be large and may be constructed to fold up easily and be moved.

Study Skills Instruction Through Learning Activity Packets (LAPs)

LAPs, which include objectives for instruction, preassessment, learning activities, and postassessment of mastery, are appropriate for independent skill instruction. More information on constructing LAPs may be found elsewhere (2). Although LAPs usually are designed for individual use by students deficient in a skill area, it is possible for some aspects of a LAP to involve group discussion, interaction, activities, and checking.

An advantage to using LAPs is that once they have been created and duplicated, they may be reused in the future. Again, a teacher's initial efforts are greatest in assembling materials for use in a LAP. Most of the drawbacks to LAPs involve their use. Although teachers could assign only specific parts of a LAP for use with a particular student, or they could provide for partial use through pretesting, the tendency is to use the complete LAP with all students, regardless of their level of skill development. Furthermore, since LAPs usually are in mimeographed form, it is tempting to include strictly paper and pencil activities. However, used creatively, LAPs can contain more involved activities like collecting a set of data and constructing a table and graph for presentation of the data.

How Prescribed Is the Content Area Curriculum?

The mode of presenting content material is another consideration in planning prescriptive teaching strategies. Some teachers favor a structured approach with objectives for instruction and assigned readings drawn primarily from a textbook. Other teachers prefer the flexibility of choosing objectives and accompanying materials. Three possibilities on the continuum of varying amounts of flexibility are discussed below.

Study skills instruction using a textbook

When the content instruction is presented primarily through the medium of a textbook, the content teacher must thoroughly review that textbook for the following information:

1. What study skills are necessary for grasping the content study?
2. What level of proficiency is necessary in each skill?
3. Which skills are taught in the material itself? Are these skills taught adequately with sufficient practice material?
4. Which skills are not taught adequately by the material, yet are necessary in using the textbook to fullest advantage in content study?

For the skills that are identified in item 4 above, the teacher should decide at which places in the textbook study skills instruction should be inserted. For example, if a given social studies textbook uses location skills with a polar map projection but does not provide instruction in these skills, the teacher should provide instruction in these skills before students are required to interpret that map in their textbook. Instruction may occur using any of the techniques discussed above.

Study skills instruction using a defined curriculum

Instead of a textbook, some schools use units of study that are defined by a curriculum guide. Although no one textbook is used, the content to be covered is specified in detail. Parts of textbooks, other books, magazines, and pamphlets are the materials used in instruction.

As in the textbook approach, the content teacher should thoroughly review each curriculum unit, asking the same questions as above. The teacher decides which study skills are necessary for studying the curriculum unit and then which ones are not taught adequately. Again, any of the prescriptive teaching strategies may be used as a vehicle for study skills instruction.

Study skills instruction using a teacher-defined approach

Some schools allow teachers considerable freedom concerning the specific objectives for instruction and the materials to be used in presenting these objectives. With this flexibility teachers may want to consider study-skill needs of the students first, using a criterion-referenced group reading inventory and short skill assessments, and then structure instruction in the content area around the skills. For example, an English teacher who has determined that students are deficient in locating information skills may plan a unit of instruction where students do research reports on various aspects of life during the Elizabethan period while also reading a Shakespearean play. But the major purpose in preparing the report would be to teach the students the use of location skills. In other words, first the teacher considers skill needs and then designs instructional activities to overcome deficiencies in skill development.

CONCLUDING REMARKS

We have emphasized in this part the use of a diagnostic-prescriptive framework for instruction. Since students differ vastly in reading abilities and study skills, diagnosis is essential to determine instructional needs. Grouping students with similar instructional needs enables the content teacher to make optimal use of diagnostic information. Since classes are generally large in content subjects, grouping provides a means for dealing with individual differences. Other techniques for individualizing instruction, such as contracts, learning centers, and LAPs, can help in providing for individual needs. The necessity for careful record keeping becomes apparent as teachers diagnose study skills needs and organize instruction to meet those needs. A chart, as described earlier, can aid teachers in learning what skills are needed by most of the group as well as by individuals.

If multiple sections of the same subject (ninth grade English, for example) are offered at the same time, teachers may coordinate their skill instruction efforts. If two teachers have overlapping periods, one teacher may provide instruction in a given set of skills for students in both classes while the other teacher handles instruction in a different set of skills needed by other students in both classes. The advantage that results is efficiency since each teacher prepares instruction for only half of the necessary skills instead of teaching all skills to one group of students. Elementary teachers frequently exchange students during reading period to narrow the wide range of capabilities in a typical class. Some also exchange students for skill development groups so that one teacher may offer instruction in a skill to all students who need it.

Even if instructional efforts cannot be combined, teachers in the same content area can work together in developing and sharing materials for skill instruction. Quality often tends to improve as teachers share ideas with colleagues. In terms of the curriculum for a subject area, it is important for teachers to do group planning anyway so that important skills and concepts are covered in each classroom.

Development of study skills should also be viewed by teachers of the same content area from a longitudinal perspective. Ideally, social studies teachers, as an example, who teach at various levels of junior and senior high school would plan together, identifying what study skills are important in grasping the social studies content and determining which skills should be taught at each level. Since most of the skills build on lower-level skills, opportunities for review and reinforcement are numerous. In keeping with this, an introduction to the use of area symbols (such as those showing the terrain of an area) in a map representation system could easily include a quick review of point and line symbols as types of nonpictorial map symbols. If skill instruction is consistent and planned throughout the curriculum of a given content area, then teachers can anticipate more accurately the backgrounds of their students. Classroom records could be passed on from year to year as a source of diagnostic information.

Furthermore, teachers who function in interdisciplinary teams (science and mathematics) can ensure skill application across subject matter lines. If interdisciplinary teams are not part of the teaching organization, individual teachers from different content areas at a given level (say, junior high school) can coordinate efforts. For example, if students study map skills in their social studies class, these skills can be reinforced and applied in their English class when a map is presented in their literature anthology. Retention of skill mastery is more likely to occur if skills can be applied frequently in various content areas.

A final consideration is that the goals of study skills instruction not only include skill mastery and application but also independence in using the skills and a positive attitude toward doing so. If, for example, students are taught the skills associated with reading graphs, then they ought to be able to study a graph independently when it appears in reading material later on. If they choose to ignore the graph in their independent reading, then the study skills instruction has been ineffective. Therefore, the task of the teacher not only is to make instruction in study skills interesting but also to demonstrate the relevancy of the skills in content study and in everyday life.

REFERENCES

1. Askov, E. N., & Lee, J. W. "The language experience approach in the content area classroom." *Journal of Language Experience*, 1980, *2*, 13-20.
2. Dupuis, M. M., & Askov, E. N. *Content area reading: An individualized approach.* Englewood Cliffs, N.J.: Prentice-Hall, 1982.
3. Shepherd, D. L. *Comprehensive high school reading methods*, 2nd ed. Columbus, Ohio: Charles E. Merrill Publishing Co., 1978.

Location of Information in Books and in the Library

3

Think back to the first time you were asked to do a research report in elementary or junior high school. Was the task easy for you? Were you able to use library tools like the card catalog and the *Reader's Guide* independently? Did you check the table of contents of books to see whether or not some information was given about your research topic?

According to many reading experts, most students do not receive focused instruction in book and library skills, yet both types of skills are important for independent learning. The reason for a lack of instruction in these two broad skill areas may be partly found by reviewing the recent history of school libraries.

OVERVIEW

The skills involved in locating information in books and in libraries are important to students' educational development. However, instruction in these skills has been insufficient, partly due to the fact that libraries have not always been an integral part of the school. Many schools did not have libraries and expanding library collections until the 1960s (5,7). Prior to that time, approximately two-thirds of the nation's elementary schools had no libraries at all. The school libraries that did exist had collections that were sparse, shabby, and old.

The expansion of school libraries can be traced to two factors. First, the launching of the Russian Sputnik in the late 1950s caused great concern about the quality of American education. Such concerns led to a movement to improve all aspects of education. Active, independent, individualized learning was emphasized, and the library became an important component of learning at all levels.

Second, in 1960 librarians responded to the challenge to advance American education with the American Association of School Librarians' publication of the national *Standards for School Libraries Program* (1). At the time the *Standards* were published, *no* U.S. school met all the criteria established in this document. The criteria emphasized quantitative standards, such as number of books, audiovisual materials, space, staff, and money. Help for meeting needs in these areas came about through the 1962 Knapp School Libraries Project which provided funds to demonstrate the educational value of school library programs that fully meet the national standards for school libraries (10).

Additional monetary support for school libraries resulted from the passage of The Elementary and Secondary Education Act of 1965. The assumption was that study skills were related to academic achievement and that study-skills programs must include use of the school library. In fact, some educators suggested that children should spend a great portion of the school day in school libraries or in other work areas where they could search for information, analyze data, and write about conclusions they had reached. Certainly, students' information searches would be aided by instruction in library and book skills.

Today, such instruction is crucial since the sheer quantity of books in school libraries or media centers has increased the difficulty of locating a single item. In addition, the number and variety of terms used to classify library materials have added to the complex task of finding particular materials. The teacher, then, must help students to master the skills necessary for locating materials in books and libraries.

Scope and Sequence of Book and Library Skills

Although school libraries have vastly improved since the early 1960s, little attention has been given to the sequencing and teaching of book and library skills. School curriculum guides reflect wide variation in the number and sequential organization of book and library skills (5,7). Also, few curriculum guides appear to offer in-depth development of these skills objectives. Drawing from textbooks, curriculum guides, and research, some investigators, however, have identified and traced the developmental sequence of essential book and library skills (7). Their findings reveal that skills are interrelated and should be developed in a spiral-like fashion. In other words, the skills should be taught at each level with increasing complexity and difficulty.

Book Skills

Book skills include the use of the table of contents, index, and glossary. The table of contents provides clues to the organization and topics in a book by indicating page numbers, chapter headings, and perhaps subheadings. This section of a book, then, gives readers a skeletal overview of the material and provides the general location of topics. Students who can use the table of contents can rapidly determine whether or not a given book contains topics of interest. They can also find the precise places where given chapters are located.

Glossaries, another book aid, are actually miniature dictionaries often found in textbooks. Instruction in the use of this textbook aid is necessary because glossary terms help students understand the textbook content. Students can find new meanings for familiar words and learn the meanings of unfamiliar words as they are used within the specific content area.

Indexes, an additional book aid, are alphabetical listings of topics and names given in the text with page numbers where these may be found. They serve the purpose of cataloging specific categories of information, thus enabling the reader to find essential material quickly. Text indexes vary in complexity. Some contain broad headings while others give subjects, authors, and subtopics. Index complexity depends on the number and type of components within each index entry (4). For example, more difficult entries may contain components like diacritical markings and abbreviations.

All three book skills are used by readers primarily to locate information in a text. They are recognized as being practical and essential by many reading experts. Authorities appear to agree that teaching the use of table of contents should occur first, followed by use of the glossary and index (2,7,8).

Library Location Skills

Library skills encompass such skills as alphabetizing and using guide words and letters, the card catalog, the Dewey Decimal System, and the *Readers' Guide.* These skills are necessary for locating and gathering information.

The ability to alphabetize is basic to many other library skills. Initially, children learn to alphabetize by attending to the first letter of the word. Gradually they learn to incorporate two, three, or more letters (6). Alphabetical order is usually taught during the primary years, but teachers should not assume that junior and senior high students have already acquired this skill.

Guide words and letters at the top of a dictionary or encyclopedia page enable students to locate words or topics that are in alphabetical order. Using the card catalog in the library also involves using alphabetical order. The card catalog contains subject, author, and title cards arranged alphabetically. In the case of the subject index within the card catalog, certain key words may have to be known to the young researcher. The ability to determine key words as a guide needs continued emphasis and should begin in the primary grades with examining the titles of books for clues to contents (3). Usually the use of the card catalog is not taught until after students have learned to use indexes and have mastered alphabetical order.

The Dewey Decimal System is a categorizing process used most often in school libraries. While the Dewey Decimal System does guide students in the location of books, periodicals, and newspapers, it does not aid students in finding specific articles. Rather, indexes such as the *Readers' Guide* help with this latter process. Since the *Readers' Guide* covers several disciplines and provides current information, it is particularly useful to the young researcher. Magazine articles are listed alphabetically under subject and author's name. Students should be able to use a book index and alphabetize prior to learning how to use the *Readers' Guide.* Usually they have also had experience in using the card catalog prior to using the *Readers' Guide.* The problem concerning appropriate subject categories in the card catalog is also pertinent to the use of the *Readers' Guide.* In fact, as students begin to use other, more specialized indexes the problem of selecting the correct descriptors becomes more difficult.

Library Resources

Library resources are necessary tools for the elementary or secondary school student. While many resource tools are available, we shall limit our discussion to the use of the dictionary, encyclopedia, atlas, and vertical file.

Students should recognize that dictionaries are fundamental to the acquisition of new words and essential for the expansion of meanings for familiar words. The knowledge of alphabetical sequence is one essential prerequisite skill for dictionary use. Other prerequisite skills may include guide words and index use (9). Although some researchers would expand the list of dictionary subskills still further (8), most dictionary subskills could probably be categorized into location, pronunciation, and meaning skills (11).

Encyclopedias are sources containing information on a variety of subjects. Topics are arranged alphabetically, usually in an index for all information provided in the series. A cautionary note is in order about teaching the use of the encyclopedia, however. Many encyclopedias are written at high readability levels. Students who are assigned reports and use the encyclopedia may tend to copy sections verbatim without really understanding the passage. Thus, the teacher must take care in giving assignments involving encyclopedia use. Students may need to use the more simply written encyclopedias for such independent projects.

Atlases are another important library resource. While mention is made of this library tool in many professional reading texts, our review revealed that authors do not usually state how this tool should be taught. Likewise, the use of the vertical file tends to receive little attention in the research or in professional texts. This last library resource is a collection of magazine, newspaper, or pamphlet clippings and small softbound materials that are not substantial enough to be placed on shelves. Arranged by subjects, the vertical file frequently contains clippings related to current events. Certainly students in search of materials unavailable elsewhere in the library need to learn how to use this resource.

BOOK SKILLS

Book skills are the first skills to be considered in locating information. Specifically, this includes the use of the table of contents, index, and glossary. Effective, efficient use of resource books is important to locating needed information. Therefore, by knowing how books are organized one can save time and energy.

Developmental Perspective

Book skills are among the first study skills taught to young children. Proper book usage is learned at home by the preschool child as he or she listens to stories read by a parent. The child learns that books have a beginning and an end, and that they are held right side up. Besides developing an interest in reading, as a preschooler the child also learns the proper handling of books by example.

When children begin formal instruction in reading, they have the opportunity to learn rudimentary book skills. The information contained in the title page and table of contents is usually taught in first grade. Children may use a table of contents to locate a particular story in the reading instructional materials or perhaps in a favorite storybook. They learn how to identify the title and author even if they do not use the other information contained on a title page.

Students usually have their first exposure to the index and glossary in content area textbooks that may be used as early as first grade, but more often by third or fourth grade. In science or social studies textbooks, the intent is not to teach students how to read, but rather to teach some specified content. Students are expected to apply reading and study skills in learning the content. If students do not know how to use the textbook, the content will either not be learned or be learned ineffectively and inefficiently. Book skills that are not difficult for most children can save them time when properly applied.

Development Activities

Development activities are presented for use after students have had some introduction to rudimentary book skills in the primary grades. These skills should be taught as the need arises in content area materials. In other words, as long as a glossary, for example, is not used in content materials, no reason exists for teaching its use. When students must consult other sources that use glossaries, however, then the skill must be taught.

Development activities are provided as a basis for developing book skills. Students should be provided not only with development activities but also, and perhaps more importantly, with appropriate skill application activities. We urge the reader to work through all activities in order to have a better understanding of the skills and to identify teaching activities that may be used with students. (The answers to these activities can be found in the appendix.)

Specialized book skills

Before considering the book skills of using the table of contents, index, and glossary, a review of various book parts is appropriate. Begin by checking your knowledge of book parts by answering the following questions:

1. The title of the book is ______________________________.
2. The author is ______________________________.
3. The publisher is ______________________________.
4. If you want to write to the publisher, to what city would you send the letter?
______________________________.

FIGURE 3-1
Title page of a content area textbook
(*From H. A. Wolf,* Managing Your Money. *Boston: Allyn and Bacon, Inc., 1977.)*

MANAGING
YOUR
MONEY

Allyn and Bacon, Inc.

Boston • Rockleigh, N. J. • Atlanta • Dallas • Belmont, Calif.

5. What very important piece of information can be found on the back of the title page?____.
6. The table of contents is found in the __________ of the book. It is arranged according to ____.
7. The index is found in the __________ of the book. It is arranged according to ____.
8. If you want to know the meaning of a word as it is used in the textbook, you would look in the ____. It is located in the __________ of the book and is arranged according to ______.
9. If the book is compiled by an editor, rather than written by an author, you can find the name of that person on the ______________________________.
10. The name of the illustrator, if there is one, may be found on the ____________.
11. Sometimes the book includes a __________ which comes __________ the main part of the book to explain why the book was written and for whom it is intended.
12. Additional material for further information may be included in an __________ at the end of the book.
13. A __________ may be included at the end of the book or at the end of each chapter to indicate sources that were consulted in writing the book.
14. __________ or __________ may be used to indicate key words and concepts in the text.
15. The indentation of headings may indicate______________________________.

Table of contents

Since use of the table of contents is usually taught in the primary grades, the focus here is on how it differs from an index and how it may be used in identifying relevant material. The table of contents should be used to locate information if the topic of interest is general and has considerable coverage in the book.

The index can help locate more specific information by listing the page numbers on which a certain topic is mentioned. If the topic is too broad, then too many pages may be listed in the index to be useful. In that case, the reader may be better to use the table of contents.

Decide whether you should look in the table of contents or index for information on the topics that follow. A sample table of contents is provided in Figure 3-2 so that you can decide which would be more appropriate. Indicate which you should consult by a check in the appropriate column:

	Topic	*Table of contents*	*Index*
16.	buying stocks	_____	_____
17.	benefits of a homeowner's policy	_____	_____

FIGURE 3-2
Table of contents of a content area textbook
(*From H. A. Wolf,* Managing Your Money. *Boston: Allyn and Bacon, Inc., 1977.*)

Table of Contents

	Topic	*Table of contents*	*Index*
18.	mortgage bonds	______	______
19.	purchasing life insurance	______	______
20.	buying traveler's checks	______	______

By using the table of contents presented in Figure 3-2, decide whether this book would be a good source for information on the topics that follow. Indicate by checking the appropriate column:

	Topic	*Yes*	*No*
21.	opening a checking account	______	______
22.	types of credit	______	______
23.	causes of inflation	______	______
24.	types of investments	______	______
25.	leisure time during retirement	______	______

Index

Main entries in an index are usually presented in the left margin with subheadings indented underneath. A comma in a page reference means *and* (22, 36 means that information on the topic may be found on pages 22 and 36). On the other hand, a hyphen between two numbers means that information on the topic is contained in the pages between those numbers (22-36) means that the topic is discussed on those fifteen pages).

List the page numbers you would consult for information in Figure 3-3 on the following topics:

	Topic	*Page numbers*
26.	coverage against hail damage	______
27.	Medicare	______
28.	personal liability insurance	______
29.	loans for home improvements	______
30.	government regulation of loan institutions	______
31.	estimating property value of your home	______
32.	fixed obligation	______

Item #32, fixed obligation, illustrates the use of *See also* (see Figure 3-3). If further information, beyond what is given in the referenced pages, is desired, the reader can find more information by looking under another topic in the index as indicated by the *See also* reference. On the other hand, sometimes the reader does not use the same topic heading as the text in the index. In that case, the index may refer the

FIGURE 3-3
Index of a content area textbook
(*From H. A. Wolf,* Managing Your Money. *Boston: Allyn and Bacon, Inc., 1977.)*

reader to a different name for the topic. If, for example, the term *fixed obligation* was not referenced with a page number, the index would have referred the reader to a more appropriate heading by *See* Bonds, corporate.

Glossary

A glossary provides only the definitions of words as they are used in the textbook. To illustrate, compare the following definition of *specialists* with that given in any dictionary. The glossary in a business textbook provides a more specialized definition:

> Members of the Exchange who specialize in buying and selling only certain specific securities that are traded at a specific location on the exchange. The commission broker, or the contract broker, will go to whatever specialist is required to execute an order.[1]

In contrast, the definition given in a dictionary includes more than one meaning that is not directly related to the use in the business textbook:

> specialist *n* 1: one who devotes himself to a special occupation or branch of learning 2. any of four enlisted ranks in the army corresponding to the grades of corporal through sergeant first class[2]

Students need to learn that the glossary in their textbook can provide definitions that are more appropriate than dictionary definitions in terms of the specific usage in the content area. The glossary, then, is a better resource for word meanings than the more general definition provided in a dictionary.

Illustrations

The illustrations demonstrate how book skills may be applied in instruction. In application the teacher stresses integration of the skills which may have been taught separately in development activities.

Illustration 1

A high school art teacher helps her students plan an exhibition of prints of famous painters for the school. She wants the students to write short descriptions of the painters' lives and of their specialized artistic techniques. Since the school library has only limited resources on this specialized subject, she brings in her own technical art history reference books. To help students locate information on specific painters and their techniques, she reviews the use of the index as the most efficient method of locating specific information. The *See also* cross reference is also explained when she notices that some of the reference books are organized in such a way that the artistic techniques may be considered in several places as aspects of other topics.

1. H. A. Wolf, *Managing Your Money* (Boston: Allyn and Bacon, Inc., 1977), p. 537.
2. *Websters' New Collegiate Dictionary* (Springfield, Mass.: G. & C. Merriam Company, 1981), p. 1107.

Illustration 2

An elementary social studies teacher is preparing his fifth grade students for writing a research report on different aspects of pioneer life. The students form groups on the basis of interest in certain topics such as transportation, housing, food, protection, and so on. He anticipates that the students may experience difficulty in locating information on their topics, although the school librarian has helped him gather together some appropriate reference sources which he takes back to the classroom for several weeks. He shows the students how to study the table of contents to determine whether their topics are treated in given reference sources. Although the students are all familiar with the use of the table of contents to locate a particular chapter in their social studies textbook, they have not used the table of contents to evaluate whether or not a particular reference source is relevant to a given topic.

Practice Exercise

Consider the following teaching situation and decide what book skills you may be teaching if they are needed by the students. Write down at least one development and one application activity that students may do to use the book skills you have selected. Third grade students are using a science textbook for the first time.

Book skills ______________________________

____

Development activity ______________________________

____

Application activity ______________________________

____

Example Lesson

Skill selected: Glossary use (other book skills are also possible)

Development activity: Students compare the definitions of key vocabulary words in the glossary and dictionary. (The purpose is to note that the glossary definition is more appropriate to the use of the word in the science textbook.)

Application activity: To reinforce word meanings, the students solve a crossword puzzle using the new vocabulary words with definitions from the glossary. In order to determine the correct meaning of the words as used in the science textbook, students must use the glossary.

LIBRARY LOCATION SKILLS

This part of the discussion of library skills focuses on the location of resources within a library. The next section, Library Resources, concerns the different types of library resources. This distinction is obviously artificial since we must locate a library resource before we can use it.

Developmental Perspective

Problems involving the location of information in library resources often can be traced to a deficit in a basic skill—alphabetizing. Perhaps because many elementary classrooms contain posters displaying the alphabet, some children never master the knowledge of alphabetical order from memory. Or some may have to sing the entire alphabet song before knowing whether *t* precedes or follows *u*.

A common procedure for teaching alphabetical order in the primary grades is to divide the alphabet into thirds. Children are asked whether a given letter falls in the first third, middle third, or last third of the alphabet. This type of practice enables young children to deal with a portion of the alphabet at a time instead of having to deal with all twenty-six letters at once.

Young children learn to alphabetize words only by the first letter. As proficiency is gained, they alphabetize by the second and third letters. After the rudiments of alphabetical order have been mastered, children can apply this knowledge in using guide letters and words in simple dictionaries and encyclopedias. Much practice is generally required before students become comfortable with using guide letters and words in the location of words or topics in dictionaries or encyclopedias. The card catalog is generally not used to locate library resources until the student is in upper elementary school. The *Readers' Guide* and other indexes are usually taught after students have learned to locate books using the card catalog.

Development Activities

Since alphabetizing is the most basic of the library skills, we first begin with an alphabetizing exercise requiring the use of the second and third letter in determining alphabetical order. Next, the reader can work through more sophisticated library skills.

Alphabetical order

Alphabetize the following words by the first three letters to describe a character:

33. chic, charming, coy, Cynthia, classy
34. Rusty, redheaded, rustic, rural, ridiculous
35. Mickey, mad, Mouse, masked, mastermind

Guide letters and words

Guide letters are most commonly used to locate a particular volume in which a given subject may be treated. Most encyclopedias have an index volume, the use of which should be encouraged as the most efficient means of locating information on a given topic. If no index volume is available, then students would need to be able to locate the correct volume by using the guide letters on the spine of the volumes. For example, if a student was interested in the subject of turtles, and if no index volume is available, she or he could look in the T-V volume of an encyclopedia for information about turtles.

Guide words are usually more difficult for students than guide letters because of the need to alphabetize by more than the first letter. The importance of efficient use of alphabetical order can be demonstrated by dictionary races in which students compete to locate a particular entry first. Those who do not use the guide words cannot win except by sheer luck.

Guide words, whether in a dictionary, encyclopedia, or other reference sources, are used in the same way. The word on the left side of the page indicates the first entry at the top of the left column. The word on the right side of the page indicates the last entry on the page located at the bottom of the right column.

In the following exercise identify the page numbers on which you would expect to find the given list of words:

Dictionary page	*Guide words*[3]	
702	master plan	material
703	material	matter-of-factness
704	mattery	Maya
705	Mayan	mealybug
706	mealymouthed	meaty

	Words	*Page*		*Words*	*Page*
36.	measure	_____	38.	MDT	_____
37.	matron	_____	39.	mastodon	_____
			40.	mauve	_____

The card catalog, basic to use of the library, also requires the knowledge of alphabetical order. The use of guide letters and words is necessary to enable the student to find the appropriate drawer containing entries on the subject of interest. The following are entries from a university card catalog (author/title section). Indicate the drawer in which you would find these entries:

Card catalog guide words	*Drawer number*
Newto—Nicaragua A	1
Nicaragua B—Nicholson, E	2
Nicholson, F—Nicholson, H	3
Nicolson, I—Nietzr	4
Nietzs—Nihon	5

3. Actual guide words taken from *Webster's New Collegiate Dictionary*, pages indicated.

Entries	Drawer number
41. Nickle, Keith Fullerton	________
42. Nicholson, David	________
43. Nietzsche, Friedrich Wilhelm	________
44. *The Nihilism of John Dewey*	________
45. Nicolson, John	________
46. *The Niagara Escarpment*	________

Card catalog

Knowledge of the card catalog is essential for efficient library use. Students need to know the types of cards in a card catalog even before they use the guide words to locate a particular drawer. One fourth grader, in looking for books on coin collecting, concluded from looking in the card catalog that the library contained only a few books on coin collecting when in reality a whole shelf of the library was filled with books on that subject. What was his mistake?

47. ____.

When using a card catalog, the first step is to get to the right section! If the student knows only the subject of interest and wants to locate books on that subject, then the subject section of the card catalog is appropriate. If he or she wants to locate a book by a particular author, or knows the title of a particular book, then the author/title section is appropriate.

Figures 3-4, 3-5 and 3-6 show three different cards. Answer the following questions using the cards depicted:

FIGURE 3-4 Card catalog entry card 1

LB1632
.R62

STUDY, METHOD OF

Robinson, H. Alan, 1921-
Teaching reading and study strategies: the content areas/H. Alan Robinson, Boston: Allyn and Bacon, © 1975

ix, 277 p.: ill.; 25 cm.
Includes bibliographies and indexes
ISBN 0-205-04714-9.

1. Reading (Secondary education)
2. Study, Method of. I. Title

FIGURE 3-5
Card catalog entry card 2

LB1573
.E84
1978 Estes, Thomas H., 1940-
Reading and learning in the content classroom: diagnostic and instructional strategies/Thomas H. Estes, Joseph L. Vaughn, Jr. Abridged
x, 277 p.: ill.; 24 cm.
Bibliography: p. 225-231
Includes index
ISBN 0-205-05986-4

1. Reading I. Vaughn,
Joseph L., 1942- joint author

FIGURE 3-6
Card catalog entry card 3

LB1050
.S596
1976 Reading activities for child involvement

Spache, Evelyn B.
Reading activities for child involvement/Evelyn B. Spache, 2d ed.
Boston: Allyn and Bacon, 1976.
xi. 243 p.: ill.; 25 cm
Includes index
ISBN 0-205-04840-4 (pbk.)

1. Reading—Handbooks, manuals, etc.
I. Title

48. Which card would you consult if you knew only the subject you were interested in?__________
49. Which card would you use if you wanted to read books by a particular author?____
50. If someone had told you the name of a useful book, which card would you use to locate it?__________
51. Which card indicates that the book was written by more than one author?______
52. Which card indicates that one book is slightly shorter in length but has slightly longer introductory material (indicated by the Roman numerals)?________
53. Which card indicates that one book is the most recently published?________

54. Which card indicates that the book has been revised and that a second edition is available?__________
55. Which cards indicate that the books contain bibliographies?__________
56. If you were interested in other books similar to *Reading Activities for Child Involvement,* under what subject heading would you look in the card catalog?__________
57. If you were interested in more books related to method of study, under what other subject heading would you look in the card catalog?__________
58. The cards indicate that all three books contain __________ and __________
59. Where on the card are the numbers that you use to locate the book in the library?__________
60. Another identification number is the ISBN which is used primarily in ordering books from publishers. What do you suppose ISBN stands for?__________

Dewey Decimal System

Most readers have probably become familiar with at least one system of classifying books in a library. Many university and public libraries have converted to the more sophisticated and newer Library of Congress classification system. However, because the Dewey Decimal System is less complex, many school libraries have retained the use of the older system. A teacher should become thoroughly acquainted with the system being used in the local school library in order to teach the skills students need in locating books.

Although the numbers (in the upper left corner) used in the sample cards from the card catalog in Figures 3-4, 3-5, and 3-6 were from the Library of Congress classification system, the following activities employ the Dewey Decimal System since school libraries still commonly use this system. Ten main classifications are used:

000 General Works
100 Philosophy
200 Religion
300 Social Sciences
400 Languages
500 Pure Sciences
600 Applied Sciences
700 Art and Music
800 Literature
900 History

Under each category are subcategories; for example, under Sciences (500) mathematics is 510. This number is used with the initial letter of the author's last name to make up the call number. A mathematics book by Webb may have the following call number: 510 W. The call number is located in the upper left corner of the card from the card catalog and on the spine of the book.

Fiction books, on the other hand, are not categorized as part of the numbering system. They are arranged alphabetically according to the author's last name. If one author has written several books, then the books by that author are alphabetized according to the first word in the titles.

Biographies are sometimes categorized separately under the letter B. They are arranged alphabetically, not according to author as fiction books are, but according to the initial letter of the last name of the person about whom the book is written. If more than one author has written a biography about a given person, then the books about that person are arranged alphabetically according to the authors' last names. Occasionally, libraries will classify biographies under the 900 number instead of B.

Call numbers designated by *R* before the numbers indicate reference books, such as dictionaries, encyclopedias, atlases, and so forth. These are usually kept in a special section for use in the library. If you needed to find information on the following subjects, write the number that you would locate if your library used the Dewey Decimal System:

Subjects	Category of the *Dewey Decimal System*
61. chemistry	__________
62. Abraham Lincoln	__________
63. poetry	__________
64, Buddhism	__________
65. Charlie Brown and the Peanuts Gang	__________
66. Civil War Battles	__________
67. French	__________
68. engineering	__________
69. books by Laura Ingalls Wilder	__________
70. law books	__________
71. almanac	__________
72. animals	__________
73. Susan B. Anthony	__________
74. education	__________
75. photography	__________

This exercise allows the reader to practice using the general categories within the Dewey Decimal System. Categories often are given greater specificity by adding a decimal after the numbers. For example, within the general category of history

(900's), the subject of history of India is 954. When more specific periods or aspects of history (such as Nehru's period) are considered in particular, the number is indicated by decimal (for example, 954.04). In order to locate the books on the shelves quickly and efficiently, students must understand how books are ordered. In the next exercise place the following call numbers in the order you would expect to find them on the shelf:

76.	590 F	589 K	590.74 A	589.2 M	589 C
77.	947.084 S	947.07 P	947 M	947.08 H	947 S
78.	333.7 E	332.6 S	332.678 B	332 B	332.6 E
79.	428.2 M	428 S	428.246 R	428.4 L	428.43 S
80.	745.2 B	745.013 E	745.1 D	745.0977 D	745.0973 C

Again, we urge you to learn the library classification system of the local school library. After the teacher is thoroughly acquainted with the system of classifying books, she or he can help students locate books for needed information. The most effective practice involves the location of actual books in the local school library by the use of call numbers. Students working in pairs can race each other to locate a list of books that the teacher has prepared or the teacher can devise a treasure hunt in which the location of one book sends the student back to the card catalog to locate another book.

Readers' Guide

While the card catalog serves as a gigantic index for books, the *Readers' Guide to Periodical Literature* provides an index for magazines. (The children's counterpart to the *Readers' Guide* is called the *Subject Index to Children's Magazines*.) The entries in the *Readers' Guide* are listed in alphabetical order by either the subject or the author's last name together in one list. *See* and *See also* references are common to enable the user to locate the greatest number of articles pertaining to a subject of interest.

Because magazines are published frequently throughout a given year, most of the issues of the *Readers' Guide* are published on a semimonthly basis. The *Readers' Guide* enables the reader to locate the most recent information on a given subject or by a given author. An abridged version is frequently used in schools while the unabridged is available in most university libraries.

FIGURE 3-7
Sample page from the *Readers' Guide*
(From Readers' Guide to Periodical Literature *80 (March 10, 1980): 74. Copyright © 1980 by the H. W. Wilson Company. Material reproduced by permission of the publisher.)*

MADEIRA
Charm of Madeira. L. Dennis and L. Dennis il map Trav/Holiday 153:60-5 F '80
MADEIRA wine. See Wine
MADOC, Prince. See Madog Ab Owain Gwynedd
MADOG Ab Owain Gwynedd
Frontier of illusion: the Welsh and the Atlantic revolution. G. A. Williams. il maps Hist Today 30:39-45 Ja '80
MAEKAWA, Haruo
Japan's new crusader for a stronger yen. por Bus W p 106 F 4 '80 •
MAFIA
Respectable Mafia. Y. Gudkov. World Press R 27:51 Ja '80
MAGAZINE stands, racks, etc
Versatile footstool doubles as sewing and magazine rack. il Workbench 36:44 Ja/F '80
MAGICIANS
On Vegas' Strip Siegfried & Roy enjoy the paws that refresh. P. Hevener. il pors People 13:112-13 F 4 '80
MAGNETIC fields (cosmic physics)
Corotation lag in Jupiter's magnetosphere: comparison of observation and theory. T. W. Hill. bibl f il Science 207:301-2 Ja 18 '80
Magnetic field of Saturn: Pioneer 11 observations. M. H. Acuna and N. F. Ness. bibl il Science 207:444-6 Ja 25 '80
Saturn's magnetic field and magnetosphere. E. J. Smith and others. bibl f il Science 207:407-10 Ja 25 '80
MAGNOTTA, Anne. See Magnotta, V. jt auth
MAGNOTTA, Vince, and Magnotta, Anne
Miami Beach. il Trav/Holiday 153:26-7+ F '80
MAGUIRE, Anne
Tragedy of a broken heart. il por Time 115:47 F 4 '80 •
MAHAN, John Henry
Inlaid wooden music box. il Workbench 36:74+ Ja/F '80
MAIL handling
See also
Friden Mailing Equipment (firm)
MAIL order business
Clock kits, parts and plans. . .where to buy them. Workbench 36:69 Ja/F '80
Where to get it [hardware or specialty tools] Fam Handy 30:42-5 F '80
MAINE
See also
Vegetable gardens and gardening—Maine
MAITRES d'hôtel. See Waiters and waitresses
MAJOR Indoor Soccer League. See Soccer, Professional
MAKE-it-yourself furniture. See Furniture
MAKE-up
Brighten up your eyes with makeup. il Mademoiselle 86:94-5 Ja '80
Getting down to beauty basics [tips from A. Grey] P. R. Jackson. por House & Gard 152:26+ F '80
MAKEOVERS, Beauty. See Beauty, Personal
MALNUTRITION
See also
United States—Presidential Commission on World Hunger
MALONE, Moses
Thou shalt not mess with Moses on the boards. por Sport 70:70 F '80 •
MALONE & Hyde Inc
Malone & Hyde: a food jobber seeks growth in nonfood retailing. il por Bus W p 117-18 Ja 28 '80
MALVEAUX, Julianne
Your financial plan for the eighties. il Essence 10:25-6+ Ja '80
MAMMALS
See also
Marine mammals
MAMMARY glands
See also
Breast
MAMMOTH Cave National Park
Mammoth Cave violates planning process, appeases local interests. Nat Parks & Con Mag 54:20 Ja '80
MAN
See also
Psychology
Origin and antiquity
See also
Man, Prehistoric
MAN, Prehistoric
At the American Museum [search for missing Peking man fossils] D. J. Preston. il Natur Hist 89:96-7+ F '80
Was the first working man a woman? P. O'Toole. il Work Wom 5:54-5+ Ja '80
MANAGEMENT
See also
Communication in management
Organization
MANAGEMENT and Budget, Office of. See United States—Management and Budget, Office of
MANAGEMENT consultants. See Business consultants
MANAGEMENT development programs. See Executives—Training
MANAGERS. See Executives; Women executives
MANATEES
Defending the defenseless. J. Kirshenbaum. Sports Illus 52:13+ F 4 '80
MANDAN Indians
Frontier of illusion: the Welsh and the Atlantic revolution. G. A. Williams. il maps Hist Today 30:39-45 Ja '80
MANDATORY retirement. See Retirement
MANGURIAN, David
Children of the Incas. il Américas 32:3-8 F '80
MANKIEWICZ, Jane
Time out [story] New Yorker 55:30-4 Ja 28 '80
MANNERS and customs
See also
Etiquette
Kissing
MANPOWERED aircraft
Flights
What it's like to fly the M.I.T. pedal-powered biplane. T. Sahagian. il Pop Mech 153:120-1+ F '80
MANUSCRIPTS
See also
Illumination of books and manuscripts
MANUSCRIPTS, Illuminated. See Illumination of books and manuscripts
MANUSCRIPTS, Persian
Gardens of the princes [exhibit of 16 century Persian illuminations] R. Hughes. il Time 115:79 Ja 28 '80
Persian paintings [exhibition Wonders of the Age: Masterpieces of Early Safavid Painting 1501-1576] S. B. Sherrill. il Antiques 117:118+ Ja '80
MAPS
See also
Atlases
MAR, Frank. See Lee, R. jt auth
MARAN, Stephen P.
Sky reporter [cont] Natur Hist 89:78-81 F '80
MARCIANO, Linda Boreman. See Lovelace, Linda
MARCUS, Leonard
Editorial [cont] Hi Fi 30:6 F '80
MARDI Gras. See Carnival (pre-Lenten festival)
MARGINAL land. See Land
MARIANI, John
Secrets of staying slim. il Seventeen 39:126-7+ F '80
MARIE and Bruce [drama] See Shawn, Wallace
MARIJUANA
Laws and regulations
Japan
Drug rap in Tokyo brings down Wings and Paul McCartney. il por People 13:111 F 4 '80
Moral and religious aspects
Make a burnt offering unto the Lord [controversy over marijuana usage by Ethiopian Zion Coptic Church in Florida] S. Sackett. Chr Cent 97:60-2 Ja 23 '80
MARINE archeology. See Archeology, Submarine
MARINE biology
See also
Marine pharmacology
Spawning
MARINE engines
See also
Motor boat engines
MARINE fauna
See also
Horseshoe crabs
Marine mammals
MARINE Mammal Protection Act. See Marine mammals—Laws and regulations
MARINE mammals
See also
Manatees
Laws and regulations
Porpoises resurface [tuna industry and Marine Mammal Protection Act] R. Cahn. Audubon 82:5-6+ Ja '80
MARINE parks and reserves
Marine sanctuaries in jeopardy. N. Karas. il Outdoor Life 165:111 Ja '80
MARINE pharmacology
Dorisdosine: a new hypotensive *N*-methylpurine riboside from the nudibranch anisodoris nobilis [methylisoguanosine] F. A. Fuhrman and others. bibl f il Science 207:193-5 Ja 11 '80
MARINE pollution
Measurement
Big bag [controlled experimental ecosystems] V. Gibson and G. Grice. il Oceans 13:21-5 Ja/F '80

To conserve space, abbreviations are used extensively. At the front of the *Readers' Guide* the abbreviation for each periodical that is indexed is provided as well as a listing of those periodicals with addresses and subscription prices. A key to other abbreviations used throughout the *Readers' Guide* is also provided in the format.

Use the page from an issue of *Readers' Guide* to answer the following questions:

81. How many articles on magnetic fields can be found in this issue?__________
82. What periodicals contain articles about Persian manuscripts?__________
83. Under what heading would you find an article by Prince Madoc?__________
84. How many subheadings are provided under the heading of marijuana?__________
85. What is the title of the most recent article on make-up?__________
86. Where would you look for information on the Mardi Gras?__________
87. Who wrote the article, "Was the first working man a woman?"__________
88. What is the title of the article about Mandan Indians?__________
89. What special graphic material does this article contain?__________
90. List the title of the periodical volume, date and page number of an article on mail ordering clocks.__________

Illustrations

Some examples follow to show how library location skills may be applied in various content areas. Application activities stress the integration of the skills.

Illustration 1

In conjunction with an emphasis on expanding students' vocabularies, an elementary teacher leads her students in making a class dictionary. As new words are introduced as part of the various content areas, such as social studies and science, students add them to the class dictionary. Based on the usage in their textbooks, they discuss the meanings and write their own definitions as a group. Then these definitions are checked for accuracy in a glossary or dictionary. The students' definitions are modified if necessary and entered in the dictionary on index cards to permit students to add the words in alphabetical order. As students learn new meanings of multiple meaning words, they add these to the class dictionary. The students who have the most difficulty with alphabetical order are asked to add the new entries.

Illustration 2

Redfield Junior High School has begun an emphasis on sustained silent reading in every content area class. Fifteen minutes of each content subject are to be devoted to silent reading related to that content area at least once per week. Mrs. Lee, the seventh grade math teacher, decides to plan cooperatively with Mrs. Warren, the science teacher who has the same students. They agree to alternate days for sustained silent reading so that the students will have a silent reading period in one of their classes three times per week. Each student must choose a book related to either math or science. To help the students in their book selection, Mrs. Lee provides instruction on the Dewey Decimal System which is used in their school library. Students are told to select books from the 500 classification number. Mrs. Warren takes the students to the library during science class for their first experience in book selection. As they finish a book, they are to write down the title, author, and some new information gained from reading the book. They are to return the book to the library during a study hall and select a different book from the 500 category.

Practice Exercise

Consider the following teaching situation and decide what library location skills you may teach if needed by your students. Write down at least one development and one application activity that students may do to use the library location skills you have selected. Assume a teaching situation of a junior high school current events class.

Library location skills ______________________________

____

Development activity ______________________________

____

Application activity ______________________________

____

Example Lesson

Skill selected: *Readers' Guide*

Development activity: Students study entries in the *Readers' Guide* to practice location of information according to the subject and author's last name.

Application activity: Students search for current information on an assigned topic, such as economic conditions caused by inflation.

LIBRARY RESOURCES

The focus of this section is on the various resources that can be found in a library. Students need to know which resource is most appropriate to consult for given demands for information.

Developmental Perspective

The first general information source that children usually learn to use is the encyclopedia. Because the encyclopedia provides general but basic information on a wide variety of topics, it is a good starting place for a child just learning to use reference sources. It is also a good starting place for older students doing library research to get an overview of a subject before consulting more specialized library resources.

Young children also learn how to use dictionaries at an early age. Even in first grade picture dictionaries commonly help children spell words used in their writing. As their need for variety in vocabulary increases, so should their dictionaries increase in the number of words and amount of information presented.

Of paramount importance in using library resources is the student's familiarity with the resources available so that the most appropriate resource can be selected.

Imagine a student who is studying the geography of an area but doesn't know that an atlas exists! Or perhaps a student who needs current statistics on a country consults an encyclopedia instead of an almanac! Accurate and appropriate information can be obtained only by consulting appropriate library resources.

Development Activities

Since dictionary skills are basic to the use of other library resources, we will begin with activities for teaching dictionary usage.

Dictionary

We have already discussed location skills in using a dictionary in the previous section, Library Location Skills. Here we are concerned with dictionary usage other than finding words in the dictionary.

Students need to use dictionaries primarily for three purposes: (1) to check the correct spelling(s) of a word; (2) to learn how to pronounce a word; and (3) to discover the meanings of a word. We will not deal with the first use as it is obvious. We are concerned, however, with using dictionaries for pronunciation and meaning.

Use of the pronunciation key is not difficult, but it can be confusing for those students who did not receive phonics training as part of their reading instructional program in the primary grades. Since the dictionary pronunciation guide keys the phonic or sound elements to specific symbols, the student's task is to sound each element according to the key and blend the sounds together. A complete pronunciation guide is usually found at the front of the dictionary and an abbreviated form at the bottom of the page.

Pronunciation symbols are frequently used in glossaries and parenthetically next to new vocabulary in content area textbooks. Students may have to refer to a dictionary pronunciation key for the sound equivalent of each symbol if a key is not provided in the textbook.

Rewrite the following sayings (some not so "tried and true") in correct spelling using the pronunciation key provided in Figure 3-8:

91. 'wächt 'päts 'nev-ər 'bȯi(ə)l.
92. ən 'ap-əl ə'dā 'kēps t͟hə 'däk-tər ə-'wā.
93. ə 'stich (')in 'tīm 'sāvz 'nīn.
94. 'wet 'bərdz 'nev-ər 'flī ət 'nīt.
95. 'wən 'sel-dəm 'fīnds ən 'em(p)-tē tə-'bas-(ˌ)kō 'bät-əl

Now pronounce the following uncommon but real words using the pronunciation key and respellings provided in a dictionary:

96. 'kyü
97. 'fäs-fə-tīz
98. 'slüs

FIGURE 3-8 Dictionary pronunciation key
(The system of indicating pronunciation is used by permission. From Webster's New Collegiate Dictionary © 1981 G. & C. Merriam Co., Publishers of the Merriam-Webster Dictionaries.)

Pronunciation Symbols

ə ......banana, collide, abut

ˈə, ˌə ......humdrum, abut

ə ......immediately preceding \l\, \n\, \m\, \ŋ\, as in battle, mitten, eaten, and sometimes cap and bells \-əm-\, lock and key \-əŋ-\; immediately following \l\, \m\, \r\, as often in French table, prisme, titre

ər ......operation, further, urger

ˈər-, ˈə-r ......as in two different pronunciations of hurry \ˈhər-ē, ˈhə-rē\

a ......mat, map, mad, gag, snap, patch

ā ......day, fade, date, aorta, drape, cape

ä ......bother, cot, and, with most American speakers, father, cart

ȧ ......father as pronounced by speakers who do not rhyme it with bother

au̇ ......now, loud, out

b ......baby, rib

ch ......chin, nature \ˈnā-chər\ (actually, this sound is \t\ + \sh\)

d ......did, adder

e ......bet, bed, peck

ˈē, ˌē ......beat, nosebleed, evenly, easy

ē ......easy, mealy

f ......fifty, cuff

g ......go, big, gift

h ......hat, ahead

hw ......whale as pronounced by those who do not have the same pronunciation for both *whale* and *wail*

i ......tip, banish, active

ī ......site, side, buy, tripe (actually, this sound is \ä\ + \i\, or \ȧ\ + \i\)

j ......job, gem, edge, join, judge (actually, this sound is \d\ + \zh\)

k ......kin, cook, ache

k̲ ......German ich, Buch

l ......lily, pool

m ......murmur, dim, nymph

n ......no, own

ⁿ ......indicates that a preceding vowel or diphthong is pronounced with the nasal passages open, as in French *un bon vin blanc* \œⁿ-bōⁿ-vaⁿ-bläⁿ\

ŋ ......sing \ˈsiŋ\, singer \ˈsiŋ-ər\, finger \ˈfiŋ-gər\, ink \ˈiŋk\

ō ......bone, know, beau

ȯ ......saw, all, gnaw

œ ......French boeuf, German Hölle

œ̄ ......French feu, German Höhle

ȯi ......coin, destroy, sawing

p ......pepper, lip

r ......red, car, rarity

s ......source, less

sh ......with nothing between, as in shy, mission, machine, special (actually, this is a single sound, not two); with a hyphen between, two sounds as in death's-head \ˈdeths-ˌhed\

t ......tie, attack

th ......with nothing between, as in thin, ether (actually, this is a single sound, not two); with a hyphen between, two sounds as in knighthood \ˈnīt-ˌhu̇d\

t̲h̲ ......then, either, this (actually, this is a single sound, not two)

ü ......rule, youth, union \ˈyün-yən\, few \ˈfyü\

u̇ ......pull, wood, book, curable \ˈkyu̇r-ə-bəl\

ue ......German füllen, hübsch

u̅e̅ ......French rue, German fühlen

v ......vivid, give

w ......we, away; in some words having final \(ˌ)ō\ a variant \ə-w\ occurs before vowels, as in \ˈfäl-ə-wiŋ\, covered by the variant \ə(-w)\ at the entry word

y ......yard, young, cue \ˈkyü\, union \ˈyün-yən\

ʸ ......indicates that during the articulation of the sound represented by the preceding character the front of the tongue has substantially the position it has for the articulation of the first sound of *yard*, as in French *digne* \dēnʸ\

yü ......youth, union, cue, few, mute

yu̇ ......curable, fury

z ......zone, raise

zh ......with nothing between, as in vision, azure \ˈazh-ər\ (actually, this is a single sound, not two); with a hyphen between, two sounds as in gazehound \ˈgāz-ˌhau̇nd\

\ ......slant line used in pairs to mark the beginning and end of a transcription: \ˈpen\

ˈ ......mark preceding a syllable with primary (strongest) stress: \ˈpen-mən-ˌship\

ˌ ......mark preceding a syllable with secondary (next-strongest) stress: \ˈpen-mən-ˌship\

\- ......mark of syllable division

( ) ......indicate that what is symbolized between is present in some utterances but not in others: *factory* \ˈfak-t(ə-)rē\

99. sə-'ner-ə-səs
100. ˌes-ə'ter-ik

One comment should be made about accent marks. An obvious example of the importance of the accent mark is the difference between the two meanings of *present* with the difference in accent changing pronunciation—*pri-'zent* versus *'prez-nt.* The pronunciation of some words seems different from what may be expected due to accent. For example, one may expect *potpourri* to be pronounced *pot-pour'-ri* rather than *pō-pu̇-'rē.* The difference in syllabic divisions and accent makes the same word in print almost unrecognizable orally if one is unfamiliar with the pronunciation of the word.

The use of the dictionary to check word meanings is not difficult; the selection of the correct word meaning appropriate for a particular usage, though, can be difficult. Sometimes definitions include unknown words due to a technical background from which a word comes. Before assigning students to look up a list of words, the teacher should do what two things:

101. ____

____

If words are presented only in list form, students will not know the context in which they are used. Students should learn early in their dictionary usage that not all meanings for a word are appropriate in a given situation. It is their task to select the correct meaning, given a particular context.

The following sentences use the words given above in the pronunciation exercise. Use the context of the sentence to select the appropriate meaning for the italicized words from any dictionary:

102. The girl's *queue* became entangled in a low branch of the mulberry tree.
103. The chemist decided to *phosphatize* the substance as the next step in the experiment.
104. The children had fun playing in the *sluice* created by the workmen repairing the dam.
105. In the child's oral reading the teacher noted several examples of *syneresis.*
106. The professor belongs to an *esoteric* club that admits only professors interested in studying water bugs.

Dictionaries provide other information in addition to the correct spelling(s) of words, their pronunciation, and meanings. Check your dictionary to see what types of information are provided:

107. ____

____

Encyclopedia

Most students have early experiences with general encyclopedias. As content area studies become more in-depth, and the need for more specialized knowledge emerges, students may need to consult special subject encyclopedias. Instead of a general encyclopedia, a student may find more technical and specialized knowledge on given topics from subject encyclopedias, such as *The Encyclopedia of Education, Encyclopedia of Educational Research, Encyclopedia for Horsemen,* and *Encyclopedia of American Foreign Policy.*

General encyclopedias are a good starting point for research on a topic. General background is provided so that the student may then select a more specialized encyclopedia or nonfiction book to gain more detailed information. For example, a student wanting to find out information on photosynthesis may first start with the encyclopedia for an overview description. If more information is needed, then nonfiction books may be located through the card catalog by checking the subject index. The *Readers' Guide* could also provide a listing of current magazines which contain articles on the subject. Thus, the student is able to move from a general overview to more specialized and technical information as the need dictates.

108. How would you find a list of the presidents of the United States?____________
109. How could you locate a brief description of James John Audubon's life?________
110. If you wanted to find out about current business trends, could you look in an encyclopedia? ____________ Why or why not?____________________________

____

Almanac, atlas, and specialized resources

Many specialized reference sources exist in a library. The teacher needs to find out which are available in the school library to guide students in finding information. Students need to be familiar with the various resources in order to pick the most suitable one(s).

Below are listed a number of research needs Next to each, list the most appropriate reference source that you would consult.

	Research need	*Resource*
111.	to locate the capital of Pennsylvania	__________
112.	to find out who won the motion picture academy awards	__________
113.	to find some pictures of cities for a report on urban renewal	__________
114.	to identify a more descriptive word for *walk*	__________
115.	to learn about a children's author's life	__________

116. to check the meaning of *mythomaniac* (if someone called you that) __________
117. to read pamphlets on children's nutrition __________
118. to find out the newsworthy events on a particular date __________
119. to prepare for probable weather conditions if traveling to another part of the country __________
120. to find out the dates of the reign of a particular British king __________

Illustrations

The illustrations show how teachers may integrate the library resource skills in instructional activities that stress application of the skills.

Illustration 1

Fourth-grade students, as part of a science unit, select an animal that they want to research. The outcome of their research will be an oral presentation on the animal accompanied by some sort of visual representation. Since the encyclopedia will be the main source of information, the teacher reviews the use of encyclopedias as a general source of information. Since the school library also has a nature encyclopedia, the teacher directs the students to locate additional information on the animal in the specialized encyclopedia. Using both sources, the students should be able to find at least one picture of their chosen animal to use in making a picture, figurine, puppet, or whatever visual representation they select.

Illustration 2

A high school English teacher discovers that some of his students cannot pronounce words that they look up in the dictionary. Since dictionary usage for pronunciation of new words is important in his class, he prepares a short Learning Activity Packet (LAP) on dictionary pronunciation skills. He administers a quick pretest to all students in his ninth-grade English classes, but only those students who do not demonstrate mastery of the skill need to work through the LAP. Afterwards, he readministers the same quick assessment to those students to determine whether or not they have mastered the skill after instruction.

Practice Exercise

Consider the following teaching situation and decide what library resources you may be teaching if needed by the students. Eighth-grade geography students need to locate information on the topography of the various parts of the United States.

Library resources ______________________________

____

Development activity ______________________________

____

Application activity ______________________________

____

Example Lesson

Library resource selected: Atlas

Development activity: Students learn to read area symbols on maps (See Part 6)

Application activity: Students use the maps in an atlas to learn about the topography of selected areas of the United States. They use area symbols on blank outline maps of the United States to show the topography of these areas.

TEACHING LOCATION OF INFORMATION IN THE CONTENT AREA

We will now provide several illustrations of how the various location and library skills may be integrated in the content areas. The strategies presented in this section should be considered as examples of how skills and content can be integrated. Before studying this section, however, the reader should have worked through all the development activities for book skills, library location skills, and library resources.

Illustrations

Illustration 1

A ninth-grade introductory Spanish class is learning not only language skills but also some of the customs of Spanish speaking countries. The Spanish teacher decides that an enjoyable method of introducing students to the various Spanish speaking countries is to have them prepare travelogs.

After permitting the students to choose which country they want to study, the teacher suggests that they may include the following sample pieces of information about these countries in their travelogs:

1. What are the weather conditions and climate?
2. What is the topography?
3. How large is the country? How many people?
4. What are the major industries?
5. What are the major imports and exports?
6. What is the form of government?
7. What are the typical customs, dress, houses, and so forth?

The teacher next reviews the almanac as a source of current information, particularly statistical and factual information. She suggests, however, that they begin their research in the encyclopedia to get a sense of historical perspective as well as a general overview of the country. Next they should check the most recent almanac for current statistical information. They should also look in the vertical file to see if they can locate pictures of the country.

The final products consist of posters advertising the country. Students present information about the countries in Spanish to the rest of the class displaying any pictures and artifacts that they were able to find.

Illustration 2

A fifth-grade social studies class in a river town is studying the water level of the river during the spring months to watch for possible flooding nearby. The students consult the atlas to determine the path of the river that runs through their town. They attempt to identify low areas where the danger of flooding is the greatest by using map elevation symbols. The students check the local newspaper daily to record the water levels of the river at their town. These figures are shown on a line graph so that daily and weekly comparisons can be made.

Illustration 3

A high school chemistry class investigates the ingredients found in a common pesticide used in the local farming area. After the students find out the ingredients in the pesticide, they research the effects of these chemicals on animal and plant life. Working in teams, with each team investigating a particular ingredient, they consult various chemistry resource books in their school library for information; they locate these using the subject cards labeled *chemistry* in the card catalog. They use the indexes of the books to find the specific references. They also consult the *Readers' Guide* looking under *pesticides* to determine whether current information is available in magazines on the effects of pesticides. The information that each team collects is shared orally with the rest of the chemistry class. The students then debate in class whether or not farmers in their area should continue to use the pesticide.

Illustration 4

Two third-grade teachers working cooperatively create a learning center on location skills. The center consists of a variety of activities that begin with alphabetical order—alphabetizing to the second and third letters. The next activity in the center is using guide letters and words to locate information in an encyclopedia and dictionary. The third activity requires application to dictionary usage of what they have learned. Given a list of related words such as words pertaining to a particular food, the students must locate these words in a dictionary and record the page number on which the entry is found. For example, given the food *potato,* related words might be *root, tuber,* and *skin.* The students should write down the definitions of any unknown words in the list such as *tuber.* The next activity requires that the students find that food in the encyclopedia. They should indicate, by a checkmark, which of the words in the list were also found in the encyclopedia description of the food. They use note-taking skills to record information about the food that they find in the encyclopedia. The information gained from the learning center also prepares the students for a nutrition unit on the four basic food groups. Students share the information that they have learned about their food with the rest of the class.

REFERENCES

1. American Association of School Librarians. *Standards for school library programs.* Chicago: American Library Association, 1960.
2. Burns, P., & Roe, B. *Teaching reading in today's elementary schools* (2nd ed.). Chicago: Rand McNally Publishing Company, 1980.

3. Carpenter, H. M. "Treasure hunt for information." *Instructor,* 1965, *74,* 27-28; 110.
4. Frinsko, W., & Drew, G. "Look it up! But can they?" *Elementary English,* 1972, *44,* 74-76.
5. Middleton, R. K. *Library skills instruction in the fifth and sixth grades.* Bloomington, Ind.: Agency for Instructional Television, 1977. (ERIC Document Reproduction Service No. 157 153).
6. Monroe, M. "The use of picture dictionaries in the primary grades." *Elementary English,* 1964, *41,* 344.
7. Otto, W., Kamm, K., & Weibel, E. *Wisconsin design for reading skill development: Rationale and objectives for the study skills element.* Working Paper No. 84. Madison: Wisconsin Research and Development Center for Cognitive Learning, 1972.
8. Ransom, G. *Preparing to teach reading.* Boston: Little, Brown and Company, 1978.
9. Smith, R., & Johnson, D. *Teaching children to read* (2nd. ed.). Reading, Mass.: Addison-Wesley Publishing Company, 1980.
10. Sullivan, P. (Ed.). *Realization: Final report of the Knapp school library project.* Chicago: American Library Association, 1968.
11. Zintz, M. *The reading process* (3rd ed.). Dubuque, Iowa: Wm. C. Brown Co., 1980.

Reading for Information in the Content Areas

4

The skills notetaking, outlining, test taking, and rate/flexibility have been grouped together because they all pertain to grasping, organizing, and using information from content area materials. Test taking is considered part of this process because students must organize information in study so that it is retrievable in a test-taking situation. In other words, study and test-taking strategies should be parallel—a student should study the content material with the test or use of the material in mind.

OVERVIEW

In this part we will look at notetaking and outlining together since they are two, related study strategies. Next we will consider the research pertaining to test taking in which the student applies what she or he has learned from the content material. Rate and flexibility are considered last as an application of the previous strategies in adjusting reading rate to the difficulty of the material and the demands of the task.

Notetaking and Outlining

For many students, the process of reading, studying, and later recalling information in a text is an overwhelming task. Indeed, students may find the process difficult because they have not mastered helpful study techniques such as notetaking and outlining. Research suggests that students do not know how to take notes or make outlines because very little attention is given to teaching these study skills (4,5,16). In order to understand how these study skills can be taught effectively, a close examination of their components is necessary.

What are the components of notetaking and outlining?

At the most basic level, notetaking and outlining demand that students detect, classify, and organize the ideas presented in a text. When children are asked to adopt a study strategy like notetaking without prior experience in organizing and classifying material, that strategy is unlikely to be of great benefit (3). Recognition and classification of ideas imply that students can distinguish the main ideas or the author's central message from significant details and that they can separate relevant from irrelevant material. In order to recognize and classify ideas successfully, students should be familiar with the organization typically found in various types of writing (such as textbooks, newspapers, narrative stories, letters, and so forth). Exposure to different types of prose materials helps students become aware of structure or organization of the content material.

Once students have been taught to identify and classify ideas, and to note the organization of passages, they must learn to recognize the relationships among the ideas that are presented (17). If students must reorganize text passages as they take notes, greater comprehension and recall are evident—especially on essay exams—when students themselves create the relationships among ideas (1). The student's active reformulation of text material into notes or outlines demands focused attention, a deep level of comprehension, and careful reasoning about the ideas and relationships expressed in the text. On the other hand, only a superficial reading is necessary if students need only to record ideas verbatim from a text.

We are suggesting, then, that during reading, notetaking, and outlining, learners must be active participants. They must rethink, reword, and reorganize text passages as they outline and make notes, thereby interacting with the text. Certainly both time and cognitive effort are necessary in order for students to take notes or to outline properly. But the time and effort spent should result in a clearer understanding and greater recall of the content.

Instructional considerations for notetaking and outlining

A basic assumption in notetaking and outlining instruction is that students' expectations about the test or use of the material will necessarily influence what material is studied and how the material is studied (1). When the type of test or exercise is made explicit to students *before* they read, students will learn more from studying than if the task is unspecified. If a student knows that an essay exam testing knowledge of main ideas will follow study, then most likely the student will focus his or her attention on the important ideas in the material. The resulting notes or outline will also reflect the main ideas. On the other hand, if the student knows that the test is composed of multiple choice questions concerning the recognition of specified details, the student's notes will encompass details. The degree of knowledge that a student has about the upcoming test or exercise is one important variable that influences study outcomes. The teacher, then, should help to ensure successful studying through notetaking and outlining by supplying students with some information about the anticipated test or exercise after study.

Helping students determine which technique to use with given reading assignments is also important in teaching notetaking and outlining. Research shows that notetaking that involves classifying and reorganizing ideas may actually be detrimental if the material to be learned is only a list of facts that is organized in a particular way

(21). The teacher needs to set clear objectives for what the students are to learn from the material.

The introduction of traditional outlining formats can also pose problems in study skills instruction. First, if students are to outline without prior training in this skill, they may use the outline format to record ideas verbatim after reading the text superficially. Second, although students can use outlines to show main ideas and details, more complex relationships such as cause/effect and comparison/contrast cannot be illustrated in outline form. While we have no perfect solution to this problem, we can suggest an alternative study skill strategy known as mapping.

Mapping: An alternative to the outline

Mapping is a method of illustrating the most important relationships among ideas in a text by visual representation (14). For example, the relations among ideas may be expressed through a flow chart, Venn diagram, sketch, or table. Mapping can be an effective comprehension and studying technique for students (2,10). We are encouraged by the possibilities that mapping holds for the improved study of texts. As research has shown, the degree to which students attend to, interact with, and elaborate on the ideas and relationships in the text influences the extent to which that text is understood and remembered (1). The student is likely to understand and accurately recall text material if mapping is used and if the anticipated test or use of the material has been defined.

Test Taking

Tests have become a part of the American life, influencing decisions that determine the futures of millions of people each year. Not only are tests used to help teachers make curricular decisions, but tests also are taken at transitional points in life, such as between high school and employment, high school and college, and so forth.

During World War II, testing gained increased credibility when the United States was faced with the need to identify individuals to serve in key defense functions (12). Psychometricians were awarded commissions to work with the Office of Strategic Services (predecessor of the CIA) to develop measurements that would identify individuals best suited to be pilots, bombardiers, or other positions. It was believed that the more characteristics that could be measured by standardized tests, the more efficient the nation would become.

Evaluation became a powerful business. Educational Testing Service, formed in 1947 by the Carnegie Foundation, was chartered to explore all areas of educational testing, develop and administer new standardized tests, and provide leadership in expansion of psychometrics. The company's growth from 276 employees in 1947 to a staff of 2,000 in 1979 and its yearly annual gross increase from $2 million to more than $50 million dollars demonstrates public acceptance of psychometric principles (12).

Standardized testing has affected all levels of the educational spectrum. Test results have been used to evaluate the effectiveness of elementary and secondary schools and to influence curriculum changes. Test results have been used by guidance counselors and teachers to track students into classes that have either increased or decreased career options. Declining SAT scores have become a political issue with irate taxpayers demanding explanations from boards of education (8). The massive scoring and analyzing of test results provided by computers has created political and social forces that have tended to control educational goals and methodology rather than provide data for decision making (6). In addition, controversies have ensued concerning the effectiveness of coaching students for standardized tests, the fairness of tests, and the validity of exams in predicting academic potential.

Research suggests that students can be prepared to take standardized tests (7,13,15,20,22). The longer the preparation and the more organized the program, the greater its success. The ability to interpret questions accurately, to understand an author's purpose in writing a paragraph, and to eliminate distractors can influence the outcome of a test. Confidence building also occurs when students are able to review the format of an exam and explain the rationale for an incorrect response in a supportive group of peers.

Test taking should not be taught as an isolated skill but as a component in all content areas. Test taking skills learned as part of classroom tests can be applied in standardized testing situations where the effect on a student's life may be greater.

Rate and Flexibility

Reading rate and flexibility are essential skills for students in the upper elementary and secondary grades. Although reading experts do not agree on the definition of rate, we take this skill to mean the speed at which materials are read. Flexibility has also been defined in various ways. However, as the term is used here, flexibility refers to the ability to adjust reading rate according to specific purposes for reading and difficulty of the material.

The interaction of these skills can be more easily understood in the context of the following example. The flexible reader is like an automobile driver who increases or decreases speed depending on weather conditions, the legal speed limits, and the reasons she or he has for taking the trip. In addition, if the driver is hurrying to arrive at a destination, the driver is apt to increase speed. Like the driver, the reader is also affected by certain conditions such as familiarity with the book, the difficulty of the written language and concepts presented, and the time available for reading. In addition, the reason or purpose for reading will influence the reader's speed. For example, if a student is studying for an exam, reading rate should decrease. On the other hand, if the reader is glancing through the newspaper simply to gather information about important events, reading rate should increase. As in the case of the driver who increases speed because he or she is late for work or decreases speed when taking a leisurely Sunday drive, the flexible reader must also adjust his or her reading rate to suit the demands of the task.

Our central concern, however, is comprehension. Flexibility and rate are of little value if the reader is not understanding what is being read. A flexible reader, in fact, is one who monitors his or her own comprehension in order to adjust reading rate to the desired level of comprehension.

The wide variety of reading purposes and conditions makes it impossible to specify one entity known as reading flexibility. Rather there are different kinds of reading flexibilities, each with different behavioral standards of success. Rate by itself becomes an inappropriate measure of flexibility when varieties of purposes and conditions are taken into account.

In discussing rate and flexibility, one researcher finds it helpful to distinguish three strategies or subclasses of reading (11). These are: (1) "rauding," (2) skimming and scanning, and (3) studying. Rauding is that type of reading behavior that is often considered typical reading. Skimming and scanning are types of rapid reading, and studying is slow, careful reading. Each of these subclasses involves a distinct reading behavior, and each requires a different set of standards for its evaluation.

Rauding, for example, may be evaluated by rate measures, such as words read per minute. On the other hand, efficient studying cannot be determined by a rate measure. Flexibility, changing from one strategy to another during a long reading assignment, also cannot be measured by rate (11, 18).

It is estimated that the average adult reads at an average speed of 200 words per minute (9). Researchers also have indicated that there are upper limits of reading speed that cannot be exceeded if the reader is to comprehend the author's message. On the other hand, it has been suggested that a very slow rate of reading can inhibit comprehension. Therefore, students should be exposed to some instruction involving flexibility, reading rate, and comprehension.

NOTETAKING AND OUTLINING

Notetaking and outlining are considered together because of their close relationship. Indeed, outlining information from written material is one form of notetaking.

Developmental Perspective

Children learn to read using narrative materials. Regardless of the approach to instruction, they practice their developing word recognition skills primarily through stories. Comprehension is important; it is aided by the use of stories set in familiar situations. In fact, at the early levels, basal readers, the most widely used beginning reading instructional materials, consist almost exclusively of narrative materials concerning children's lives in the home and neighborhood setting.

As children begin the use of content area materials, perhaps even in first grade, these materials are often written in the narrative form to enhance comprehension of the material. By third grade, however, most children are expected to read expository content materials. Many children have difficulty at this point for two reasons. First, they no longer have the familiar story organization. Instead, presentation of main ideas with supporting details characterizes expository organization. Second, the content may not be as familiar to them as in their narrative stories. In fact, the purpose of content reading materials is to present new information. Along with new information are new vocabulary and concepts.

So, simply the task of reading content materials can cause difficulty for many students. By providing study guides teachers try to help their students become accustomed to comprehending content materials. The study guide asks the student to answer questions that help identify the main ideas of the selection. Some inferential questions, those for which the answer is not directly stated, help students learn to think about the material—to predict, infer, compare, contrast, and so forth.

When used with young students, the study guide becomes a form of notetaking. The teacher, however, is directing the students to the important aspects of the material. Very often study guide questions are rewordings of the headings used in the material. The students learn to read the headings to help them identify the main ideas. Therefore, study guides are a good way to begin to teach notetaking.

As students become accustomed to study guides, they also need opportunities for independent notetaking. The teacher can help students by alerting them to what is important for them to remember from the material. If they are not guided, they may tend to try to write down everything verbatim, or they may record very little. While not as explicit as study guide questions, the teacher's directions help the students pick out what is important in the material.

Eventually, however, students do have to make notes independently. At that point they must clearly have in mind the purpose for their notetaking. In other words, they have to know the use for the material, whether for a test, research project, or some other sort of application. The teacher can help by establishing the purpose for reading material.

The students' notes, of course, should reflect that purpose. If the teacher has directed students to read for the main ideas, then students' notes should contain the main ideas of the content materials. On the other hand, if details are important, then details should be included in the notes. As a part of teaching notetaking, the teacher should check students' notes to see whether they have recorded the proper type of information.

Outlining is a type of notetaking that organizes the material in a particular way. By outlining the student must place ideas in hierarchical order. The value of outlining is that the student must think about relationships. She or he simply cannot list facts verbatim. Mapping, likewise, forces the student to think about relationships as they are portrayed in a visual representation. Usually outlining and mapping are not taught until students are able to take notes independently.

As discussed in the Overview, regardless of whether students are taking notes or making outlines, they must paraphrase or reword the material. Simply writing down the author's words is insufficient. Unless the student "translates" the material, he or she will not remember it as well. The process of rewording material forces the student to think about the meaning. The active thought process is what aids comprehension.

Some students use underlining as a study technique. We have not included this technique in our book because underlining does not force the reader to rework, rephrase, and think about the material. In our opinion, a student can use underlining effectively only if processes of notetaking and outlining have already been mastered. Then, underlining usually is more than mere rote underscoring. It may include such activities as designation of importance of ideas, listing by numerals which details fit under a main idea, and marginal notes. We see underlining as a study technique more appropriate for the college student who has already learned to take notes effectively.

Taking notes while listening is another important aspect of notetaking. While elementary teachers do not (and should not, in our opinion) lecture, high school students frequently need to take notes while the teacher is presenting information orally. Basically, the same procedures apply.

Development Activities
Notetaking

As discussed above, the first step in teaching notetaking is to provide students with study guides to help them identify the main ideas in a selection. The study guide can teach students to attend to headings that often express the main ideas. The simplest study guide, therefore, makes the headings, or main topics, into questions. The study guide usually consists of questions that the students answer in the spaces provided. Using the following selection from an English textbook on expository writing, make up a study guide consisting of questions about the main ideas.

FIGURE 4-1 Study guide questions *(Excerpt from H. Hickler and C. L. May,* Expository Writing: From Thought to Action. *Boston: Allyn and Bacon, 1980, pp. 52–53. Used by permission.)*

You have already learned that you don't write down everything you hear during an interview. You jot down reminders of the important information. You do the same thing when you are getting material from a book, magazine, or encyclopedia. If you copy every word you read, you might as well carry the encyclopedia with you and pass it in as your paper; furthermore, you will have to move into the library with food enough to last a week. This is how long it would take you to copy down every word.

Here is a list of tips that will help you take notes from your sources:

1. **You mustn't write too many words,** because it will take you too long, and it will be difficult later on to organize your notes.
2. **Be sure you have enough facts and details.** If you take too few notes, you won't have enough information for your paper. Writers usually collect more than they actually need.
3. **Don't get off the track.** When you take notes, remember what your topic is. Don't add information that has nothing to do with your subject.

(continued)

FIGURE 4–1
continued

You have to learn to write the information you think you will need. To do this, it is important to use more than one source. Young writers often make the mistake of sitting down with an encyclopedia or article, and using only that one source for their papers. If you do this, you will run into several problems:

1. **You run the risk of plagiarizing.** When you plagiarize, you are using someone else's words and thoughts as your own. You can avoid plagiarizing by reading several people's thoughts and experiences on the same subject. Then you can use this information to form your own opinions and draw your own conclusions.
2. **You miss other interesting information.** It is much more interesting to gather different people's thoughts and ideas on the same subject than to concentrate on only one person's ideas.
3. **You will not learn important skills.** You won't have practice sorting out information. You won't learn to separate information that is useful to you from unnecessary material. You won't learn to organize your thoughts and compare your ideas to the ideas of others. You can't draw your own conclusions as easily from only one source.

Now write two questions that could be used as part of a study guide on this text passage.

1. a. ______________________________
   b. ______________________________

In the next passage the main ideas are not so readily apparent. Write questions that bring out the main ideas in the passage.

FIGURE 4–2
Study guide questions
Excerpt from H. D. Drummond, The Western Hemisphere. *Boston: Allyn and Bacon, 1978, p. 193. Used by permission.)*

Throughout Central America many people are demanding a higher standard of living. Living conditions are slowly getting better. A major question, however, is whether changes will be rapid enough. When change is slow, people sometimes adopt communist methods of bringing about change. The countries will have to make very rapid progress, or the standard of living will fall. The region has one of the highest rates of population growth in the world. Cities in Central America are growing very rapidly. Most of the countries suffer from unemployment and inflation. Most of the wealth is in the hands of a few people. Often these people do not wish to invest their wealth in new industries that are needed.

A middle class is growing, nevertheless, in Central America. As educational levels are raised, the number of people in this class will probably increase. Governments are trying to encourage people from other lands to invest money in new plants. Roads are being built to isolated areas. New farming methods are being tried.

2. a. ______________________
   b. ______________________
   c. ______________________

Having students write a summary of assigned reading material is another way to check on their ability to grasp the main ideas. Students should be encouraged to create summaries *in their own words* in addition to the notes that they take. The summary, then, expresses only the main ideas. Notes, on the other hand, express both main ideas and important details.

Write a summary for the passage presented in Figure 4-2. Remember that rewording indicates that you have assimilated the material as you express the main ideas in different language.

3. ______________________
____
____

Students also need to learn a consistent notetaking strategy after they have had experience with a teacher's study guides. The particular format may not be so important as the student's consistent use of the selected format. One style is to place main ideas flush with the left margin. Indent to show a subheading and indent still further to show details under a subheading. The advantage of this style is that it shows the relationship of main ideas and supporting details as well as prepares students for outlining. If you were directed to remember main ideas and important details, take notes on a passage from the same high school geography textbook as presented above, using the format we have described.

> The early settlers on the eastern coast of the United States found a land of dense forests. These forests seemed to extend forever toward the west. These forests were of great value to the colonists. They provided a source of building material and fuel. Forest resources also were important in the development of early industry and trade. The forests furnished lumber for ships, homes, and stores. They also were the home of valuable meat and fur-bearing animals. But the settlers needed land for raising crops. They cleared the forests with axes and with fire. Vast areas of forest land were cleared with little thought given to its worth. Trees seemed so plentiful that the settlers thought the supply would last forever.

FIGURE 4-3
Notetaking: Main ideas
(Excerpt from H. D. Drummond, The Western Hemisphere. *Boston: Allyn and Bacon, 1978, p. 361. Used by permission.)*

4. ______________________
____
____
____

Be sure to check to see whether you have used the author's words verbatim or whether you have paraphrased what he said. Students have better retention if they reword the material because they must think about it in order to place it in their own words.

Not all paragraphs and passages are organized according to a main idea and supporting details. Notes should reflect the organization of the material. In the following passage the purpose of the material is to provide step-by-step procedures or directions. This type of listing is commonly found in textbooks for science, mathematics, industrial arts, home economics, and so forth.

FIGURE 4-4 Notetaking: Procedures
(Excerpt from R. B. Sund, B. W. Tillery, and L. W. Trowbridge, Elementary Science Discovery Lessons: The Earth Sciences. *Boston: Allyn and Bacon, 1980, pp. 67–68. Used by permission.)*

1. Fill two small cans with sand to a depth of 1 inch.
2. To one can add 2 tablespoons of calcium hydroxide (hydrated lime). Mix the substances by stirring. Add enough water to moisten the mixture. Evaporate the water by slowly heating the solution over a flame.
3. Mix a tablespoon of sodium silicate with the other can of sand.
4. Your teacher will add 2 teaspoonsful of dilute hydrocholoric acid to the can. CAUTION: *Acid will burn you and your clothing. If you spill any acid, wash with water and a solution of bicarbonate of soda.*
5. Heat the mixture over a flame until it is dry.
6. After the cans have cooled, compare the two sandstones you have made. Hit them to break the sandstone apart. Record your comparison of the sandstones. Look at them with a magnifying glass. Compare your sandstone with natural sandstone. How are they different? How are they similar? Why do different sandstones "hold together" better than other sandstones? What is one reason sand in a sandstone stays together?

List the procedures for making sandstone trying not to use the author's exact words.

5. ______________________________

____

____

____

____

Note in the suggested answer (see answer section in the appendix) that we have listed seven steps instead of the authors' six steps. We rearranged the material in the steps to make it clearer to us. The number of steps in a set of procedures is unimportant. Also note that we use abbreviations wherever possible.

Another type of listing, although not a set of procedures, is a description. Students need to note the important details and disregard the unimportant ones. This distinction may be difficult at first. In the following passage from a business textbook a concept is described.

> The simplest form of business organization is that which is owned by one person. It is called a *sole* or *single proprietorship*. This form of organization is the most numerous in our country. It includes most farmers and professional people, as well as many retailers. Retailers sell directly to the public. Wholesale firms which buy from manufacturers and sell only to retailers are frequently organized as sole proprietorships. In this form of business organization, only one individual is the owner, although there may be numerous employees. Usually, however, the size of the sole proprietor's business and the amount produced is quite small.
>
> Sole proprietorships make up more than 80 percent of all businesses in our economy. The large number of existing sole proprietorships indicates that they play an important role in linking consumers with resources. A community's pharmacist, for example, makes available to customers a variety of drugs from all over the nation. An individual farmer, with but a few acres of land to cultivate, contributes to the satisfaction of human wants by using the factors of production to raise vegetables.
>
> The single proprietorship is the easiest and quickest to enter. The business assets are commingled with the personal assets of the owners. Business debt and personal debt, too, are commingled. This form of business is fine for some small firms, but it cannot grow very large, as we shall see below.

FIGURE 4-5 Notetaking: Descriptive details
(Excerpt from H. A. Wolf, Managing Your Money. *Boston: Allyn and Bacon, 1977, pp. 340–341. Used by permission.)*

List the important aspects that ought to be retained in a student's notes.

6. ____

____

____

____

____

Similarly, with narrative material, such as a novel assigned for an English class, the teacher may ask students to take notes on descriptions of characters or settings. Notes would look similar to those in Figure 4-5 noting the characteristics of a business concept. Notes about the chronology of events in a narrative would be similar to those from the elementary science book in which the sequence of events is listed.

Students need to learn convenient symbols for other types of paragraph organizations. An arrow, for example, drawn from cause to effect is useful. The cause/effect relationship is important to note in terms of developing content area concepts. Take notes on the following paragraph from a high school biology textbook. Pretend that you are preparing for a multiple choice test in which details as well as main ideas are important.

FIGURE 4-6
Notetaking: Cause/effect
(Excerpt from S. L. Weinberg, Biology: An Inquiry into the Nature of Life. *Boston: Allyn and Bacon, 1974, p. 273. Used by permission.)*

Diabetes. From ancient times **diabetes,** also called *sugar diabetes,* has been a dreaded disease. *It is characterized by partial inability of the cells to use glucose.* Unused sugar remains in the blood and is excreted in the urine.

Unable fully to utilize sugar for energy, the diabetic loses weight and becomes weak. Circulation is poor, the blood clots with abnormal slowness, and minor infections flare up into serious illnesses. Slow healing of wounds may lead to tissue death or *gangrene.* Fat respiration is upset. Instead of yielding CO_2 and water, fats are changed to poisonous *acetone* and to acids that may dangerously lower the blood pH.

7. ______________________________
____
____
____

Note that one effect may be the cause for another chaining of events. Now read a longer passage dealing with the effects of the French and Indian Wars from a high school history textbook. Read for the main ideas and take notes.

FIGURE 4-7
Notetaking: Cause/effect
(Excerpt from G. Leinwand, The Pageant of American History. *Boston: Allyn and Bacon, 1975, pp. 54–56. Used by permission.)*

Military action ended in America in 1760. The war in Europe and elsewhere dragged on until 1763. In that year the Treaty of Paris was signed. By its terms England won a spectacular victory. Except for two West Indian islands, France lost nearly all her land in the New World. Canada went to Britain. Britain also got the French territory east of the Mississippi River. New Orleans, however, remained in French hands. The French territory west of the Mississippi River, known as Louisiana, went to Spain. Spain, an ally of France, gave Florida to Britain. Britain gave Cuba and the Philippines to Spain. Britain won not only land in North America, but also a dominant position in India. With almost one stroke of a pen, the treaty destroyed the French empire and gave rise to a mighty British empire.

The colonists felt they had gained as a result of the war. They felt they had contributed a lot to the British victory. They thought the victory would have been impossible without them. Colonial morale was high and most colonists were proud to be on the winning side. They felt they were part of a great empire. The elimination of France from the continent of North America opened to them the opportunities of the West. There they could lay out new cities or begin new farms.

The Indians recognized that English westward expansion, so long held back, was about to be let loose. The Indians tried to stop the English. They were unsuccessful.

FIGURE 4-7
continued

Under the Ottawa Chief Pontiac, the Indians tried to take Detroit. They were defeated. Still determined to continue his attacks, Pontiac destroyed almost every other British outpost in the West in just a few weeks. Despite early success, the conspiracy of Pontiac was finally put down. The Indian uprisings did bring two issues forward. First, what responsibility did England have to protect western settlers? Second, the people of the East rarely took the raids in the West seriously, and differences about what was important began to grow between East and West. It would not be the last time that eastern interests and western interests conflicted.

Victory over the French brought problems—as well as opportunities—for the colonists and the English. Up to 1763, the British followed a policy of "salutary neglect" toward the colonists. Up to then, the colonies played "second fiddle" to the events in Europe. This policy of neglect seemed salutary (good for, healthy) to the colonies. It seemed healthy because it gave the colonies a chance to develop their own traditions. Up to 1763 the colonies had experienced only limited interference from England. After 1763, the situation had to change. England's colonial empire in America was much bigger now. This required closer management. The English realized for the first time how valuable the 13 colonies could be. The colonies contributed to British wealth. They were also useful strategically and militarily against the French and Spanish in the New World. The English reasoned that they had better not neglect the colonies any longer.

The wars had been costly for England. Its war debt was large. Since part of that debt was spent on the colonies, shouldn't the colonies be asked to pay back their share? If the colonies needed defense, shouldn't the cost of that defense be paid by the colonies? If the colonies were to add to the wealth of the mother country (as good colonies were supposed to), were the American colonies giving as much as they could? These were the kinds of questions that Englishmen and their government asked in the years which followed the French and Indian Wars.

8. ____
____
____
____
____

Note in the passage in Figure 4-7 that the student is left to speculate about the effects of the English war debt. We indicated our inference in the answer by a question mark to show that the textbook did not actually state the effect. Notes become more meaningful as the student uses them to record hunches. Accuracy of these hunches can be checked as the student reads more material.

Another type of organization that should be indicated in a student's notes is comparison/contrast. Notes can show this type of organization by listing the two or more items being compared or contrasted as headings on the same line. Underneath the heading in the left column list the important characteristics. In the right column indicate whether the characteristic is the same by an *S* (in case of a comparison) or different by a *D* (in a contrast). Try to take notes on the main ideas from paragraphs organized by comparison/contrast from a math textbook.

FIGURE 4–8 Notetaking: Comparison/contrast *(Excerpt from D. M. Miller and D. G. Baker,* Understanding the METRIC System: A Programed Approach. *Boston: Allyn and Bacon, 1979, p. 8. Used by permission.)*

Like the English system, the metric system uses three basic units for everyday measurements, one for length, one for volume, and one for mass or weight. But unlike the English system, the units in the metric system are related to each other.

9. ______________________________

____

____

Now apply the same format to a longer passage from a high school science textbook. Pretend that you are studying in preparation for a multiple choice test of important details as well as main ideas.

FIGURE 4–9 Notetaking: Comparison/contrast *(Excerpt from S. L. Weinberg,* Biology: An Inquiry into the Nature of Life. *Boston: Allyn and Bacon, 1974, p. 169. Used by permission.)*

Birds. By the scales on their legs and their turtle-like beaks, chickens show the relationship between birds and reptiles. No organisms live entirely in the air, as many do on land or in water. But soaring vultures and migrating hummingbirds, which stay aloft for many hours, come as close to achieving this end as any creature. All birds are remarkably alike in basic structure, and many of their adaptations are related to flight.

Feathers are one such adaptation. The large breastbone and strong breast muscles are others. The efficient lungs connect with auxiliary air sacs that extend into hollow bones. Birds do not retain their excretions as land animals do, but eliminate them constantly, even in flight. They have keen eyesight and hearing, a good sense of balance, and a well-developed brain to coordinate these senses.

Flying requires concentrated energy, and birds' metabolism releases energy at a high rate. Most birds have a temperature several degrees higher than man. The four-chambered heart beats faster than ours. Like mammals, birds are *warm-blooded:* that is, they maintain a constant body temperature even in the cold. Feathers, built to provide good insulation, help in this regulation.

10. ______________________________

____

____

____

____

Taking notes while listening, rather than reading, is essentially the same task. Many students, however, have difficulty because they lack a systematic format for taking notes. We recommend basically the same format as used for notetaking with reading materials with one difference, however. Instead of placing main ideas flush left on the margin, indent at least one inch. Place main ideas on this imaginary margin and indent to show subheadings.

Because the pace of a lecture is set by the teacher, not the listener, the student usually does not have the opportunity to reword what the teacher says. Instead, she or he should jot down key phrases. Listen for words that indicate the main ideas, such as "The most important thing . . . " or "It is necessary to remember that . . . ". Words such as *first, second,* and so forth indicate a list or steps in a procedure. These should be listed under the appropriate heading. Words such as *since, because,* and *therefore* indicate causation which should be indicated by arrows in the notes.

After the lecture the student has not yet completed the notetaking process. As soon as possible, sometime during the same day, the student should reread the notes that were taken during class. Using pen or pencil of a different color, the student should underline the important points. Key vocabulary such as technical terms should be circled. In the empty space in the left column the student should now reword the main ideas that have been recorded primarily in the teacher's words. Unless the student takes the time to paraphrase and write down the main idea in his or her own words, the notes will not make sense at a later time. Only by reworking the material does the student make it memorable.

Try this procedure during the next opportunity you have to take notes while listening. After a time interval, check to see whether or not your retention of the material was enhanced by these procedures.

Outlining

Outlining while reading material is a specialized form of notetaking. In teaching outlining the objectives are to help students see relationships while reading and to organize their own ideas in preparing a written or oral report. Outlining is probably more useful for the second purpose—helping students organize their own ideas for presentation to others. However, teachers often use outlining of reading material as a way of teaching students the process of outlining. In other words, the first step is to learn how to outline what someone else has written; the next step is to create an outline in order to present information to others. The first step is of concern here as outlining is a form of notetaking.

Students can learn to outline material in the upper elementary grades by being given a partial outline that they are to complete. The teacher may provide the main headings and some supporting details, requiring students to fill in most of the subheadings that represent the important details. Fill in the supporting details that are omitted from the partial outline structure provided for a paragraph from a mathematics textbook. (This represents only the first part of an outline on a longer reading assignment.)

FIGURE 4-10
Outlining
(Excerpt from E. I. Stein, First Course in Fundamentals of Mathematics. *Boston: Allyn and Bacon, 1978, p. 259. Used by permission.)*

The three thermometer scales that are used to measure temperature are the *Celsius*, the *Fahrenheit*, and the *Kelvin*. The Celsius scale (formerly called centigrade) is based on 100 divisions, each called a *degree*. On the Celsius scale the freezing point of water is indicated as 0° and the boiling point as 100°. On the Fahrenheit scale the freezing point and the boiling point of water are indicated as 32° and 212° respectively for a 180° interval. It now appears that the Celsius scale will soon replace the Fahrenheit scale in the United States.

The Kelvin temperature scale, used in SI measurement, is related to the Celsius scale. One degree Celsius is exactly equal to one *kelvin* (the name used to mean degree Kelvin). The reading of a specific temperature on the Kelvin scale is approximately 273 kelvins more than its reading on the Celsius scale.

11. I. Temperature scales
    - A. ______________________
        1. ______________________
        2. Freezing = 0°; boiling = 100°
    - B. ______________________
        1. ______________________
        2. ______________________
    - C. ______________________
        1. 1 degree Celsius = 1 degree Kelvin
        2. ______________________

Note that in Figure 4-10 we have provided only the first main heading of the outline; other main headings would follow if more material had been provided. Nevertheless we are not overly concerned about formal outlining in notetaking. In formal outlining each heading and subheading should be presented in the same form class or part of speech. In other words, all headings and subheadings should consist of noun phrases or verb phrases, but the two constructions should not be mixed. While formal outlining may be of some value in teaching logical thinking and organization, it does not seem necessary when outlining is used as a form of notetaking.

Outlining shows the logical relationships when main ideas and supporting details are clearly presented. A newer system, mapping, may be more effective in presenting relationships when the organization does not consist of main ideas and supporting details.

Mapping

Mapping is a visual representation of the relationship in a passage. Since it can become quite complex and time-consuming to try to show all relationships within a passage, we recommend that students use mapping only when a visual representation is particularly helpful in understanding the meaning of a passage. If the intent of a passage is to describe a concept or idea, then mapping can show the relationship of descriptive characterizations to that concept.

In mapping we usually place the main idea or concept in the center with other relationships represented visually. For example, the characteristics of amphibians are represented below; the visual picture helps students see relationships and thereby aids retention.

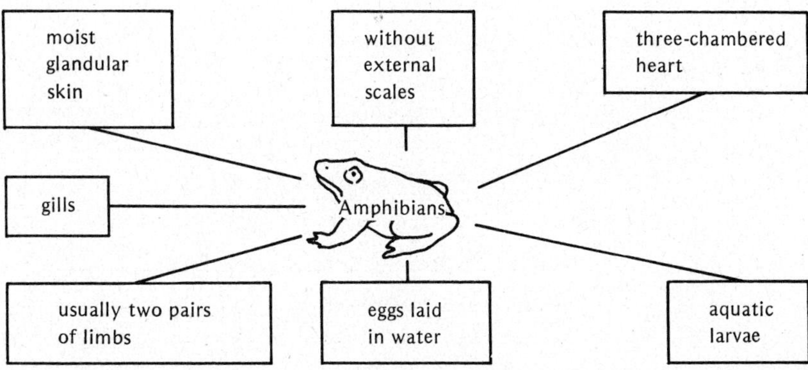

Even procedures, as in a recipe, or events, as in a narrative, can be represented in a map by a series of boxes showing the chain of events. Arrows connect the boxes to show their order by time sequence or causality. Examples of a particular concept can be shown by boxes with a box. The passage in Figure 4-9 could be represented by the following map:

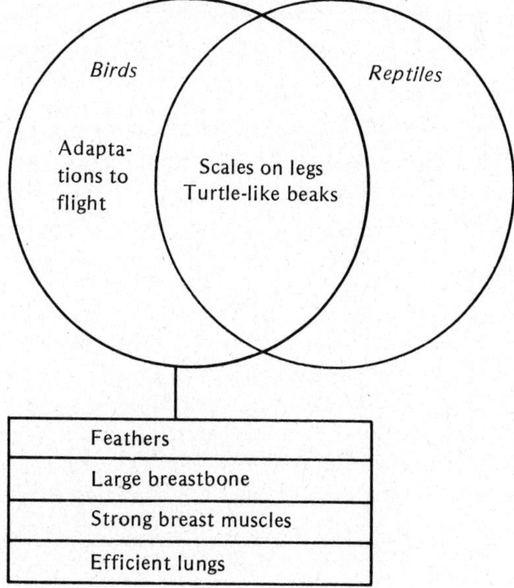

Other representations of the same material are possible. In fact, the teacher should encourage creativity on the part of the students in devising visual representations of important material. The material is more easily remembered not only because the student has a visual representation in mind but also because she or he has applied time and effort in thinking about the relationships expressed in order to portray them in a map. Because mapping does require considerable time and effort, it ought to be used only for significant passages, especially those developing important concepts for the content area study.

Try to map the following passage concerning inflation from a business textbook. First, however, read the entire passage to determine the organization and relationships expressed within the passage. Any map that expresses the correct relationships is appropriate.

FIGURE 4-11 Mapping *(Excerpt from H. A. Wolf,* Managing Your Money. *Boston: Allyn and Bacon, 1977, pp. 10–13. Used by permission.)*

Personal income is affected by *inflation*. During periods of inflation each dollar of income buys less and less. Inflation is a persistant rise in prices. When prices rise it takes more dollars to buy goods. During periods of inflation, people who have fixed incomes find themselves with less and less buying power. Individuals who receive wage or salary increases may have rising money incomes. But not many have an income which rises more rapidly than prices. However, a few may, and they will be better off. Inflation is inequitable; it harms many although a few may benefit.

In addition to reducing most people's incomes, inflation also erodes savings. The dollar held in bank accounts will buy less and less as prices rise. The interest earned on savings will also provide less buying power. For example, if savings accounts earn an annual 5 percent interest, but prices rise by 3 percent per year, the savings are really earning only 2 percent per year. In some years, prices have risen more rapidly than the earnings on savings accounts.

Inflation changes the relationship between the borrower and the lender. For example, an individual may buy a house with a $20,000 mortgage in 1976 at the 1976 price level. If prices then double, the borrower pays off the debt with dollars that buy only one-half as much as the dollars that were borrowed. The borrower benefits from this inflation, while the lender's position is worsened. The lender does not receive dollars that have the same buying power as the dollars that were loaned.

There are many causes of inflation. If there are too few goods and a great demand for those goods, prices are forced up. This was the situation immediately following World War II. Another cause of inflation is the easy availability of credit. If banks make too many loans, an oversupply of money may result. If there is a large increase in the supply of money without an equal increase in production, prices are bid up. People with too many dollars try to buy too few goods. An additional factor could be a rise in the costs of production. A manufacturer or producer of goods may be forced to raise the price of the product. Finally, inflation may be caused by excessive government spending. If the government spends more money than it receives in taxes, it creates a deficit in the national budget. The government must then borrow money from lending institutions to pay for the goods and services which it buys. This greater government demand helps to increase prices.

12. ____

____

Illustrations

The illustrations demonstrate how notetaking and outlining skills may be applied in content area instruction.

Illustration 1

As part of a third grade science unit on animals, students are to read several selected nonfiction books at appropriate reading levels. Accompanying each book is a study guide that helps students focus on the main ideas related to the animal unit. The questions consist primarily of reworded headings used in the book. (In that way students become used to reading headings in search of the main ideas.) The last item on each study guide requires students to summarize what they have learned about the particular animal that they had not known before reading the book. As the teacher corrects the study guides, she is particularly interested in whether the students were able to write their summaries using their own words.

Illustration 2

A seventh grade math teacher requires his students to take notes on the written work that he places on the chalkboard. Because this written work supplements the textbook, students are required to copy the information from the chalkboard verbatim with the idea that an accurate transcription will lead to understanding of the material. The teacher is dismayed when on a quiz he discovers that his students have retained little of his chalkboard presentation. On checking their notes, the teacher discovers tremendous inaccuracies in copying the information. He realizes if the students had understood the concepts he was presenting they could not have copied the material as they did. The next day he again places supplementary information on the chalkboard. This time he instructs his students not to take notes, but instead to listen, think, and answer his questions. He encourages students to ask for clarifications where they do not understand the material. At the end of his presentation he asks all students to summarize on paper what they have learned. Their summaries, which are then discussed, corrected, and amplified, now become their notes. Students are also instructed to copy a few of the problems as examples for their future reference. Scores on the next quiz indicate that most students have grasped the information presented in class.

Illustration 3

A high school home economics teacher wants students to learn to follow directions in sewing clothes by using a pattern. She notices that some students skip steps or parts of steps while assembling their pattern. She decides, therefore, to require students to map the directions on the pattern, using arrows to indicate the sequence. Once the students have completed the mapping exercise, they are to follow their maps in making their clothing. As they do each step in the procedure, they are to check that box on their maps.

Practice Exercise

A sixth grade social studies teacher checks his students' notes following a reading assignment in which the students were directed to read for the main ideas. He discovers that one student has copied verbatim many phrases from the assigned reading selection while another student has written only one or two words.

Notetaking and Outlining Skills ______________________________

____

Development Activity ______________________________

____

Application Activity ______________________________

____

Example Lesson

Skill Selected: Notetaking

Development Activity: The teacher instructs his students to list main ideas in their own words flush left at the margin of their paper. Any important supporting details are to be indented underneath. He provides students with several paragraphs for practice in notetaking. They work in pairs to take notes on material that they have already read. He particularly checks to see whether they have reworded the language of the passages in stating the main ideas.

Application Activity: The students work independently to take notes on assigned reading material in preparation for writing a research report. Afterwards, the teacher checks each student's notes for accuracy in identifying the main ideas and expressing them in their own words. Next the students are to go to the library to read at least one additional source and take notes on it before writing their reports.

TEST TAKING SKILLS

Many students have the frustrating experience of spending long hours preparing for an exam and feeling confident that they know the material only to find out later that they have failed. Poor test scores can be caused by ineffectual preparation or inability to take tests. To do well on an exam students must be able to understand the test format, be able to organize the assigned content, interpret the questions accurately, eliminate distractors, and express responses in a coherent written form.

Developmental Perspective

Since exams are based on expository writing, students should have a clear understanding of main ideas and supporting details. Young children can be taught to identify details or facts by associating a fact with an inquiry. Facts tell *who, what, when,* and *where.* Main ideas bring facts together by telling what happened, *why* or *how.*

Teaching children to respond to essay questions begins in kindergarten when the teacher asks pupils to synthesize ideas in order to select a title for the experience story they have written.

Essay questions require the student to identify the main idea (predict the question), outline the response (preparation), interpret the question correctly in the testing situation, sequence the content for the response, and write in an acceptable form. To study for an essay exam a student begins with a main idea and supports this idea with details.

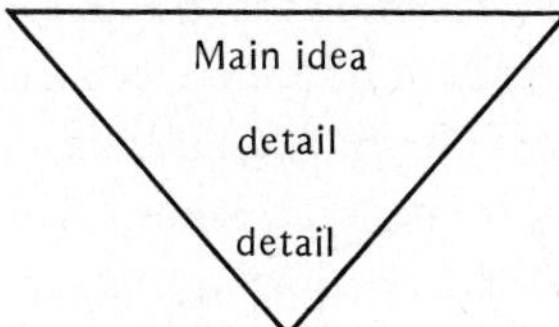

Objective exams (true-false, multiple-choice, fill-in-the-blank) challenge the student to discriminate or recall in the testing situation but not organize like the essay exam. To prepare for an objective exam, the student needs to begin with details leading into a major synthesis of the content.

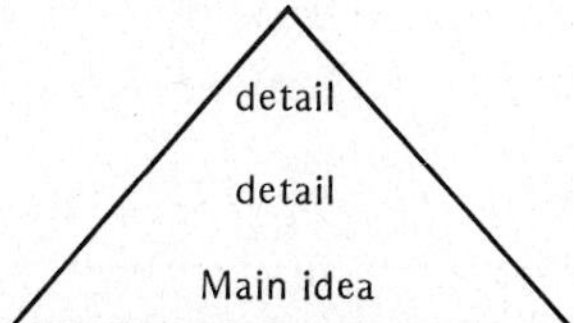

One of the most basic, obvious, and frequent problems with test taking is students' inability to follow directions. Often students fail exams simply because they did not answer the question. Giving students the opportunity to go over an exam afterwards in order to point out errors in following directions is important. Asking students to make up questions for other students can help them analyze the demands of test taking more carefully. As the students are encouraged to discover their own errors in test taking, patterns of strengths and weaknesses may emerge.

Organization is of vital importance to memory in the preparation stage of test taking; therefore classroom instruction should include categorizing, comparing, contrasting, summarizing, and listing information prior to the exam. Class preparation should focus on those types of skills that will be needed for the test.

Fill-in-the-blank questions are usually based on vocabulary knowledge. To eliminate the distractors in a multiple-choice question or to judge a question true or false, the student needs to identify the issue, mentally state what he or she knows to be correct, and compare this concept to the responses. Multple-choice distractors should be eliminated in the order of least correct eliminated first.

Careful attention should be given to the vocabulary used in exams. Words such as *always*, *never*, and *sometimes* can change the meaning of a question. *List* and *summarize* call for a smaller task in the essay format than words like *trace*, *discuss*, or *explain*. Students should underline these words in the directions so that they are considered in answering the question. Students should also circle key content words to help them remember their study of related concepts.

Students should be instructed to read through the entire test and answer easy questions first in order to build their self-confidence. They should, if possible, allow time at the end of the exam to reread their test paper to check accuracy. On an essay exam they should correct spelling and grammar or clarify wording as they reread.

Many publishing houses provide study guides for standardized tests. These study guides can be used to help students develop realistic expectations of tests such as the SAT and Service Exams. Directed reading activities can be developed from the sample exercises.

Test taking instruction should be taught throughout the curriculum with emphasis on student identification of the cause of errors and structured instruction to teach the lacking skills.

Development Activities

Main ideas and details

Being able to identify the main ideas and important details of a paragraph is an important skill and it is a prerequisite to successful test taking.

FIGURE 4–12 Main ideas and details *(Excerpt from H. A. Wolf,* Managing Your Money. *Boston: Allyn and Bacon, 1977, p. 87. Used by permission.)*

> More than forty separate federal agencies perform significant consumer functions. Most of the agencies regulate the actions of business and professional groups. They do not work directly with consumers. While they protect the consumer interest, they work only with the groups they can regulate. These agencies see to it that some competition exists in the marketplace. In cases like utilities and public transportation they actually set the price which the seller may charge. They are also involved in safety. Minimum standards are set and potentially harmful products controlled.

Make up a title from the main idea in the paragraph.

13. ______________________________

Read the paragraph and tell the details.

14. who ______________________________
15. where ______________________________
16. what ______________________________
17. how ______________________________

Categorizing information

Students need to learn how to categorize information in different ways. They especially need to be flexible in categorizing the same information in a variety of ways. How many categories can you identify for the following?

train	submarine	buggy
airplane	trolly	bicycle
boat	horse	roller skates
sled	dog sled	skateboard

18. List the categories for these methods of transportation.________________

Explicit and inferential questions

Explicit questions call for detailed answers which are clearly stated in the paragraphs. Inferential questions are concerned with main ideas, inferences, relationships, and evaluations. They require the student to go beyond what is explicitly stated and make a judgment about what he or she has read. Students need to determine the nature of the question in order to answer appropriately.

FIGURE 4-13 Explicit and inferential questions

Jones joins list of injured Rhinos

Cornerback Ray Jones has joined the ever growing list of injured Rhinos, as Sunday's showdown with the Dallas Dogies in Philadelphia nears. Jones pulled a muscle in practice, but is expected to play Sunday, along with Sam Leads, who has a sore knee, and Pete Prowse, who has a jammed toe. For a look at the injured Rhinos, plus stories on coaches Harry Coates and Joe Smith and Dallas quarterback Al Bonner, turn to page 9.

Read the article, answer the questions, and identify each question as explicit or inferential.

19. What two teams will be playing on Sunday?________________
____
Circle *explicit* or *inferential.*
20. How many Eagles are mentioned in the article?________________
Circle *explicit* or *inferential.*
21. Based on the information stated in the article, which team has the advantage?___
Circle *explicit* or *inferential.*

Read a passage from a high school science textbook. Answer hypothetical test questions and identify each as explicit or inferential.

FIGURE 4-14
Explicit and inferential questions
(Except from S. L. Weinberg, Biology: An Inquiry into the Nature of Life. *Boston: Allyn and Bacon, 1974, pp. 86–88, Used by permission.)*

The changing earth. The earth itself changes. In 1883 the explosion of Krakatoa blew to pieces the East Indies island on which this volcano stood. By contrast, Mexican families in 1943 watched a brand new volcano, particutin, push itself from the earth in the midst of their cornfields.

You surely have seen after a rain, a little stream on some nearby hillside washing *sediment*—sand and mud—down the slope, and depositing it in a small fan at the foot of the hill.

This is the process of **erosion.** On a larger scale and over a vastly longer period, erosion wears down mountains and continents. Niagara Falls recedes at the rate of five feet a year. The rivers of the United States each year wash an estimated 800 million tons of sediment into the seas. The Grand Canyon of the Colorado River was produced by 12 million years of such erosion. The river now lies a mile below the land surface in a channel it has dug itself.

Agents other than streams also help in the work of erosion. These include ice, wind, rain, and waves of the sea. You have seen winter ice crack sidewalks and concrete pavement. It does the same to rock and soil.

Geological processes build up as well as tear down. Sediment carried down the Mississippi River, and deposited at its mouth at the rate of almost half a billion tons a year, has built 200 miles of fertile delta. Earthquakes and similar processes raise up large blocks of the earth's surface. In the long run the wearing down of the surface of the earth is matched by an equal amount of uplift. Earth changes of many kinds, however, are always with us.

Some of the processes of change, like earthquakes and volcanic eruptions, take place swiftly. Others occur gradually over millions of years. In the end it is slower, less perceptible processes that produce the greater effect on the earth's surface.

The American Midwest and Southwest lay under the sea many times in geological history. The Northern Hemisphere has been partly covered with glaciers four times. They left the Great Lakes behind in their last northward retreat. The ice-covered Antarctic at one time was warm, tropical, and ice-free, as revealed by coal deposits discovered on that continent.

A great geologist, Sir Charles Lyell, pointed out in 1830 that such striking changes result, after long ages, from processes no more dramatic than the little stream washing silt down the hillside.

22. What is erosion?____________________
    Circle *explicit* or *inferential.* (Is a definition actually provided?)
23. What two actions do geological processes do?____________________
    Circle *explicit* or *inferential.*
24. Which processes of change have greater impact—fast ones or gradual ones?____
    Circle *explicit* or *inferential.*
25. Using *who, what, where,* or *when,* write a detail question about this passage. ___
    ____

26. Using the word *why*, write an inferential question that asks for a statement of the main idea. ____

____

Essay questions should tap the main ideas learned in a content area rather than the details. Make up an essay question from the following chapter titles: *Essay questions*

Chapter I	The Theory of Reading
Chapter II	Adolescent Reading Interests
Chapter III	Stages of Reading Development

An essay question should be the broadest main idea linking the chapters. An example of a response could be: Explain how reading theory and stages of reading development affect the adolescent's reading interests.

The topic sentence in an essay answer should always respond directly to the question and if possible order the response. After reading the question carefully, the student should underline the limiting words in the directions, circle key vocabulary, and list and order in a phrase outline the issues she or he plans to discuss. Sometimes it helps to jot down quickly examples or illustrations that can be used for clarification.

27. Invert the essay question just presented on adolescent's reading interests into the topic sentence of the answer. ____

The vocabulary used in essay questions can call for a broad or a very limited response. Terms used in directions can be categorized as:

Identification terms	ask for a name, phrase, or a date
Description terms	ask for a specific detail about a topic
Relationship terms	ask for similarities, differences, or associations
Demonstration terms	ask for data to show why something is true or false

28. Categorize these terms under the headings listed on page 76:

cite	describe	sketch	distinguish
diagram	contrast	support	justify
demonstrate	list	summarize	give
illustrate	outline	review	indicate
define	enumerate	discuss	trace
analyze	compare	prove	show

Identification Terms	*Description Terms*	*Relationship Terms*	*Demonstration Terms*
______	______	______	______
______	______	______	______
______	______	______	______
______	______	______	______
______	______		______
______	______		
	______		
	______		

29. Using the passage presented in Figure 4-14, write an essay question using each category of the terms provided.
Identification______________________________
Description______________________________
Relationship______________________________
Demonstration______________________________

Multiple-choice questions

Students need to learn how to eliminate distractors in this type of question. Limiting words, such as *always* and *never,* should be underlined. Key vocabulary should be circled. Read the following paragraph.

FIGURE 4-15 Multiple choice questions

> Preliminary figures show that 51,900 people died on the nation's highways during 1980. In 1979, the government reported 51,083 highway deaths. The National Highway Traffic Safety Administration said Friday, the deaths are alarming in view of the fuel shortage and reduced speed limits.

Which alternatives can be eliminated from the following question?

30. What was the source of the Traffic Safety Administration's alarm?
    a. Highway deaths have increased from 1979 to 1980.
    b. Speed limits are still too high and are contributing to the statistics.
    c. Americans are driving less and slower but the death rates are increasing.
    d. all of the above
    e. none of the above

The vocabulary used in questions can change the meaning and limit or extend the response. Again, underline the limiting words and circle key vocabulary used in following multiple choice question and response. Which alternatives can be eliminated?

31. Teenagers of the 1980s live in a highly stimulated world due to the media and their active lives. For this reason teenagers' reading interests:
    a. are very diverse and cannot be compared.
    b. are generated from personal and social needs.
    c. are never problem induced.
    d. are always advancing from one developmental stage to another.

Try to write a good multiple-choice question on the passage presented in Figure 4-14. Show it to a friend and see if she or he can answer it simply by eliminating distractors, *without* reading the passage. If your friend is successful, you need to rewrite your question so that she or he must have read the material in order to answer the question correctly. (It is possible that your friend's correct answer may be due to knowledge of the content area rather than a faulty multiple-choice question.) Remember to assess important information, not trivial facts.

32. Multiple choice question on Figure 4-14:______________________________
____

The purpose of multiple-choice tests is often to assess whether or not students have mastered specific content knowledge. If your test questions can be answered without reading the material in which the content is presented, then your test items have not been well constructed. On the other hand, we do want students to become "test wise"—to use their knowledge of test construction to help them answer multiple-choice questions. In teaching them test-taking skills, we must emphasize that these skills do not eliminate the necessity for studying the content material. In fact, close inspection of a teacher's test items can help them study content material because they can see what is important and ought to be remembered.

Illustration

A junior high school, life science teacher had her students analyze some of the test questions that her students had missed on an exam. The students worked in groups of three to analyze what problems thay had with the test items. After the students had attempted to identify problem areas, the teacher again went through the samples and emphasized the information following each item in parentheses:

Directions: *Identify whether each statement is true or false.*

F 1. Most insects have six legs and go through several stages before reaching the adult stage. (The term *most* is true concerning the developmental stages of insects; however, *all* insects have six legs. If one part of the question is false, the whole answer must be considered false.)

T 2. There are five groups of animals with backbones: mammals, reptiles, amphibians, birds, and fish. (The question is true; therefore, the error was caused through not understanding the concept.)

F 3. All mammals have lungs, are warm blooded, and feed their young with milk; however they can be different in size, shape, and whether or not they have hair covering. (The term *can* makes the response false since all mammals have hair of some type.)

T 4. Birds and reptiles are alike in the way they breathe; however, birds are warm blooded and reptiles are cold blooded. (The question requires students to categorize and compare characteristics of birds and reptiles in the following manner:

Birds	*Reptiles*
Breathe air—yes	breathe air—yes
warm blooded—yes	cold blooded—yes

An error could result from inadequate knowledge of the concept or inability to compare and contrast information.)

F 5. Both amphibians and fish have skin with scales, are cold blooded, and breathe through gills. (Students must classify information to judge whether it is true or false.

Amphibians	*Fish*
scales—no	scales—yes
cold blooded—yes	cold blooded—yes
gills—yes	gills—yes

Error could be the result of the inability to categorize information or inadequate concept development.)

With the aid of the text and the classroom notes, the students, working in small groups, can identify the major concepts and make up questions. Students should generate questions to clarify the issues that caused errors on the test. Sample questions could include the following:

A. How many legs do insects have? Do insects go through several stages of development?

B. How many groups of animals have backbones? Name them.

C. How are mammals alike? How are they different?
D. How are birds and reptiles alike? How are they different?
E. List the names of several amphibians. Compare characteristics of amphibians to those of fish. How are they alike? How are they different?

After each group has completed a set of questions, the groups can exchange questions and try to answer another group's questions.

Practice Exercise

Consider the following teaching situation and decide what skills are necessary to teach to best prepare your students.

Fourth grade students need to be able to order information when given a main idea.

Test Taking Skills____

____

Development Activity______________________________________

____

Application Activity_______________________________________

____

Example Lesson

Skill Selected: Main ideas and details.

Development Activity: Working in small groups, students identify a topic and prepare to conduct an interview. The main idea is listed and the group formulates questions using the question words *who, what, when, where.*

If a gasoline shortage was selected for the main idea, students may interview various school personnel to determine the impact. They may ask their questions in terms of *who, what, when,* and *where.* Students may ask the cafeteria workers what would happen if the trucks couldn't bring the food to school; the principal—what would happen if the teachers had no transportation; and the bus drivers—how would students be transported if there was no gasoline. The opinions of the school personnel can be discussed and students can agree on the main ideas and supporting details.

Application Activity: After the main ideas and supporting details have been identified and ordered, the students can use the information from the interviews to write a classroom newspaper.

RATE AND FLEXIBILITY

As with any other practice that is done frequently, reading becomes a habit. In a sense this is good because we usually want to use reading as a tool rather than an end in itself, particularly when it is related to the content areas. The problem is that we tend to read all material at the same rate. Obviously, it is inefficient to read a movie magazine and a science textbook at the same rate! Yet, by habit we usually do this unless we consciously think about what we are reading and why.

Developmental Perspective

Training to increase reading rate is not appropriate until students have acquired fluency in reading. That is, until students recognize instantly most of the words at their reading level by sight, they are not fluent readers. If they have to stop and think about many of the words, they are not ready to increase their reading rate.

Mainly readers acquire reading fluency through practice. They learn to apply word recognition skills easily and automatically by reading materials at their independent reading level, which is the level at which almost all words are known and comprehension is excellent. On the other hand, if they always read materials that are too difficult and have to struggle to recognize words, then fluency doesn't develop as it should which begins at about third grade for the average reader.

Unfortunately, some teachers think that poor readers can be helped by speed reading devices. Pacing devices are intended for habitually slow readers, not for those who lack fluency in applying word recognition skills. Readers of any age who lack fluency only become frustrated when mechanically forced to read faster. More appropriate and less expensive is the provision of high interest reading material at the student's independent reading level so that he or she may practice instant word recognition.

The study skill of adjusting rate flexibly to the demands of the reading task is for the student who reads fluently at his or her independent reading level. Students in the upper elementary grades have usually achieved this and can benefit from instruction in rate flexibility. Typically, they tend to read all material at the same rate, regardless of the difficulty of the material or their purpose for reading.

Our intent is to teach students to read all materials more flexibly rather than faster. Speed reading, on the other hand, has become a big business. While commercial companies can teach clients some techniques for rapid reading, for the most part they are teaching the process of skimming or reading very rapidly to pick out the main ideas. This type of reading is appropriate for previewing materials quickly in order to get a general notion of the contents. This type of reading is also appropriate for light material which is read for pleasure. It is not appropriate for *studying* in-depth content area material.

In general, we do not advocate mechanical devices for teaching students to read flexibly. While mechanical devices do force us to read faster, the same effect can be achieved by timing how long it takes to read a selection of given length and recording the progress in rate (words read per minute) and comprehension. Some commercial speed reading programs are quite expensive; the time and money may better be spent in recreational reading with a conscious effort to increase speed. Set an egg timer to see how many pages you can read in three minutes. The next day try to read more than you read the previous day again in three minutes. Be sure to think about what you read. Could you tell someone else about the ideas in the passage? Self-study kits, such as *Speedway* (Learning Multi-Systems, Inc., Madison, Wis.), are also available for those who need more structure.

Since reading at a certain rate is a habit, it may be hard to break the habit. Conscious effort and regular practice are necessary. We recommend daily practice for those who want to increase their reading rate; keeping progress records on rate and comprehension encourages setting higher goals and continued progress.

Development Activities

We need to know something about eye movements in order to understand how reading rate may be increased. Have a friend read a book while holding it up so that you may observe his or her eye movements. Draw what you see, pretending that these lines are lines of print.

____

____

____

You should have placed three or four x's (or other symbols) to represent stops that the eyes make while reading. During these stops, called fixations, the eyes take in several words at a time. Reading occurs during these fixations. You probably also saw the return sweep of the eyes at the end of the line to the beginning of the next line. You may have also seen regressions in which the eyes backed up and reread some of the same line. Excessive regressions are inefficient; they may be due to reading material that is too difficult (at the frustration level) or poor reading habits. A few regressions are normal. The reader stops when comprehension is not occurring and rereads for better understanding.

Now read the following selection from a high school geography textbook. Time yourself in minutes and seconds. Also answer the comprehension questions since rate is not meaningful without understanding.

FIGURE 4–16
Reading rate
(Excerpt from H. D. Drummond, The Western Hemisphere. *Boston: Allyn and Bacon, 1978, pp. 268–273. Used by permission.)*

The people of the United States and Canada are alike in many ways. They are similar in their *language and religion*. Most of the people in the United States and Canada speak English. In the Canadian province of Quebec, however, most of the people are French-speaking. In the American Southwest, many U.S. citizens speak Spanish. Most of them also speak English. Minor differences in pronunciation and speech habits exist from one place to another in the two countries. Almost everyone, however, can understand and speak to everyone else. This ability to communicate helps tie the countries of Northern North America together.

FIGURE 4-16
continued

Many different religions are found in both the United States and Canada. There are more Protestants than Catholics in both countries. Among the largest churches in Canada are the Roman Catholic, the United Church of Canada, and the Anglican Church of Canada. In the United States the largest church groups are the Roman Catholic, Baptist, Methodist, and Lutheran. Many Jewish people also live in the United States and Canada. Religious freedom is provided every person in both countries.

Economic life is similar throughout Northern North America. Most city *dwellers* work in manufacturing plants or in service or sales occupations. Most people living in rural areas use power-driven tools and machines. They also use scientific methods of farming. People who live in rural areas have most of the comforts of living that city dwellers have. Both groups have mail service, radio and television sets, canned and frozen foods, automobiles and trucks, electric appliances, and telephones. You will remember that great differences in living standards between urban and rural areas exist in Latin America. Such differences are not common in the United States and Canada.

Both the United States and Canada use a **monetary**, or money, system based on dollars and cents. In recent years a dollar usually has been worth about the same amount in both countries. Tourists who travel across the border may use the money of their own country, but it may be worth a few cents more or less than at home.

In contrast to most countries in Latin America, both the United States and Canada enjoy *political stability*. The governments of both countries are federal systems-with national governments and state or provincial governments. Canada has a parliamentary system of national government, with a House of Commons and a Senate. Members of the House of Commons are elected by the people. That body has much more power than the Senate, whose members are appointed for life. Canada is a member of the Commonwealth of Nations. The people, therefore, recognize Queen Elizabeth II as their queen. The prime minister, however, is the head of the Canadian government. He is elected as the leader of the party with the most members in the House of Commons. The prime minister has a Cabinet of Ministers to help him administer the government. These usually are members of his own party. If the party in power loses an election, the prime minister and the cabinet ministers lose their positions. The leader of the victorious party then becomes prime minister. The two major parties are the Progressive Conservative and the Liberal. Changes in political leadership are almost always made with good will and cooperation.

The national government of the United States has two Houses of Congress. Members of the larger body, the House of Representatives, are elected every two years. Membership of the House is determined on the basis of population. Members of the Senate are elected for six-year terms. Each state has two senators regardless of its population. Executive power in the United States government is centered in the office of the president. The president and vice-president are elected every four years. After the election, presidents select people to serve as advisors in the Cabinet. Usually, but not always, presidents choose members of their own party. Changes in the government of the United States are almost always made smoothly.

Both countries have Supreme Courts that head the judicial systems. Both nations have had fairly stable government for many years. Why do you suppose that is true?

Both the United States and Canada have developed a high standard of living by making *efficient use of available natural resources*. There are two main reasons for this efficiency. First, science and technology have been used whenever possible. Second,

FIGURE 4-16 *continued*

companies and farmers who wish to make money must operate efficiently. Some resources in both countries are being used up at alarming rates, however. The timber resources of Canada seem limitless and those of the United States vast. Easily harvested trees, however, are being cut more rapidly than they are being replaced. Many mineral resources, too, are being used very rapidly. Some people wonder whether the high standard of living enjoyed today in both countries can be maintained. Certainly both nations must be concerned about wise use and conservation of air, water, soil, forests, and mineral resources.

Differences between the countries and the two people do, of course, exist. Some of these were discussed as the likenesses were presented. Although Canada has fewer people than the United States, the Canadians are proud of their country and their independence. The people of the two nations usually get along quite well. Their governments sometimes take quite different positions on world affairs, however. A good way to show this is to note the different positions taken toward Castro's government in Cuba. The United States has not had diplomatic relations with Communist Cuba. For many years all official trade with that country has been stopped. Canada, on the other hand, has maintained relations and has increased its trade with Cuba. Perhaps the two positions were good ones for both governments to take. The example shows that the governments sometimes do not agree.

Now answer the following comprehension questions on the selection in Figure 4-16 *without* referring to the passage.

33. List the ways in which the United States and Canada are alike ____________
____

34. List the ways in which the two countries are different ____________
____
____

Now figure your reading rate, the number of words you read per minute. The selection contains 977 words. Divide the number of words (977) by the number of minutes (round seconds to the nearest fraction) to find your reading rate. Next figure your comprehension percentage score. Seven likenesses were discussed in the passage and five differences. Divide 12 into the number of correct likenesses and differences that you listed and multiply by 100 to determine your comprehension percentage score.

$$\text{Rate} = \frac{977 \text{ (words)}}{\text{(minutes)}} = \_\_\_\_ \text{ words per minute}$$

$$\text{Comprehension score} = \frac{\_\_\_\_ \text{ (number you listed)}}{12 \text{ (total likenesses and differences)}} \times 100 = \_\_\_\_\%.$$

How did you do? A high rate of, say, above 250 words per minute for this type of reading material is not necessarily good unless your comprehension score is also high. This type of content material ought not to be read too rapidly if the purpose for reading is study. On the other hand, if your purpose is only to preview the passage to see what information it contains, then rapid reading would be appropriate. What piece of information was missing when you were asked to read the passage in Figure 4-16? You need to know the purpose for reading the material in order to know what type of reading is appropriate.

Most content area reading assignments consist of study-type reading. The teacher should define the reading assignment still further by indicating whether students should read only for the main ideas or whether important details, such as the description of Canadian government, should also be remembered. Although the teacher helps define the reader's purpose, the student must also judge the difficulty of the assigned reading material in terms of his or her own background. If the student is familiar with the content due to background experiences or prior learning, he or she may read faster than when the concepts and information being presented are unfamiliar.

Some reading material, such as in science and math, cannot be read as rapidly as ordinary study material. When the material contains many facts or procedures that are to be remembered, then the student must decrease reading speed still further in order to comprehend what is important to be remembered. On the other hand, when the student reads for recreation, the rate may increase to perhaps 400-500 words per minute with comprehension of the main ideas.

We next discuss two specialized types of rapid reading because of their usefulness in content area study. These are skimming and scanning.

Skimming

When we are selecting information for our own studies, we frequently skim material. We read only the introductory and summary paragraphs, boldface print, and the headings. We glance at the visual material such as graphs, charts, or maps. We skip much of the text and read only what is highlighted. Since our purpose is only to preview the material for possible study later, at this point we do not read it with any care. If we had to explain what we had read, we could provide only a general overview of the material.

Skimming capitalizes on the reader's knowledge of paragraph structure in expository writing. Usually the main idea is embedded in the topic sentence, often found at the beginning of a paragraph. The reader seeks out key words, such as *first, next,* and *therefore,* in determining the structure of the paragraph. Not all paragraphs, of course, contain main ideas. Some provide descriptive information which may be skipped in the skimming process.

We may also skim a whole book to determine whether or not we want to read it, or parts of it, in-depth. We first look at the title page to see if the title indicates appropriateness of coverage. We check to see who the author is; perhaps we may be familiar with some of the authors who have written other materials on the subject of interest. Next we check the copyright date to see how recent the book is in terms of information on the subject. Then we skim the table of contents to see if the topics we are interested in are covered. Finally we may even skim a selected chapter or two, reading introductory and summary paragraphs, boldface print, and headings, to see if the book contains the information we anticipate.

In most study systems skimming is the first step toward giving the reader an overview of the nature of the material. It helps the reader formulate expectations about what will be covered in the material. These expectations may be expressed as guide questions which the reader formulates. The reader then engages in study-type reading to answer the questions that he or she has posed. The questions and answers form the basis of the student's notes which are to be reviewed and remembered.

Skimming, therefore, is important in helping students anticipate what will be covered. An active, not passive, orientation toward reading is essential. An active orientation adjusts reading rate to seek out information. The reader does not plod through all material at the same rate.

Look back at the passage in Figure 4-16. Although no headings are provided, you have other guides to use in skimming. Using Figure 4-16, answer the following questions.

35. What typographical aid is provided to assist the reader in skimming?__________
36. Instead of headings, the student can read the topic sentences, which contain the main ideas, to get an overview of the coverage of the material. Underline these in the passage.

Scanning

Another form of very rapid reading is called scanning. The purpose of scanning is to locate a particular item, such as a name in a telephone directory or a word in a dictionary. Scanning ought to be the most rapid form of reading since we are really not reading at all. If we find ourselves reading some sentences, then we are no longer scanning. Using the sample page from the *Readers' Guide* presented in Figure 3-7 time yourself to see how long it takes you to locate the following entries:

37. Maran, Stephen P. Time:______
38. Magicians Time:______
39. Marine pharmacology Time:______

Scanning, although frequently performed with listed material, may be used with prose writing. For example, the reader may want to know the date of a particular historical event; he or she scans the material to locate that fact. Or perhaps the reader needs to locate a particular chemical formula. The key word or phrase must be kept in mind with all other material ignored during scanning.

Using the passage in Figure 4-16, scan to answer the following questions. Record the time it took you to locate the answers to these questions.

40. What are the two major political parties in Canada?____________ Time:______
41. What is said about timber resources in Canada and the U.S.?______ Time:______

Your times for scanning should be only a few seconds for scanning list material, especially since it is in alphabetical order. You should be able to locate specific facts within the text provided in Figure 4-16 in less than 30 seconds.

Flexibility

It should be obvious by now that we can't talk about a person's reading rate. We have to talk about reading *rates*. Rapid reading by itself is not adequate. It must be accompanied by comprehension that is appropriate for the intended use for the material.

In order to be a flexible reader, we *consciously* must decide on an appropriate reading rate. We *constantly* must monitor our own comprehension. When we don't understand, we must adjust our reading speed accordingly.

In making the decision about the appropriate reading rate for any given reading assignment, show students how to ask themselves a series of questions in making a decision.

1. Why am I reading this material? What purpose has my teacher set? Am I to read only for main ideas, or am I also to note important details? If my teacher provided no guidance in reading this material, what type of use does she or he usually make of assigned reading? If I will be tested on the material, will main ideas be emphasized as on an essay test, or details as on a multiple choice exam? If I am to use this information in some sort of project, what type of informatiion do I need? Beyond the purposes of this course of what value is this material to me? Will I use or need this information when I am no longer in school?

2. How difficult is this material? Are long words and complex sentences used? How much do I already know about this subject? Am I familiar with the vocabulary and concepts that are used? What was the author's purpose in writing the material? Has his or her purpose affected the difficulty level of this material?

A quick review of these questions *before* reading helps a student decide on an appropriate rate for reading a given selection. The teacher can help students answer these questions, but ultimately students must learn to make conscious and active decisions themselves. Flexibility, then, is really the result of the decision-making process.

To check your ability to read flexibly, match reading rate to various reading tasks. Assume a moderate difficulty level of the material. Indicate the letter of your choice of reading rate.

Task	*Rate*
42. You are selecting nonfiction books for use in a research report.____	a. Scanning
43. You pick up a novel for recreational reading before bedtime.____	b. Skimming
44. You need to find out the dates of Alexander Graham Bell's life.____	c. Rapid reading
45. You are comparing several accounts of the same historical happening, evaluating different points of view.____	d. Study type reading
46. You are studying your science textbook which describes the procedures for conducting an experiment that you are going to do.____	e. Slow careful reading
47. Your teacher has told you to read for the main ideas in your social studies textbook.____	
48. You are reading a Shakespearean play for English class.____	
49. You are locating the definition of a word used in your chemistry textbook in the glossary.____	
50. You are writing a paper on a poem by Yeats.____	
51. You are preparing to read your biology textbook. Your first step is to preview the material to formulate questions for yourself to be answered in reading.____	
52. You are reading the directions for assembling a model airplane.____	

Illustrations

The following illustrations show how teachers may apply rate and flexibility skills in their content area instruction. In application the skills are integrated rather than taught separately.

Illustration 1

Mrs. Robinson, an upper elementary teacher, notices that her students are slow in locating words in the dictionary. Because her students need to use the dictionary efficiently, she reviews alphabetizing and guide words. But she notes that even once the students have located the correct page on which the word appears, they seem slow in finding the specific word. She teaches her students how to scan by having them form a mental picture of the word and then seeing how quickly they can locate it when it is embedded within other words on a worksheet. She also has them scan a page from a telephone directory to locate a given name, and scan a newspaper advertisement to find out the price of a given item. Sports fans locate the name of their favorite player on the newspaper sports page. The students also race to see who can find given words in a dictionary.

Illustration 2

Students in a junior high school honors English class complain that their teacher has assigned too many novels for them to read in studying the novel as a literary form. The teacher is surprised because the novels are written at a readability level that should be at the independent level for all his students. He decides to have them read in class so that he may observe their reading habits. He notices that some of the better readers are able to read the novel quickly as he had anticipated. However, some other students are plodding slowly through the book though their tested reading levels are far above that of the difficulty level of the novel. The problem appears to be that the students are reading at a rate that is appropriate for studying science, instead of adjusting their rate to the easy material. He shows those students who are reading too slowly how to increase their rate by deliberately letting their eyes fixate on a line of print no more than three times. Then he times them as they read several pages. He is careful to check their comprehension, however, to be sure that they are still understanding what they are reading. He suggests that the students time themselves as they continue their reading and try to read each chapter a little faster than the preceding one. He stresses that good readers are flexible readers.

Practice Exercise

Junior high school students in a combined social studies/English block are preparing to do independent research papers on topics of their choice related to the study of the U.S. and foreign governments. The teacher wants them to use nonfiction books as resource material in addition to an overview which they may get from an encyclopedia.

Rate and Flexibility Skill ____

____

Development Activity ____

____

Application Activity ____

____

Example Lesson

Skill Selected: Skimming

Development Activity: The teacher selects books that he knows from the school library. He demonstrates for the students how to skim to find out what may be the content of a given book. He distributes books to the students and instructs them to read only the table of contents, chapter introductions, and conclusions. He allows the students five minutes for skimming after which they must write down what they expect to learn from that book. Because the teacher is familiar with the books, he can check the accuracy of their previewing.

Application Activity: The students go to the school library to select nonfiction books for their research papers. They use skimming to determine if a given book is relevant to their topic.

TEACHING READING FOR INFORMATION IN THE CONTENT AREA

Teacher guidance is important in helping students learn to read for information in content area textbooks. The teacher especially needs to be aware of the differences in reading abilities among the students. If a textbook is written at the frustration level for a given group of students, the teacher must find more appropriate alternative reading material or adapt the textbook material in some way. Likewise, those students who are reading at an independent level wth regard to the textbook need to have their skills extended. They need to learn and apply more advanced reading and study skills. The students for whom the textbook is at an instructional level can read the text with teacher guidance, such as preteaching new vocabulary, concepts, establishing purposes for the students' reading, and asking follow-up comprehension questions. The first illustration focuses on accommodating these different reading levels in a reading assignment.

Illustrations

The skills in this part may be integrated and applied in the content areas. The following illustrations stress application of the skills.

Illustration 1

A junior high school science textbook presents the structure of the atom through a historical account of what scientists have believed to be the composition of matter. In other words, the description of the nature of the atom as it is known today is presented last, with historical views provided first. The teacher is primarily concerned that his students learn the modern construct of the atom and understand how theories evolve over a long period of time through scientific inquiry and experimentation. For his instructional and independent readers he prepares a grid in which the various scientists are listed across the top as shown on page 90.

The students who can read the textbook are to fill in the grid after they have read the assignment. Thus the grid serves as a study guide and helps the students in notetaking. In addition to the reading assignment, the independent readers, in a group project, are to draw the models of the atom as the various scientists have envisioned them throughout history.

Since a small group of students would be unable to understand the material if they read it because it is written at their frustration level, the teacher rewrites the last page of the assignment in which the modern concept of the atom is described. By substituting difficult and long vocabulary with simpler terms and shortening the long, complex sentences, he is able to make the material understandable. After reading this rewritten version, the poorer readers then study the pictures of the atom as drawn by the

	Democritus	Empedocles	Aristotle	Etc.
Description of theory				
Scientific proof?				
Strengths and weaknesses of theory				

independent readers. As the independent readers briefly explain the evolution of the theory of the atom to the frustration level readers, the teacher jots down what they say. When this is typed on ditto paper, the frustration level students then have a version of the text that has been rewritten by their peers. They are then able to fill in the grid using the rewritten version as dictated by the independent readers.

Illustration 2

In a high school American history class students seem to comprehend material when they are provided with a study guide, especially when the teacher introduces new vocabulary and concepts to the students *before* giving them the guide. When he has not provided a guide, however, the students have had difficulty focusing on the important aspects of the content, even though he introduced the new vocabulary and concepts beforehand as usual. The teacher decides that the students need help in learning a systematic independent study technique. He decides to teach them SQ3R(19) as one of several study techniques that have been thought to improve reading comprehension.

The first S stands for *survey,* skimming the material to get an overview. He shows his students how to read the introduction, main headings, boldface print, and study questions. He also suggests that they look at graphic material, such as maps and graphs, for the information they convey. To determine if his students have learned how to skim, on their next reading assignment he asks them to skim the material for no longer than three minutes. Then they are to close their books and jot down what they think the assigned reading concerns. The students compare answers, focusing on how they reached their conclusions.

Students then learn the rest of the steps in SQ3R. They learn to turn the headings in the selection into guide questions. They discover that the more general headings, such as *Declaration of Independence,* may lead to rather superficial questions, such as "What is the Declaration of Independence?" A more specific heading, such as *Signers of the Declaration of Independence,* can be converted into a more helpful question, such as "Who were the signers of the Declaration of Independence?" The skimming that preceded formulating questions is crucial because it helps the students identify what is important to learn in the material.

The three R's stand for *read, recite,* and *review.* The students, after having written down guide questions based on the headings, are now ready to answer the questions. But they read actively, not passively, in search of the answers to the questions posed. The students write down (or recite) the answers to the questions they have formulated. These questions and answers become the written notes the students use in reviewing the material in preparation for a test. In studying, the teacher encourages them to use their notes, which he routinely checks for accuracy, instead of rereading the material. The teacher points out that they have created their own study guide and that they cannot depend on the teacher's guidance when they are doing independent research.

Illustration 3

Sixth graders are learning to take different types of tests and to adjust their study and preparation to the different types of tasks. Their teacher directs them to read for main ideas only in assigned social studies reading materials. She checks their notes to be sure they have recorded only the main ideas and a few supporting details. She gives them short essay questions that focus on the main ideas.

In assigning science reading material, however, she advises them to read for details as well as for the main ideas. She again checks their notes for appropriate notations and tests their understanding of the material with a multiple-choice test. In making a math assignment she suggests that they read very carefully because they will need to apply the steps described in working a set of problems. If they are able to work the problems using the proper set of steps, she is satisfied that they have understood the assignment.

REFERENCES

1. Anderson, T. H., & Armbruster, B. B. "Reader and text—studying strategies." In *Reading expository material,* edited by W. Otto and S. White. New York: Academic Press, 1982.
2. Armbruster, B. B., & Anderson, T. H. *The effect of mapping on the free recall of expository text.* Technical Report No. 160. Urbana, Ill.: University of Illinois, Center for the Study of Reading, 1980.
3. Brown, A. L., & Smiley, S. *The development of strategies for studying prose passages.* Technical Report No. 66. Urbana, Ill.: University of Illinois, Center for the Study of Reading, 1977.
4. Butcofsky, D. "Any learning skills taught in high school?" *Journal of Reading,* 1971, *15,* 195-198.

5. Dunkeld, C. "Students' notetaking and teachers' expectations." *Journal of Reading,* 1978, *21,* 542-546.
6. Fitzgerald, S. "What are the effects of tests?" *Childhood Education,* 1980, *56,* 216-217.
7. Frankel, E. "Effects of growth, practice, and coaching on the scholastic aptitude test scores." *Personnel and Guidance Journal,* 1960, *38,* 713-719.
8. Gallagher, E. "Preparing for the SAT applications of a research project?" *Clearing House,* 1980, *53,* 230-232.
9. Gibson, E. J., & Levin, H. *The psychology of reading.* Cambridge, Mass.: The M.I.T. Press, 1975.
10. Hansell, T. "Stepping up to outlining." *Journal of Reading,* 1978, *22,* 248-252.
11. Hoffman, J. V. "The relationship between rate and reading flexibility." *Reading World,* 1978, *17,* 325-328.
12. Levy, S. "E. T. S. and the 'coaching' cover-up." *National Association of College Admissions,* 1979, *23,* 14-21.
13. Marrow, J. E. *Preparatory school test preparation: Special test preparation, its effects on college board scores and the relationship of affected scores to subsequent college performance.* Study No. 1-A1.02-63-001. West Point, New York: United States Military Academy, 1965.
14. Merritt, J., Prior, D., Grugeon, E., & Grugeon, D. *Developing independence in reading.* Milton Keynes: The Open University Press, 1977.
15. Pallone, N. J. "Effects of short- and long-term developmental reading courses upon SAT verbal scores." *Personnel and Guidance Journal,* 1961, *39,* 654-657.
16. Palmatier, R. A., & Bennett, J. M. "Notetaking habits of college students." *Journal of Reading,* 1974, *18,* 215-218.
17. Policastro, M. "Notetaking: The key to college success." *Journal of Reading,* 1975, *18,* 372-375.
18. Rankin, E. F. *The measurement of reading flexibility: Problems and perspectives. Reading information series: Where do we go from here?* Newark, Del.: International Reading Association, 1974.
19. Robinson, F. P. *Effective Study.* (Rev. ed.) New York: Harper and Row, 1961.
20. Roberts, S. O., & Oppenheim, D. B. *The effect of special instruction upon test performance of high school students in Tennessee.* Research and Development Report 66 7, No. 1. Princeton: Educational Testing Service, 1966.
21. Schultz, C. B., & Divesta, F. J. "Effects of passage organization and notetaking on the selection of clustering strategies and on recall of textual materials." *Journal of Educational Psychology,* 1972, *63,* 244-252.
22. Slack, W. V., & Porter, D. "The scholastic aptitude test: A critical appraisal." *Harvard Educational Review,* 1980, *50,* 154-175.

Graphic Skills: Graphs, Tables, Charts

5

One of our main reasons for including a discussion of graphic skills is that many readers are unfamiliar with the idea that specific skills are necessary in order to read and interpret graphic displays. Understanding these displays contributes significantly to effective reading, particularly in the content areas, where authors may use displays extensively to help present their facts and information in a clear and concise way.

The term *graphic display* refers to essentially any configuration that is not made up of conventional lines of print. The graphic skills themselves are specific tools for determining a wide range of information from a display—from identifying numerous isolated facts to gaining a perspective on the entire presentation. In both Parts 5 and 6 we describe the skills and displays in detail so that teachers will feel well-informed and, in turn, encourage their students to use these skills to read and understand displays they encounter in their daily reading.

The skills discussed in Part 5 pertain to graphic displays other than maps. Because they are highly specialized forms for presenting information and require a very different set of skills to interpret them, maps are discussed separately in Part 6.

OVERVIEW

A variety of graphic displays can be found in content area texts. Usually displays enhance the material they accompany in one of three ways. They may restate the information in a more concise way; show additional, related information; or simply illustrate one of the author's ideas.

Because the function of graphic displays is to condense information, frequently they are difficult to interpret, and, therefore, are overlooked by students who do not have experience in reading them and relating the information to the accompanying text material. To correctly interpret the displays, students must acquire certain graphic skills and then learn to use them independently. Applying the skills will enhance the students' comprehension because, typically, authors use visual displays to further explain and reinforce their ideas in their text.

We have identified a specific set of skills that are important to students' abilities to read graphic displays. In the Overview we review how these skills were identified and why they are important. We also explain the various types of displays and make some suggestions for carrying out skill instruction.

Historical Perspective

The ability to interpret graphic displays has not always been viewed as important as it is today. In the past, little interest existed among curriculum planners for developing a way to acquaint students with the multitude of graphic displays and related skills. Linke has noted that patterns of sequential instruction generally have been based on the intuitive reasoning of individual curriculum writers or teachers, rather than on research in the developmental learning capacities of children, or on the structure of the skills involved in graph construction and interpretation (2).

The heightened interest in the graphic materials today is related to the worldwide changes taking place in the greatly increased scientific and statistical communications. The role of graphic materials in these communications is great, and understanding them is becoming a priority in many school curricula.

Nature of Graphic Materials

As more emphasis is placed on teaching graphic materials, their complexity becomes more apparent. Weintraub (5) observes, "Graphs present concepts in a concise manner and give at a glance information which would require a great deal of descriptive writing. They distill a wealth of information into a small amount of space. It is because graphic materials can do this that they are often quite difficult to interpret. Their very strength thus creates a problem" (p. 345). Taking this complexity into account, educators have begun to question what is the best approach for learning to interpret these materials. Some researchers have advocated sequencing types of graphs (for example, picture, bar, circle, and line graphs) in terms of their relative difficulty. However, each type of graph can be presented in a more or less complex fashion. For this reason, other researchers have held that the central issue is not the sequencing of the types of graphs, themselves, but rather the sequencing of the skills involved in interpreting any particular graph (2,3,4).

Our position is that the skills are the basis for reading and understanding graphic materials, and that the attainment of them permits a student to correctly interpret a wide variety of displays.

Instruction in Graphic Materials

When skills have been incorporated into a curriculum as the basis for instruction in graphic materials, a teacher needs to be informed about the skills themselves and the best way to teach them. Teachers should be familiar with the variety of graphic displays and be able to determine the relevant skills for interpreting the different presentations. These important aspects to graphic skill instruction are discussed in the remainder of this overview section.

Graphic skills

The graphic skills we identified include comparing relative amounts, extracting directly and interpolating, determining differences, determining purpose and summarizing, making projections and relating information, and solving problems. Our decision to choose skills, as opposed to specific graphic displays, as a framework for instruction is based on indications from a field test study: Students who had attained the skills were generally able to interpret a variety of graphic displays; but those students who did generally well answering questions about one type of display, say a line graph, did not necessarily do well in answering questions about other graphic displays (4).

Although no particular sequential order for teaching the skills has been empirically defined, a logical progression does exist. In fact, for instructional purposes we have designated the first three skills—comparing relative amounts, and extracting directly and interpolating as the "preliminary" skills—which will be discussed below. The remaining skills—determining differences, determining purpose and summarizing, making projections and relating information, and solving problems—are more advanced and are explained in the Developmental perspective and activity sections following the Overview.

The skill designated as comparing relative amounts does not involve actual computation. A student merely compares two or more amounts and decides which one is greater, lesser, or the same. The skill is generally most useful in reading graphs and tables. It is an important beginning skill, because it familiarizes the student with the scope of the data, before he or she is required to note the exact amounts indicated by the corresponding labels on the vertical and horizontal axes. In Figure 5-1 the student compares relative amounts to answer the question.

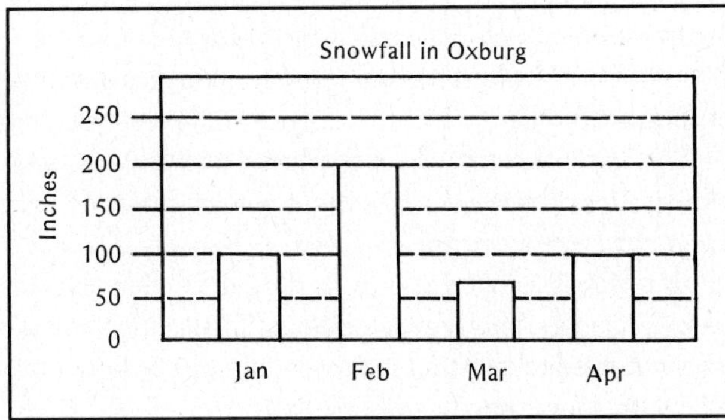

FIGURE 5-1
Which two months had about the same amount of snowfall?

The skill, extracting directly, involves having the student note on a graph the exact line to which a bar or dot is placed, and reading the corresponding stated amount. In a table the student can note the amount represented at the intersection of a row and column. Using Figure 5-1, the question, "How much snow fell in February?" illustrates the use of this skill. When a student becomes independent in using this skill, he or she is able to derive factual information that is stated explicitly on a graph or table.

The skill, interpolating, is similar to extracting directly, only the student derives facts that are represented on graphs by bars or dots *inbetween* specifically stated amounts. The student must usually use some judgment in order to derive correct information. Using Figure 5-1, again, the student interpolates to answer the question, How much snow fell in March? (*Ans.:* About 60".)

Interpolating may also be used to derive information from certain tables and charts, but this use of the skill is not as frequent. When the advanced graphic skills are examined later, the reader may want to review this discussion of the preliminary skills.

Graphic displays

The term, graphic display, refers to presentations of information that are arranged differently from than, say, conventional lines of print in a book. With this broad definition it is no wonder that displays take on a wide variety of shapes and forms. Authors can present their information virtually in any format they think is appealing and easy to read and understand. Perhaps only when drawing up lists of amounts, such as in graphs and tables, are authors encouraged by their publishers to use a standard format.

Along with having a variable format, graphic displays have a variety of names. Graphs, tables, charts, schedules, diagrams, and pictures are the usual terms, but frequently these terms may pertain to more than one type of display. For example, a presentation listing types of foods and corresponding nutritional values may be termed a chart by some people and a table by others. The important aspect of dealing with graphic materials, however, is not so much to decide on a good name for a display but to be able to read and understand it.

When teachers teach graphic materials, they must take into account their complexity and be able to identify the skills necessary to interpret them. All types of displays range from simple to complex. Picture graphs can represent a simple one-to-one correspondence or a many-to-one correspondence; line and bar graphs may show only one or several groups of data over a ten-year period; tables and charts may show only a few rows and columns or several rows and columns, and so on. When teachers select a graphic display for skill instruction, they should try to match the complexity of it to the students' experience in interpreting displays. That is, students with little experience should not be expected to interpret the most difficult displays until they have had substantial practice with some simpler presentations.

To identify the skills necessary for reading a graphic display, first teachers should examine the display(s), and then determine what procedures are necessary to derive the desired information from it. Not all skills are pertinent to all displays and types of information. For example, to study a table showing cost of living increases over a five-year period, the skill, Determining differences, may be most important if the teacher wishes to compare this year with last year. The skill, Projecting and relating information, in this case, would not be appropriate to teach.

The importance of having a context

Helping students see a reason for learning to interpret graphic displays is important if students are to eventually use the skills independently. One researcher, Linke, for example, has noted that although graph instruction is closely related to instruction in mathematics in the elementary grades and to science instruction in the secondary grades, the modes of instruction and skills involved have not been well integrated (2).

One approach to teaching skills in context is to teach them as the need arises as in a content text. In this situation the teacher points out how the graphic information relates to the accompanying text. For example, the students may determine whether facts are simply restated or additional information is also provided. Another approach to teaching the skills in context is to teach them in a sequence of lessons that focuses primarily on developing the skills. With this approach, practical materials from current homework assignments in one or more content areas should be included, as well as follow-up work pointing out the relevance of the skills. We offer more emphasis on the importance of teaching the skills in context in our discussions of the development activities.

The importance of constructing graphic materials

Another aspect to instruction in graphic materials is the importance of students constructing their own displays. The survey of literature by Otto, Kamm, and Weibel pertaining to the teaching of graphs emphasizes the need for the student to be involved in the actual construction of graphs in order to thoroughly understand them (3). More recent literature also supports this view (1, 2, 6), and both investigators and teachers who use this procedure in the classroom give it wide acclaim. Many of these teachers feel that gathering and organizing factual information helps students to more easily detect the organization of other materials already constructed.

Despite the apparent acceptance of this instructional strategy, however, construction of graphic materials is not widely included as a classroom activity. One investigator (6) notes, " . . .With few exceptions, students are rarely involved with collecting data and making decisions about scales or in more than superficial interpretation of information contained in a graph or chart" (p. 392).

We encourage those teachers who do not routinely incorporate graphic construction into their lessons to do so. It is one activity that teachers can count on to increase students' familiarity and understanding and general appreciation of graphic displays. And, the activities need not be complicated. Students—first as a group and then individually—can gather data in a single classroom, for example, that is sufficient for gaining the necessary experience in constructing graphic materials. Interpreting displays made by friends also offers a good opportunity for skill reinforcement.

Our discussion of the preliminary graphic skills, the types of displays, and important instructional aspects should help prepare the reader to examine the following Developmental perspective and activity sections for the advanced graphic skills. Teachers may want to review this discussion later, when they begin to organize their skill instruction materials.

DETERMINING DIFFERENCES

Developmental Perspective

The skill of determining differences on graphic materials involves the comparison of at least two different amounts that have been determined by using either or both of the preliminary skills, extracting directly and interpolating (see Overview). The amounts may be compared by adding, subtracting, multiplying, or dividing. This skill is important to have when interpreting graphs and tables in particular, because it allows a student to relate different parts of a graph or table to one another and to glean additional, specific information (as opposed to general information obtained by using the preliminary skill, comparing relative amounts [see Overview]) that is not explicitly stated in the display. Making such comparisons also helps a student examine data with some perspective, as opposed to simply looking at the information one piece at a time. A sample question that requires a student to determine differences on, say, a graph showing the number of pencils Mrs. Jones' students have is: Who has about one-half as many pencils as Tom? In the following section, Development Activities, practice in determining differences is offered.

Development Activities

Development activities for learning to determine differences are provided so that the reader can work through them to ensure his or her understanding of the skill and to identify some teaching ideas for use with students. Students should be introduced to these activities after they have had some introduction to the rudimentary graphic skills discussed in the Overview section.

Determining differences should be taught as the need arises in the content area materials. For example, if the students are not required to interpret any graphic materials, no need exists to teach this skill. If, however, graphs and/or tables are presented in conjunction with the text the students are studying, then this skill should be taught since it is important to the students' comprehension of the display(s).

Before beginning the activities, we urge the reader to recall the distinction made between skill development and application activities in our discussion of "Study Skills Instruction" in Part 1. Keeping the differences between the types of activities in mind helps lend perspective to each activity. We also urge readers to review the Remarks section following the questions for each skill. They point out why the items are appropriate for development instruction. The remarks are particularly helpful to teachers who adapt their own materials to teach the skills, because they serve as reminders of the kinds of questions to include.

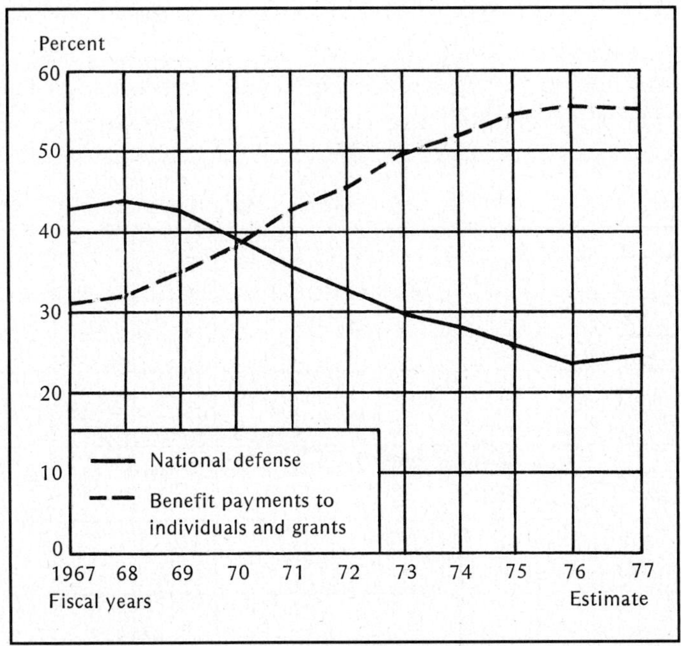

FIGURE 5-2 Changing priorities since 1967
(From the U.S. Budget in Brief Fiscal Year 1977, Office of Management and Budget, *p. 2.)*

1. (a) (See Figure 5-2) In what year was 20% more spent for benefit payments than for national defense?____________________ *Determining differences*

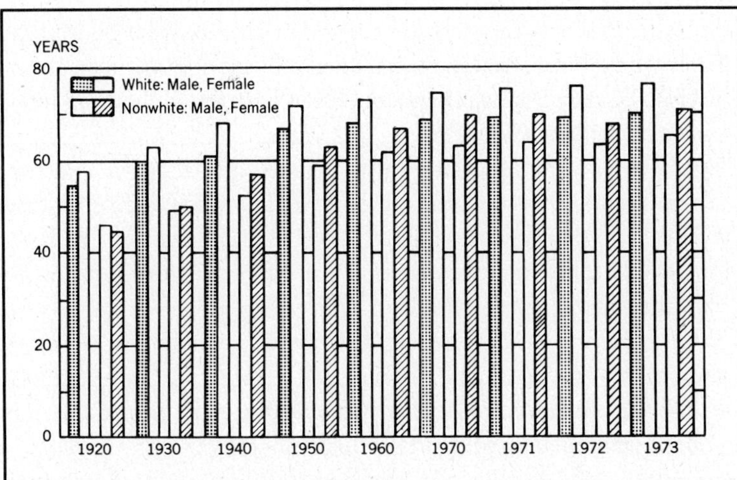

FIGURE 5-3 Expectation of life at birth: 1929–1973
(From U.S. Bureau of the Census, Statistical Abstract of the United States: 1975. *Washington, D.C.: U.S. Government Printing Office, 1975, Table 82, p. 59.)*

(b) (See Figure 5.2) In what year(s) shown was there over two times as much spent for national benefit payments as for national defense payments? ____

____

2. (See Figure 5-3)
   (a) In what year were there about ten more years of life expectancy for male nonwhites than in 1940? ____
   (b) About how many years of life expectancy were added to female whites between 1920 and 1973? ____

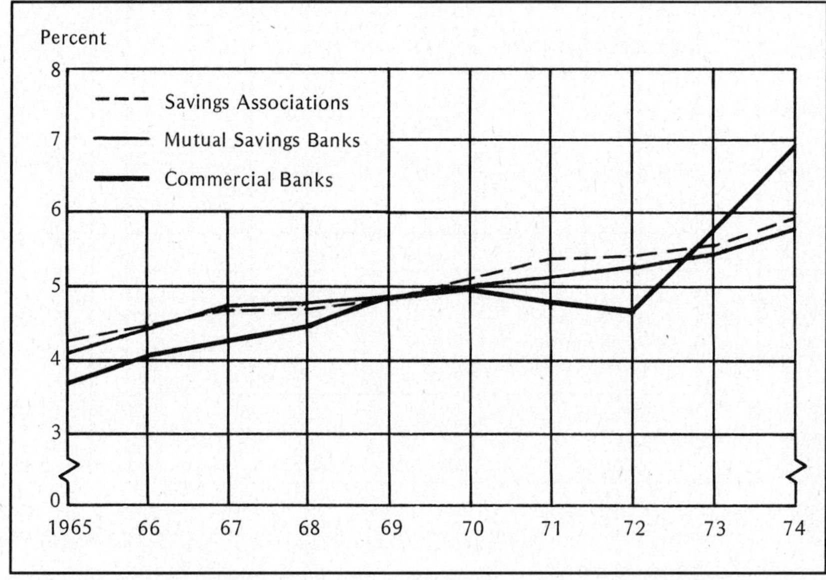

FIGURE 5-4 Rates of return paid on time deposits and savings *(From* Savings and Loan Fact Book, 1975, *Chicago: United States League of Savings Association, p. 22.)*

3. (See Figure 5-4)
   (a) In 1966 what was the difference in percent being paid by Mutual Savings Banks and Commercial Banks on time deposits and savings? ____
   (b) In 1974 Savings Associations paid about how much more on time deposits and savings than in 1965? ____
4. (See Figure 5-5)
   (a) In what age group is the death rate for heart/vessels about 100 times what it is for the 15-24 age group? ____
   (b) For 30-year-olds how does the death rate compare for cancer and diabetes?
5. (See Figure 5-6)
   (a) About how many more persons held the Supplementary Group policies in 1967 than in 1961? ____
   (b) In 1968 the Insurance Company total represented about four times more persons with major medical than which other policy? ____

Age groups	1-4	5-14	15-24	25-44	45-64	Over 64
Heart/vessels	1	2	5	50	504	3812
Cancer/Leukemia	7	6	8	39	285	926
Motor vehicle accidents	12	10	51	29	27	38
Not motor vehicle accidents	20	10	21	22	32	106
Flu/Pneumonia	8	2	3	7	27	226
Diabetes	*	*	*	4	22	136
Suicide	*	*	8	15	20	*
Homicide	2	1	11	15	8	*
Cirrhosis of the liver	*	*	*	12	11	36
Emphysema/Bronchitis	1	*	*	*	*	106
Birth defects	10	3	2	*	*	*

*Cause not one of top 10 for age group.

FIGURE 5-5 Deaths per 1,000,000 people in 1969 *(From DHEW data. Cited in W. Thurber, R. Kilburn, and P. Howell,* Exploring Life Sciences. *Boston: Allyn and Bacon, 1975, p. 197. Used by permission.)*

End of year	Insurance company total	Group policies			Individual and family policies
		Net total	Supplementary	Comprehensive	
1951	108	96	96	—	12
1955	5,241	4,759	3,928	831	482
1960	25,371	24,429	17,991	8,463	1,607
1961	32,334	30,729	24,488	9,851	2,372
1962	37,130	35,002	28,445	10,636	2,949
1963	42,003	39,446	32,307	11,699	3,459
1964	47,338	44,087	36,925	12,241	4,185
1965	53,020	49,700	42,450	12,962	4,456
1966	57,881	54,732	46,830	14,154	4,516
1967	63,428	60,517	51,824	15,570	4,552
1968	68,171	65,076	55,422	17,014	4,873
1969	73,752	70,272	58,905	19,260	5,377
1970	77,061	73,702	61,718	20,244	5,414
1971	80,252	76,971	63,442	22,111	5,479
1972	83,668	79,025	64,443	23,363	6,630
1973:					
Under 65	86,223	81,256	65,005	25,279	7,098
65 and over	1,616	1,468	1,220	411	212
Total	87,839	82,724	66,225	25,690	7,310

(continued)

FIGURE 5-6 Number of persons with major medical (000 omitted) *(From* Source Book of Health Insurance Data, 1975–1976. *New York: Health Insurance Institute, p. 27.)*

FIGURE 5-6
continued

End of year	*Insurance company total*	*Group policies*			*Individual and family policies*
		Net total	*Supplementary*	*Comprehensive*	
1974:					
Under 65	89,555	84,642	66,856	27,191	7,018
65 and over	1,766	1,614	1,266	527	217
Total	91,321	86,256	68,122	27,718	7,235

FIGURE 5-7
Motor vehicle registrations in United States (in millions)
(From W. Thurber, R. Kilburn, and P. Howell, Exploring Earth Sciences. *Boston: Allyn and Bacon, 1977, p. 329. Used by permission.)*

Type of vehicle	*1950*	*1955*	*1960*	*1965*	*1970*	*1975 (est)*
Cars, taxis	40.3	52.1	61.7	75.2	84.4	92.8
Trucks, buses	8.8	10.5	12.7	15.1	18.1	21.7
Motorcycles	0.4	0.4	0.6	1.4	2.5	4.5

6. (See Figure 5-7)
   (a) How many more car registrations were there in 1970 than in 1950?________
   (b) In 1965 how did the registration for cars and trucks compare?____________

Remarks on determining differences items

- To answer the questions students must have a knowledge of such beginning graph skills as comparing relative amounts, extracting directly, and interpolating from a simple bar and line graph.
- Graphs and tables are the main types of displays to which Determining differences is applicable. A variety of graphs and tables is used.
- The questions, together, ask about different parts of each graphic display.
- The questions ask about both subtractive and multiplicative differences. (Additive differences are not as commonly determined.)

DETERMINING PURPOSE AND SUMMARIZING
Developmental Perspective

The skills of determining a purpose of a graphic display and summarizing—or making a concluding statement about—the information may trouble students primarily because students simply have not formed the habit of using these skills. When confronted with a graphic display that is related to the text she or he is reading, a student should determine the purpose of the display first, and then later, after interpreting certain information from it, take the time to summarize the facts or main features so that he or she has a clear idea about what the display represented.

To determine the purpose, a student should note not only the title but each of the labels on the bottom and sides of the display. For example, in a table showing the number of cars produced by several companies over several years, the student should carefully note what the numbers in the various rows and columns stand for. That is, does an entry of "2" indicate that 2, 200, 2,000 or 2,000,000 cars were produced? Such important subheadings as "Millions of cars" can easily be overlooked in studying a table or graph, and yet be critical to a student's determining the purpose of the presentation.

To summarize graphic information a student should first note either all the entries (on a graph, table, chart, or schedule) or the entire scope of information (in a diagram or picture). Then he or she should try to identify a trend or main characteristic and relate it to the information in the accompanying text. For example, a trend on a bar graph may signify that production in about half the companies listed decreased, while it increased or stayed the same in the other companies; or, a main characteristic of a diagram may indicate that the nitrogen cycle is based on numerous and complex relationships.

Development Activities

The reader should proceed with the development activities for determining the purpose and summarizing just as he or she did with the activities for determining differences. We recommend working through the activities to ensure understanding of the skill and to identify some teaching ideas for use with students. Students should be introduced to these activities after they have had some introduction to the rudimentary graphic skills discussed in the Overview section.

Determining the purpose and summarizing should be taught as the need arises in the content area materials. For example, if the students are not required to interpret any graphic material, no need exists to teach the skill. If, however, graphs and/or tables are presented in conjunction with text the students are studying, then this skill should be taught since it is important to the students' comprehension of the display(s).

Amt. smoked	Deaths/year/100,000 men
Never	13
½ pck/day	95
½–1 pck/day	108
1–2 pck/day	229
2 pck/day	264

FIGURE 5-8 Death rates from lung cancer *(From W. Thurber, R. Kilburn, and P. Howell,* Exploring Life Science. *Boston: Allyn and Bacon, 1975, p. 185. Used by permission.)*

Determining purpose and summarizing

7. (See Figure 5-8) What is the purpose of this graph? ________________________

____

FIGURE 5-9 Combining risk factors (in any order) *(From W. Thurber, R. Kilburn, and P. Howell,* Exploring Life Science. *Boston: Allyn and Bacon, 1975, p. 201. Used by permission.)*

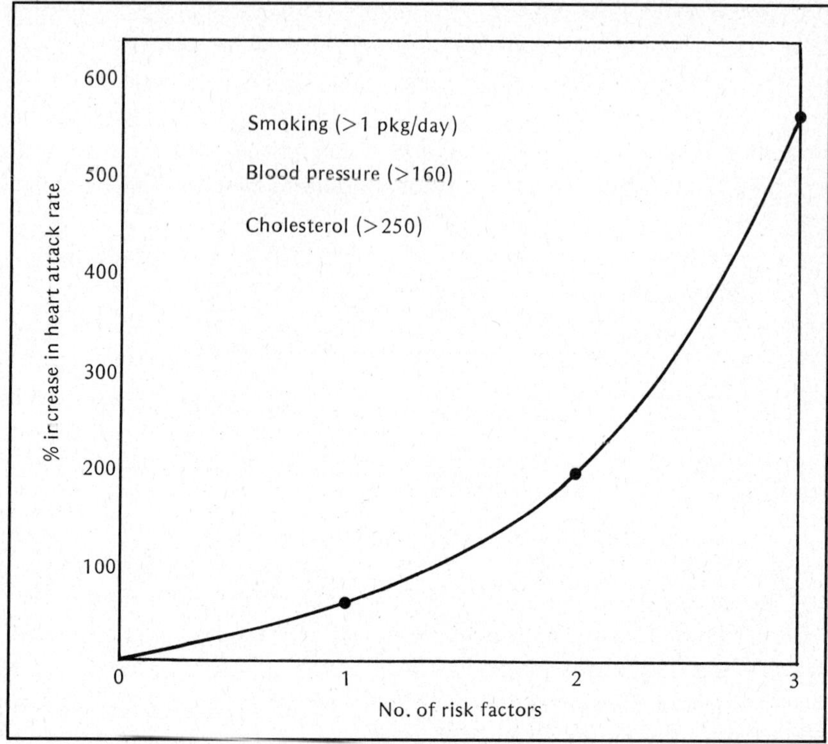

8. (See Figure 5-9) What is one conclusion that can be drawn from this graph?____

9. (See Figure 5—10) What is one conclusion that can be drawn from this table?____

10. (See Figure 5-11) What is the purpose of this timeline?____

FIGURE 5-10 Effect of smoking on chances for a long life (30-year-old men) *(From W. Thurber, R. Kilburn, and P. Howell,* Exploring Life Science. *Boston: Allyn and Bacon, 1975, p. 185. Used by permission.)*

Age	*Non-smoker*	*Moderate smoker*	*Heavy smoker*
40	92%	91%	81%
50	81%	72%	63%
60	67%	62%	46%
70	46%	41%	30%
80	22%	20%	14%

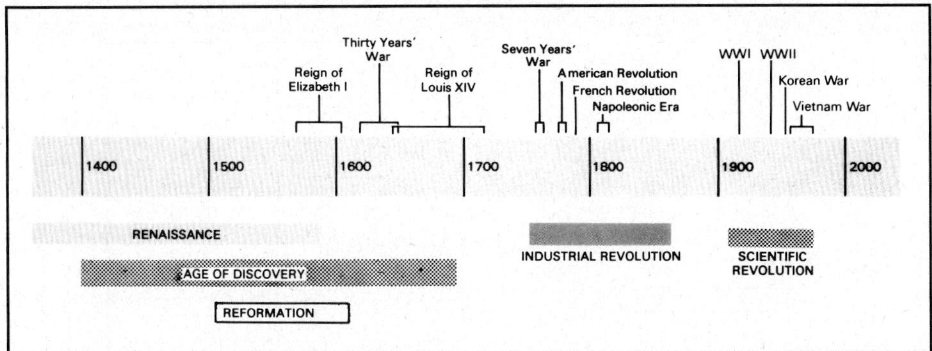

FIGURE 5-11 Modern history —1500–present *(From G. Leinwand,* Pageant of World History. *Boston: Allyn and Bacon, 1975, p. 450. Used with permission.)*

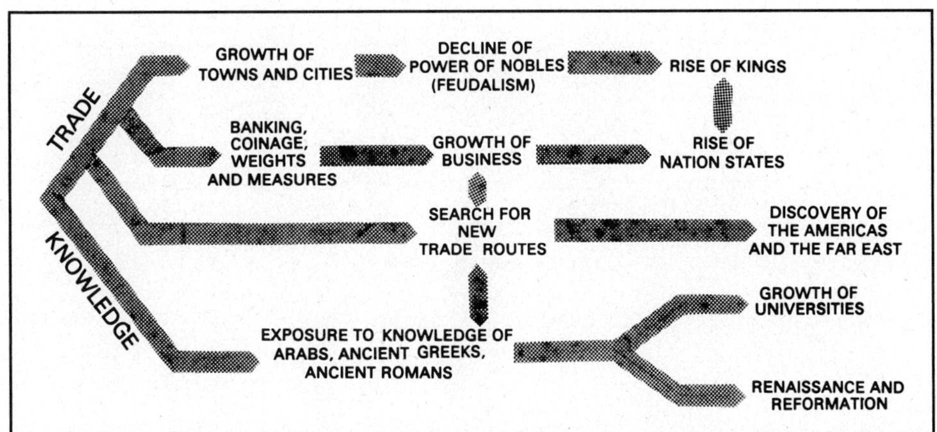

FIGURE 5-12 Results of the crusades *(From G. Leinwand,* Pageant of World History. *Boston: Allyn and Bacon, 1975, p. 140. Used by permission.)*

11. (See Figure 5-12) What is one conclusion that can be drawn from this diagram? ______________________________

12. (See Figure 5-13) What is the purpose of this diagram? ______________________________

13. (See Figure 5-14) What is the purpose of this picture in conjunction with the text? ______________________________

14. (See Figure 5-15) What is the purpose of the cartoon in conjunction with the text? ______________________________

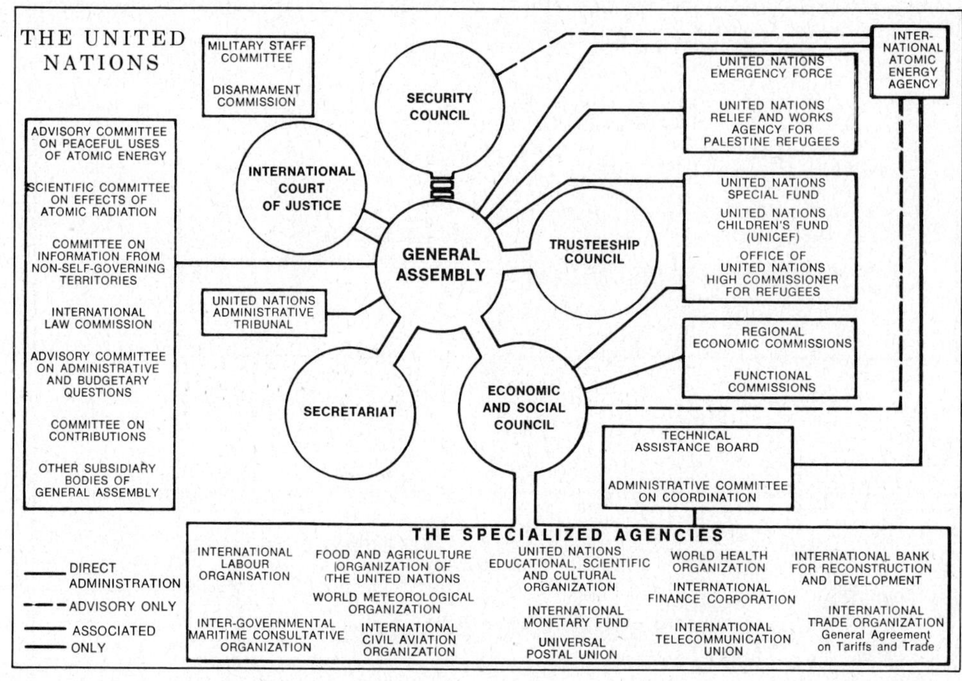

FIGURE 5-13
The United Nations
(From G. Leinwand, Pageant of World History. *Boston: Allyn and Bacon, 1975, p. 247. Used by permission.)*

Jazz from New Orleans made its way North. New dances brought "the bodies of men and women in unusual relations to each other," as a bishop complained. The American woman and the American girls sought and won freedom. This was true politically as it was socially and sexually. The "flapper age," as it was called, was dominated by mini-skirted women. They wanted to be skinny and to appear flat-chested. In 1919 the skirt was six inches above the ground. By 1927 it had reached the knees. Painted in "kiss-proof" lipstick and wearing unbuckled galoshes, the flapper tried to look feminine, masculine, and casual—all at the same time.

FIGURE 5-14
A "flapper girl" of the early 1920s
(Excerpt from G. Leinwand, Pageant of American History. *Boston: Allyn and Bacon, 1975, p. 475. Used by permission.)*

WELL—?

President Truman, who had become President on Roosevelt's death, ordered the use of the atomic bomb. When he took office the defeat of Japan seemed close. His military advisers, however, informed him that the final defeat of Japan would require an invasion of Japan. They estimated that an invasion would result in the loss of a staggering number of American lives. President Truman felt that dropping the atomic bomb on Japan would hasten the end of the war in the Pacific. On August 6, 1945, the first atomic bomb used in warfare was dropped on Hiroshima. Three days later a second bomb was dropped on Nagasaki. These were proof enough that Japan could not possibly win. With the army and its leaders in disgrace, Japan prepared to give up the fight. In Tokyo Bay on September 2, 1945, the Japanese surrendered to General MacArthur aboard the battleship Missouri. World War II was over.

FIGURE 5-15 Picture of atomic bomb
(Excerpt from G. Leinwand, Pageant of American History. *Boston: Allyn and Bacon, 1975, pp. 543–544. Used by permission.)*

Type	*Typical stars*	*Temp.*	*Color*	*Spectrum*
O	Zeta Puppis	33,000°C	Blue-white	Helium lines
B	Rigel, Spica	22,000°C	Blue-white	Helium lines
A	Sirius, Vega	11,000°C	White	Hydrogen lines; metals appear
F	Canopus, Procyon	7700°C	Yellowish-white	Metals stronger
G	Sun, Capella	6100°C	Yellow	Many metallic lines
K	Aldebaran, Arcturus	4400°C	Orange	Calcium lines very strong

(continued)

FIGURE 5-16 Stars
(From W. Thurber, R. Kilburn, and P. Howell, Exploring Physical Sciences. *Boston: Allyn and Bacon, 1977, p. 77. Used by permission.)*

FIGURE 5-16
continued

Type	*Typical stars*	*Temp.*	*Color*	*Spectrum*
M	Betelgeuse, Antares	2200°C to 3300°C	Red	Titanium oxide
R	U Cygni			Carbon compounds
N	Y Canum Venaticorum			Carbon compounds
S	R Andromadae			Zirconium oxide

FIGURE 5-17
Was Nixon's victory reflected in the number of seats his party won in Congress?
(From W. Thurber, R. Kilburn, and P. Howell, Exploring Physical Sciences. *Boston: Allyn and Bacon, 1977, p. 656. Used by permission.)*

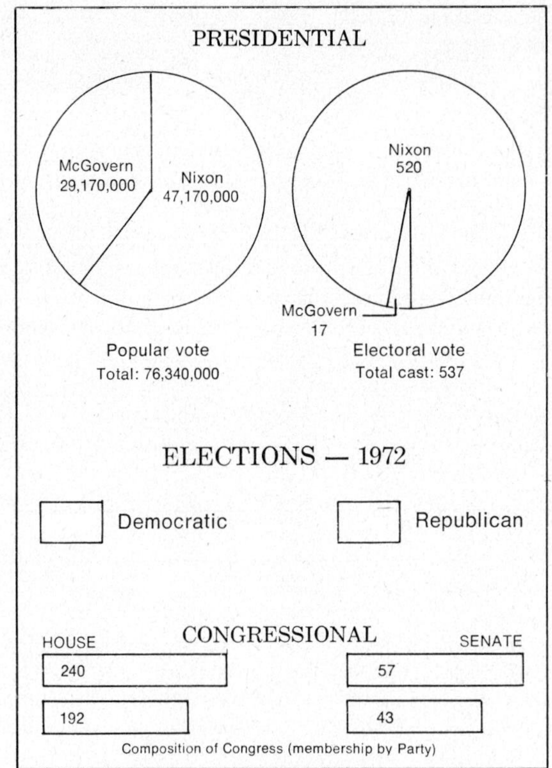

15. (See Figure 5-16) What is one conclusion that can be drawn from this chart?____

16. (See Figure 5-17) What is one conclusion that can be drawn from these two circle graphs?____

Remarks on determining purpose and summarizing items

- Both purpose and summary questions are included.
- A variety of graphic materials—which are of different types and from several subject areas—are used.

MAKING PROJECTIONS AND RELATING INFORMATION

Developmental Perspective

Making a projection based on information in a graph or table is similar to making a conclusion about the information, but the student must go beyond "drawing the facts together," and make a statement about facts that are not included in the display. To do so, the student must carefully note all of the trends suggested in the data. For example, on a graph showing the number of bushels of corn harvested per acre for several farms over a ten-year period, a student may project that one farmer will get an even greater yield in the eleventh year, since his ten-year record has shown a steady increase. For another farmer, the reverse may be true; and for another, perhaps an increase could be predicted, based on the fact that every other year the crop yield was up.

This skill is particularly useful when the teacher wants students to compare past and present events and to give some interpretations to them instead of viewing them as unrelated incidents. Many such comparisons are made when, for example, students study economic conditions, climate variations, or even political situations.

Relating information from a display to background knowledge is very closely tied with making projections since calling on such knowledge is often helpful in actually making the prediction. And, too, once a prediction is made, the implications should be considered. Typically, in a graph showing the rainfall for a certain area over several years, based on the data, a student may make a prediction that the rainfall will be slightly less the next year. If the student also knows from background information, however, that the procedure of seeding clouds in that area has been fairly unsuccessful, then he or she may have more confidence in the prediction. To consider the implications, the student would again relate the information to his or her experience and conclude, for example, that local crop growth would be affected, and, subsequently, market prices may change.

When students are practicing this skill they perhaps may find it interesting to look at certain events within a specific period of time that ends five or ten years before the current year, make their predictions and relate the information, and then check a current events source (an almanac) to see what has actually happened (or is happening). When students are first exposed to this skill, however, teachers may find hypothetical instructional materials very helpful, since the data can be construed to provide easily detectable trends about familiar topics. The initial success can give students a sense of accomplishment with the skill before they tackle real data, which is often more difficult to interpret.

Development Activities

The reader should proceed with the development activities for making projections and relating information just as he or she did with the activities for both determining differences and determining the purpose and summarizing. Remember! While "real" graphs are often more interesting to study and use as examples, frequently, hypothetical graphs are more useful in initially teaching the skill. The information in them can be manipulated to emphasize many different aspects of using the skill.

FIGURE 5-18 Population of Lake Erie
(From W. Thurber, R. Kilburn, and P. Howell, Exploring Life Science. *Boston: Allyn and Bacon, 1975, p. 406. Used by permission.)*

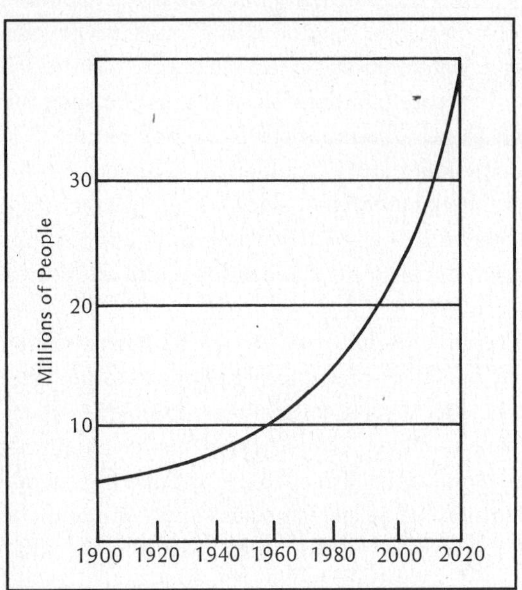

Projecting and relating information

17. (See Figure 5-18)
    (a) In 1880 the population of Lake Erie basin was probably
        a. close to zero.
        b. less than 10 million people.
        c. about 20 million people.
        d. over 30 million people.
    (b) If the projection on this graph proves correct, what will be happening to the basin about the turn of the century?______________________

    ____

18. (See Figure 5-19)
    (a) What was most likely the crime rate per 100,000 persons in 1973?
        a. About 1,000
        b. About 2,000
        c. Between 2,500 and 3,000
        d. Over 3,000

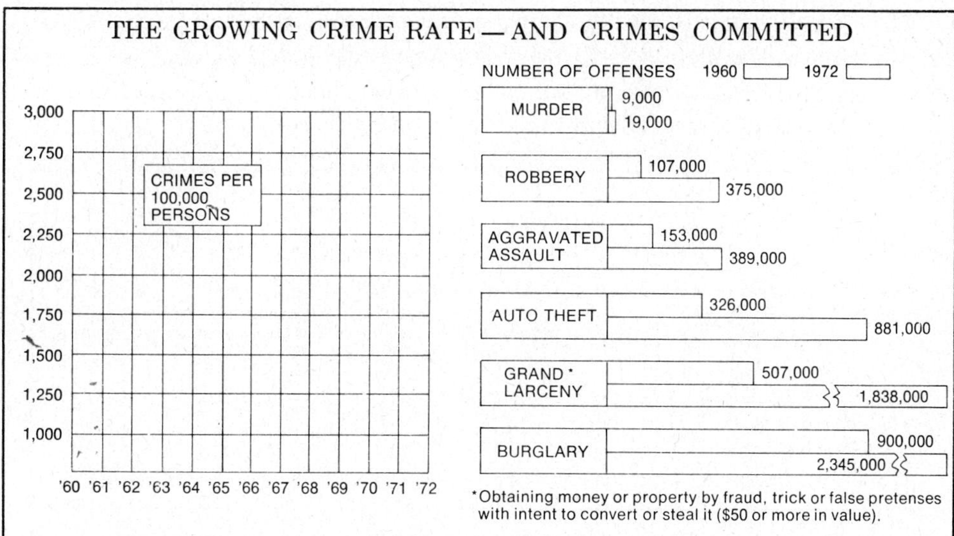

FIGURE 5-19 The growing crime rate—and crimes committed *(From G. Leinwand,* Pageant of American History. *Boston: Allyn and Bacon, 1975, p. 675. Used by permission.)*

(b) What is (are) some probable reasons for several neighborhood vigilante groups forming for the first time in one city in 1970?
   a. The crime rate was higher than it had ever been.
   b. The crime rate was high, but on its way down and the groups would help it decrease faster.
   c. The crime rate was about the same as in other years, but the people were better educated in how to handle it.
   d. Few of the "fight-crime" programs were considered effective.

	Cars per hour				
Streets	*1940*	*1950*	*1960*	*1970*	*1980*
Cedar	500	350	200	125	70
Maple	900	1100	1200	1000	800
Oak	25	100	350	680	1000
Pine	400	350	380	500	470
Willow	1000	1050	1100	1200	1300

FIGURE 5-20 Traffic patterns in Cedarburg over a 40-year period

19. (See Figure 5-20)
   (a) Based on the information in this table, what will the traffic probably be like on Pine Street in 1990? ________________________

(b) Based on the information in this table, which street has most likely changed from a side street in 1940 to a thoroughfare in 1980?__________

(c) Which street has become less often used than previously?__________

(d) Which street has probably been the busiest for the last 40 years?__________

FIGURE 5-21 How much are you worth *(From The Prudential Life Insurance Co. Cited in H. Wolf, Managing Your Money. Boston: Allyn and Bacon, 1977, p. 266. Used by permission.)*

Amount you will earn between now and 65 if your average income per month is

Age at present	*$300*	*$400*	*$600*	*$800*	*$1,000*	*$1,500*
20	$162,000	$216,000	$324,000	$432,000	$540,000	$810,000
25	144,000	192,000	288,000	387,000	480,000	720,000
30	126,000	168,000	252,000	336,000	420,000	630,000
35	108,000	144,000	216,000	288,000	360,000	540,000
40	90,000	120,000	180,000	240,000	300,000	450,000
45	72,000	96,000	144,000	192,000	240,000	360,000

20. (See Figure 5-21)
Based on this table, if you were a teenager and earning $500 per month, about how much would you earn between now and age 65?
(a) Under $200,000
(b) A little over $200,000
(c) About $300,000
(d) Probably over $350,000

Remarks on making projections and relating information items

- Both projecting and relating questions are included.
- Different types of graphic materials from different subject areas are included.
- Where open-ended questions might be confusing, choices are provided to give the reader a range from which to choose a suitable answer. (Choices with numbers are listed in numerical order.)
- A hypothetical table is used as a basis for several questions, so the student does not have to examine a new graphic display for every question.

SOLVING PROBLEMS

Developmental Perspective

Using graphic materials to solve problems is a skill perhaps most closely associated with reading schedules and various tables. It is a very practical skill and experience in using it can be rewarding when a student is planning to, say, travel according to a train schedule; work out a particular diet and/or menu according to a table of food groups and nutritional values; or, to make a sizeable purchase, based on a table or chart with a multitude of facts about alternative products.

Mainly the skill involves examining a display to determine the scope of the information presented, and then selecting various parts of that information to solve a problem or satisfy an inquiry. While this skill may sound similar to Determining differences, it is usually more complex, because many more than two entries need to be consulted and compared, and often the entries are not parallel, for example, as on an airplane schedule where departure times and flight numbers are given next to each other, they do not all convey the same information.

One use of this skill is to consider how two people, living in two different cities, would plan to travel by train to meet each other in a third city. To read and understand their schedules, a variety of factors should be taken into account: leaving/arriving/a.m./p.m. times, the different trains with different routes, the different daily and weekend times, the different stations for different trains, the different fares for different times and ages and dates of purchase, and the different accommodations available.

The main point to consider in teaching the problem-solving skill with graphic materials is that the students' ability to interpret various displays will increase as they gain experience in working with different formats. With practice in the skill, students will become better at manipulating the data to find solutions and, in turn, become more independent in acquiring information.

Development Activities

The development activities for solving problems are presented for use after students have had some introduction to the rudimentary graphic skills discussed in the Overview section. While the displays presented here represent but a select few, students' exposure to them can be helpful in making other schedules seem less formidable. Once these types of charts and tables are familiar, students are more likely to consult and use them on their own.

Solving problems

21. (See Figure 5-22)
    (a) If you left the Dearborn station in Chicago, going eastbound, on the Mohawk 164, when would you arrive in Pontiac?________________
    (b) How long would the above trip take if the train was on schedule?________
    (c) If you left Detroit going eastbound on the Maple Leaf 158 and got off the train five hours later, where would you be?________________
    (d) If you wanted to travel from Battle Creek to Chicago early in the morning, which train would you take?________________
    (e) John and Peter plan to meet in Durand. John is from London and will take the Maple Leaf 159 on Wednesday. What train should Peter take from South Bend so that he will arrive within a short time of when John does?____
    (f) (See question e.) Who will arrive first and how long will he have to wait for the other boy?________________

FIGURE 5-22
Train schedule
(Courtesy Grand Trunk Western/Canadian National Railways.)

READ DOWN EASTBOUND — **CHICAGO—DETROIT—PORT HURON—TORONTO** — READ UP WESTWARD

International 156	Mohawk 164	Maple-Leaf 158	Miles	TABLE 1	International 155	Maple-Leaf 159	Mohawk 165
Daily	Daily	Daily		**Central Standard Time**	Daily	Daily	Daily
PM	PM	AM			AM	PM	PM
8.40	**4.30**	10.10	0.0	Lv **Chicago, Ill.** (Dearborn Station) Ar	8.35	**6.15**	**9.10**
9.05		10.32	10.3	Lv Chicago Lawn (63rd St. & Central Park Ave.) Lv	8.10	**5.50**	
10.00		11.22	56.8	Lv Valparaiso, Ind. Lv	7.17	**4.58**	
10.45	**6.11**	**12.01**	100.2	Ar **South Bend** Lv	6.29	**4.10**	**7.15**
10.49	**6.14**	**12.07**	100.2	Lv **South Bend** Ar	6.24	**4.05**	**7.11**
				Eastern Standard Time			
		f 1.34	122.9	Lv Cassopolis, Mich. Lv		**4.42**	
		f 1.45	135.8	Lv Marcellus Lv		**4.28**	
		2.02	152.2	Lv Vicksburg Lv		**4.10**	
1.10	**8.23**	**2.30**	176.6	Ar **Battle Creek** Lv	6.10	**3.47**	**7.04**
1.20	**8.26**	**2.40**	176.6	Lv **Battle Creek** Ar	6.00	**3.37**	**7.01**
		3.04	202.4	Lv Charlotte Lv		**3.10**	
2.03	**9.12**	**3.35**	220.9	Ar **Lansing** Lv	5.14	**2.50**	**6.20**
2.15	**9.14**	**3.45**	220.9	Lv **Lansing** Ar	5.04	**2.45**	**6.18**
	9.45	**4.16**	253.3	Ar **Durand** Lv		**2.15**	**5.50**
	9.48	**4.30**	253.3	Lv **Durand** Ar		**2.00**	**5.48**
		f 4.49	269.5	Lv Fenton Lv		**1.39**	
		f 4.54	273.7	Lv Holly Lv		**1.34**	
	10.25	**5.15**	293.9	Ar **Pontiac** Lv		**1.15**	**5.08**
	10.27	**5.16**	293.9	Lv **Pontiac** Ar		**1.13**	**5.06**
	10.38	**5.29**	302.4	Lv Birmingham Lv		**1.01**	**4.55**
	10.42	**5.35**	307.0	Lv Royal Oak Lv		**12.55**	**4.51**
		d 5.42	313.6	Lv Highland Park Lv		**f 12.45**	
		5.46	316.1	Lv Milwaukee Junction Lv		**12.40**	
	11.10	**5.55**	320.5	Ar **Detroit** (Brush St. Sta.) Lv		**12.30**	**4.30**
		4.20	253.3	Lv **Durand** Ar		**2.12**	
3.03		**4.36**	270.4	Ar **Flint** Lv	4.20	**1.53**	
3.15		**4.47**	270.4	Lv **Flint** Ar	4.10	**1.51**	
		5.08	290.0	Lv Lapeer Lv		**1.30**	
		f 5.20	302.0	Lv Imlay City Lv		**1.16**	
4.25		**6.00**	333.9	Ar **Port Huron** Lv	3.15	**12.45**	
4.50		**6.25**	333.9	Lv **Port Huron** Ar	2.55	**12.27**	
5.02		**6.37**		Ar **Sarnia** Lv	2.43	**12.15**	
5.10		**6.50**		Lv **Sarnia** Ar	2.30	**12.07**	
6.05		**7.45**	405.7	Ar **London** Lv	1.35	11.05	
6.15		**7.55**	405.7	Lv **London** Ar	1.30	11.00	
		8.45	448.5	Ar Stratford Lv		10.15	
7.37		**A 9.32**	**469.2**	Ar **Dundas** Lv			
B		**C**	**476.3**	Ar **Hamilton** Lv	**E 11.15**		
7.52		**A 9.48**	**483.6**	Ar **Burlington** Lv	**11.56**		
8.30		**10.55**	515.6	Ar **Toronto** (Union Station) Lv	**11.20**	8.00	

(g) (See question e.) Which boy traveled the farthest? How much farther?______

22. (See Figure 5-23)
   (a) If you want to leave Los Angeles in the early afternoon for Denver, how many flights do you have to choose from?______
   (b) If you leave New Orleans at 3:20 p.m., what time will you arrive in Denver?______ Is the flight nonstop?______ Will a meal have been provided?______
   (c) Sue is flying from Albuquerque to El Paso. Her friend, Joan, plans to take a nonstop flight from Chicago and arrive there at the same time. What time will each girl have to depart?______

FIGURE 5-23
Plane schedule
(Courtesy Continental Airlines)

To Denver cont. from previous page	Leave	Leave Airport Code	Arrive	Arrive Airport Code	Originating Flight	Connect at	Connecting Flight	Stops	Meals	Frequency	Remarks
FROM LOS ANGELES, CALIF.	12 45 a	LAX	3 38 a	DEN	712			0			
	8 00 a	LAX	11 00 a	DEN	18			0	Brkfst		
	9 00 a	ONT	11 49 a	DEN	86			0	Snack		
	11 25 a	LAX	2 23 p	DEN	26			0	Lunch		
	2 00 p	LAX	5 00 p	DEN	10			0	Snack		
	5 00 p	LAX	7 57 p	DEN	16			0	Dinner		
	7 00 p	LAX	9 57 p	DEN	44			0	Dinner	Ex Sat	Eff Nov 1
	7 00 p	LAX	9 57 p	DEN	44			0	Dinner		Dis Nov 1
	10 00 p	LAX	12 55 a	DEN	42			0			
LUBBOCK, TEXAS	8 25 a	LBB	12 45 p	DEN	181	El Paso	146	3	Brkfst		
	1 00 p	LBB	2 40 p	DEN	153			2	Lun/Snk		
	2 00 p	LBB	4 20 p	DEN	111			2			
	3 30 p	LBB	5 32 p	DEN	191	Mid/Ods	155	1	Snack		
MIDLAND/ODESSA, TEXAS	12 20 p	MAF	2 40 p	DEN	153			3	Lun/Snk		
	2 05 p	MAF	4 20 p	DEN	171	El Paso	111	2			
	5 05 p	MAF	5 32 p	DEN	155			0	Snack		
NEW ORLEANS, LA.	7 00 a	MSY	9 22 a	DEN	443	Houston	423	1	Brkfst		
	7 00 a	MSY	11 00 a	DEN	443			3	Brkfst		
	7 20 a	MSY	9 33 a	DEN	451			1	Brk/Snk		
	12 15 p	MSY	4 25 p	DEN	425			3	Snack		
	3 20 p	MSY	5 52 p	DEN	429			1	Dinner		
	5 00 p	MSY	10 15 p	DEN	431	Houston	427	3	Snack		
OKLAHOMA CITY, OKLA.	9 10 a	OKC	9 33 a	DEN	451			0	Snack		
	3 15 p	OKC	4 25 p	DEN	425			1			
ONTARIO, CALIF.	9 00 a	ONT	11 49 a	DEN	86			0	Snack		
PHOENIX, ARIZ.	1 20 p	PHX	6 30 p	DEN	160	El Paso	144	3	Dinner		
PORTLAND, ORE.	7 00 a	PDX	10 03 a	DEN	420			0	Brkfst		
	11 45 a	PDX	2 48 p	DEN	426			0	Lunch		
	3 25 p	PDX	6 27 p	DEN	452			0	Dinner		
SAN ANTONIO, TEXAS	5 45 a	SAT	9 22 a	DEN	54	Houston	423	1	Snk/Brk		
	8 50 a	SAT	12 45 p	DEN	93	Albuquer	146	2	Brkfst		
	11 15 a	SAT	2 40 p	DEN	153			4	Lun/Snk		
	1 00 p	SAT	4 20 p	DEN	171	El Paso	111	3	Snack		
	4 00 p	SAT	5 32 p	DEN	155			1	Snack		
	6 45 p	SAT	10 15 p	DEN	166	Houston	427	3	Snack		
SEATTLE/TACOMA, WASH.	12 50 a	SEA	3 58 a	DEN	430			0			
	6 05 a	SEA	10 03 a	DEN	420			1	Snk/Brk		
	7 00 a	SEA	10 08 a	DEN	432			0	Brkfst		
	11 45 a	SEA	2 53 p	DEN	428			0	Lunch		
	2 30 p	SEA	6 27 p	DEN	452			1	Dinner		
	3 30 p	SEA	6 38 p	DEN	424			0	Snack		
TUCSON, ARIZ.	2 05 p	TUS	6 30 p	DEN	160	El Paso	144	2	Dinner		
TULSA, OKLA.	7 40 a	TUL	8 42 a	DEN	147			1	Brkfst		
	9 55 a	TUL	11 00 a	DEN	443			1			
	1 30 p	TUL	2 32 p	DEN	145			1			
	5 35 p	TUL	6 03 p	DEN	143			0	Dinner		
	9 10 p	TUL	10 15 p	DEN	427			1			
WICHITA, KANSAS	8 30 a	ICT	8 42 a	DEN	147			0	Brkfst		
	10 50 a	ICT	11 00 a	DEN	443			0			
	2 20 p	ICT	2 32 p	DEN	145			0			
	4 15 p	ICT	4 25 p	DEN	425			0			
	10 05 p	ICT	10 15 p	DEN	427			0			
To El Paso											
FROM ALBUQUERQUE, N.M.	12 25 a	ABQ	1 09 a	ELP	151			0			
	12 40 p	ABQ	1 24 p	ELP	133			0			
	1 15 p	ABQ	1 58 p	ELP	99			0			
	4 25 p	ABQ	5 09 p	ELP	145			0			
	9 20 p	ABQ	10 03 p	ELP	94			0			
AMARILLO, TEXAS	6 20 a	AMA	8 16 a	ELP	180	Lubbock	181	1	Brkfst		
AUSTIN, TEXAS	7 20 a	AUS	8 10 a	ELP	129			1	Brkfst		
	10 50 a	AUS	1 05 p	ELP	157	Mid/Ods	193	1			
	4 05 p	AUS	4 28 p	ELP	127			0			
CHICAGO, ILL.	9 05 a	ORD	1 24 p	ELP	21	Denver	133	2	Bk/Lu/Sn		
	11 10 a	ORD	1 58 p	ELP	99			1	Lunch		
	9 00 p	ORD	1 09 a	ELP	23	Denver	151	3	Snack		
COLORADO SPRINGS, COLO.	9 40 a	COS	1 24 p	ELP	124	Denver	133	2	Lun/Snk		
	2 15 p	COS	5 09 p	ELP	153	Denver	145	2			
7 continued on next page	11 20 p	COS	1 09 a	ELP	151			1			

23. (See Figure 5-24)
    (a) If you ate one slice of cheese, one egg, and one pat of butter, how many grams of saturated fat would you have eaten?______________
    (b) If you needed to take in a total of about 12 grams of polyunsaturated fats each day, and needed to choose at least one serving from each food group

FIGURE 5-24
Fat values table
(From W. Thurber, R. Kilburn, and P. Howell, Exploring Life Science. *Boston: Allyn and Bacon, 1975, p. 205. Used by permission.)*

Food	Amount	*Saturated fat (grams)*	*Polyunsaturated fat (grams)*	*Cholesterol (milligrams)*
DAILY DIET FACTOR				
(Rice, potatoes, etc.)	1 serving	1.7	1.0	0
MEAT				
Beef (steak, hamburg),		2.2	0.1	47 very lean
veal, lamb	1 serving	3.7	0.2	81 med.
		7.4	0.3	162 fatty
Ham, pork (bacon),		3.7	0.5	84 very lean
hot dogs, cold cuts	1 serving	5.3	0.8	115 med.
		9.0	1.4	190 fatty
Fish	1 serving	0.3	0.4	63
Egg	1	2.1	0.7	224
DAIRY PRODUCTS				
Whole Milk	1 cup	4.9	0.4	25
99% Fat Free Milk	1 cup	1.4	0.1	7
Skim Milk	1 cup	0.0	0.0	
Coffee Cream	14 g	1.8	0.2	10
Cheese	1 slice	5.2	0.5	27
FATS				
Butter	1 pat	2.4	0.2	12
Margarine-stick	1 pat	0.9	0.7	0
Margarine-soft	1 pat	0.7	1.6	0
Oil	1 tsp.	0.7	2.7	0
Mayonnaise	1 tbls.	1.8	5.2	(0) Trace
DESSERTS, SNACKS				
Potato or corn chips	10	2.0	4.0	0
Doughnut	1	1.0	0.0	15
Cookie	1	1.0	0.0	0
Pie	1 piece	5.0	2.0	0
Ice Cream	1 scoop	4.8	0.4	24
Cake (with icing)	1 piece	3.0	1.0	0
Chocolate Candy	1 candy bar	5.0	0.0	0
Cocoa	1 tbls.	0.3	0.0	0
Chocolate Milk Drink	1 glass	2.4	0.0	0

listed, what may be included on your day's menu?____________________

____

24. (See Figure 5-25)
    (a) Based on this diagram, can you determine the relationships that produce the nitrogen cycle? Begin with the green plants.____________________

____

____

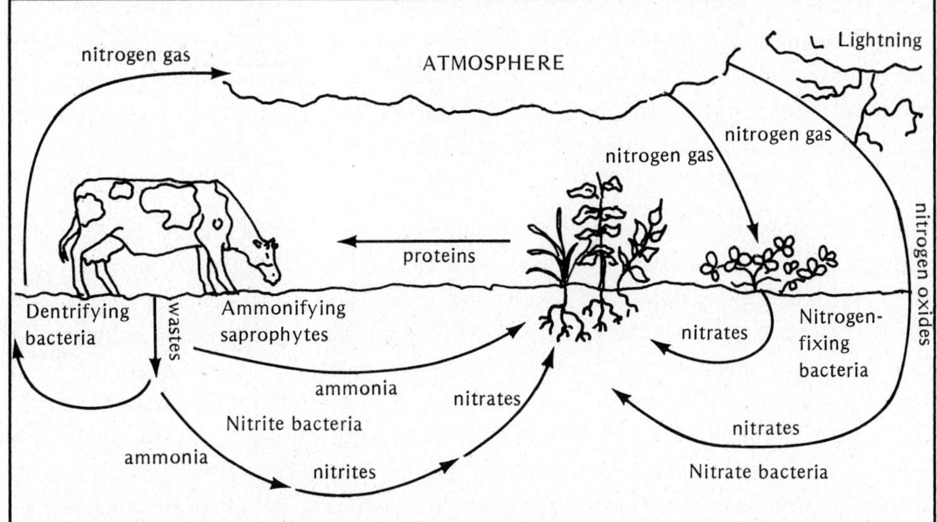

FIGURE 5-25
Nitrogen cycle
(From W. Thurber, R. Kilburn, and P. Howell, Exploring Life Science. *Boston: Allyn and Bacon, 1975, p. 361. Used by permission.)*

Remarks on solving problem items

- A variety of realistic problems are posed.
- A variety of displays are used.
- The initial question about each display is intended to help the students become familiar with the display, that is, it is not the most difficult one.

TEACHING GRAPHIC SKILLS IN THE CONTENT AREAS

The ideas presented in the following sample activities pertain to the *application* phase of skill instruction. As teachers review the activities, they should think about how to incorporate the graphic skills into their own content study, that is, use the ideas to best suit their own needs.

In order to integrate skills and content effectively, however, teachers must be familiar with the development phase of learning each skill. We recommend that teachers review our discussion of "Study Skills instruction" in Part 1 and the Developmental perspective and activities for the (Part 5) graphic skills before proceeding with the illustrations and the follow-up "Practice exercise" which are aimed at helping teachers present the skills in an appropriate context.

Illustrations

Illustration 1

In a sociology class the students were doing a unit on urban sites. The teacher planned for them to divide into groups, each one selecting one urban site, and then locate some demographic data, such as: the population changes over five or ten years; the majority and minority races; main religions; economic growth; income per family; and educational levels. After gathering the data, the teacher planned for the students to spend some time constructing graphs and tables and reviewing the skills of determining subtractive and multiplicative differences. When the graphs and tables were complete, the students would pose certain questions about them, such as, How much larger had a minority group grown over the past decade and how does its size relate to that of the majority group? Forming and answering the questions to each group's graphs help students to learn about the information they gathered and to sort out the important aspects of it. A follow-up activity may include making comparisons among the urban sites, according to one or more statistics.

Illustration 2

In an elementary school health unit the teacher was presenting a unit on nutrition and decided to tie in some graphic problem-solving skills. She copied some charts that listed the basic food groups, some individual foods, and their respective caloric and nutritional values. The teacher then divided the class into small groups and assigned each group two "patients" for whom it would have to prepare a two-day menu. Each patient was thoroughly described as to his or her caloric and nutritional needs, inabilities to digest certain foods, etc. The teacher planned to review the menus with each group and then select certain ones to share with the whole class. She hoped the exercise would provide practice in manipulating information on a chart to solve problems, assigning foods to the appropriate basic groups, and planning a well-balanced diet.

Illustration 3

In a sports history unit of a junior high school health class the students were looking up a great deal of information in reference sources, such as the *Almanac*. They were attempting to find facts and records of achievements that related to some recent and/or ongoing events, such as the Kentucky Derby and Indianapolis 500 races. The teacher decided to integrate the graphic skills—determining a purpose and summarizing—since he felt the students could benefit from using these skills in their searches. He reviewed the skills and reminded the students to always note, first, the title and labels of a graphic display to determine whether or not the display is appropriate to the students' needs.

To provide practice, the teacher directed the students to briefly write out the purpose of each display they selected in their search for facts and records. After the students jotted down the purpose and examined the set of data presented, he also told them to draw one conclusion that summarized several facts. He emphasized that making a summary statement is helpful in gaining perspective on the data and in remembering a main idea or trend. Without drawing conclusions, students often try to memorize unrelated facts which are easily forgotten.

Illustration 4

In a high school economics class the teacher outlined several lessons on the industrial and agricultural growth of the country over the past 25 years. When she realized that many of her planned discussions would focus on events in the future, the teacher decided to incorporate the skills of projecting and relating. She assembled a number of graphic displays—graphs, tables, charts—and posed questions about them that would help students gain experience in detecting trends, making projections based on them, and relating that information to background knowledge. In one lesson, for example, she planned to present some background facts on the auto industry and then have the students make some predictions about the future role of the industry in relation to the total economy.

Illustration 5

Mr. Peters is a high school instructor of a practical course in managing money. The course covers such topics as making investments, buying stocks, getting loans, buying insurance and a house, and operating within a specific budget. Because so much of his course requires that students be able to read graphic displays, Mr. Peters planned several review lessons at the beginning on the very basic skills (comparing relative amounts and extracting directly and interpolating). Then, as he introduced each of the graphs in the students' ensuing lessons, he asked relevant (to the text) questions that required the students to determine differences and the purpose and to draw conclusions from the facts presented. Mr. Peters felt that if the students gained confidence in their ability to read the graphs, they would do so independently. He believed that when the students did read the graphs, their comprehension of the text improved, because many of the important ideas expressed in narrative material were reinforced in "picture" form. Frequently, too, the students gleaned additional information from the displays, because extra, but related, facts were often presented in conjunction with the ones discussed in the text.

Practice Exercise

For Lesson A examine the table in Figure 5-26 which is part of a science unit. Then decide which graphic skill(s) may be appropriately taught in conjunction with it and write down at least one suitable development activity and one application activity that the students may do to learn to use those graphic skills you selected. In Lesson B, Figure 5-27 is a timeline that is part of a history assignment. Decide which skill(s) may be appropriately taught in conjunction with the timeline, and then write down a suitable application activity.

FIGURE 5–26
Sky data
(From W. Thurber, R. Kilburn, and P. Howell, Exploring Earth Science. *Boston: Allyn and Bacon, 1977, p. 294. Used by permission.)*

Planet	*Diameter (kilometers)*	*Distance from sun (kilometers)*
Sun	1,380,000	
Mercury	4,800	57,500,000
Venus	12,200	107,000,000
Earth	12,700	149,000,000
Mars	6,700	228,000,000
Jupiter	142,000	775,000,000
Saturn	120,000	1,430,000,000
Uranus	46,500	2,860,000,000
Neptune	44,500	4,480,000,000
Pluto	6,400	5,900,000,000

Graphic skill(s) ______________________________
Development activity ______________________________
Application activity ______________________________
____

Example lesson A

Skills selected: Determining differences, determining purpose and summarizing

Development activity:

a. About how much larger in diameter is the sun than Earth? (About 100 times)
b. What is the purpose of this table? (It presents data on the planets—their size and distance from the sun.)
c. What is one conclusion that you can draw from this information? (One of the smallest planets is closest to the sun and another is one of the farthest away.)

Application activity: As part of an astronomy unit, direct the students to draw or set up a scale model of the solar system based on the table. The students should be provided with separate, common scales for the planet diameters and for the distances from the sun. The teacher should point out the value of a table of figures when carrying out this type of an activity.

Events	President	Events
1867 National Grange established	JOHNSON	
1869 Knights of Labor organized		1869 First transcontinental railroad completed
	1870	
1873 Minting of silver coins ceases Panic sweeps country	GRANT	
		1875 Custer defeated at Little Big Horn River
1876 *Munn v. Illinois* (Granger cases)		1877 Bell Telephone Company formed
1878 Bland-Allison Act	HAYES	
	1880	
1881 Garfield assassinated	GARFIELD	
1882 Chinese Exclusion Act	ARTHUR	
		1883 Pendleton Act
1886 Haymarket Riot	CLEVELAND	
1887 Interstate Commerce Act		1887 Dawes Act
		1889 Pan-American Conference
	1890	
1890 Sherman Antitrust Act	HARRISON	
1892 Populist party organized Deep depression begins		1892 Homestead Strike
1894 Pullman Strike	CLEVELAND	
		1896 Bryan defeated in free silver campaign
1898 Spanish-American War U.S. acquires Puerto Rico, Philippines, Guam in Treaty of Paris	McKINLEY	
	1900	
1900 Open Door policy toward China		1901 McKinley assassinated
1902 Anthracite Coal Strike		
		1903 U.S. acquires Canal Zone
1904 Roosevelt Corollary announced	ROOSEVELT	
		1906 Pure Food and Drug Act Meat Inspection Act
1908 U.S. fleet circles globe	TAFT	
	1910	
1910 "Dollar diplomacy" advanced		
		1912 Marines landed in Nicaragua
1913 16th and 17th Amendments adopted		1914 Panama Canal opened World War I begins
1915 Lusitania sunk by U-boat	WILSON	
1917 U.S. enters World War I Virgin Islands acquired		1918 Armistice ends World War I
1919 Prohibition amendment adopted		
	1920	
1920 League of Nations rejected by Senate	HARDING	1921 Sacco-Vanzetti trial Washington Disarmament conference
1923 Harding dies Teapot Dome scandal erupts	COOLIDGE	1924 Immigration sharply restricted
		1928 Hoover elected President
	HOOVER	

Party in Power

- Democratic
- Republican

FIGURE 5-27
Timeline
(From G. Leinwand, Pageant of American History. *Boston: Allyn and Bacon, 1975, p. 396. Used by permission.)*

Graphic skill(s) ____

____

Application activity ____

____

Example lesson B

Skills selected: Solving problems

Application activity: Present the students with a narrative (or list) of events between 1867 and 1928, preferably without dates, and instruct them to place the events correctly on the timeline. For example, McKinley's inauguration would be placed after the entry, "1896 Bryan defeated in the free silver campaign," but before the 1898 Spanish-American war, during which McKinley was already president.

As a follow-up activity, students should construct their own timeline from a narrative about a different period of history or about a sequence of events told in a story.

REFERENCES

1. Kamm, K., Askov, E., & Klumb, R. *Study skills mastery among middle and high school students.* Paper presented at the annual meeting of the International Reading Association, 1977. (ERIC Document Reproduction Service No. ED 141 780)
2. Linke, R. D. *The effects of certain personal and situational variables on the acquisition sequence of graphical interpretation skills,* Vols. 1, 2, and 3. (ERIC Document Reproduction Service No. ED 110 317)
3. Otto, W., Kamm, K., & Weibel, E. *Wisconsin design for reading skill development: Rationale and objectives for the study skills element.* Working Paper No. 84. Madison, Wis.: Wisconsin Research and Development Center for Cognitive Learning.
4. Sals, D. *Revisions of the Type I field test: Study skills.* Working Paper No. 128. Madison, Wisconsin: Wisconsin Research and Development Center for Cognitive Learning.
5. Weintraub, S. "What research says to the reading teacher." *Reading Teacher,* 1967, *20,* 345-349.
6. Wesson, J. "Graphs and charts: An important topic for the middle grades," *School Science and Mathematics,* 1979, *79,* 592-596.

Graphic Skills: Maps

6

The most specialized of the graphic skills are the skills needed to read maps. Because traditionally these skills have not been taught in school curricula, we have found that of the four study skill areas, teachers are most unfamiliar with these skills.

OVERVIEW

The emphasis on map skills began to increase in the early 1950s. Previously, little attention had been paid to these skills. The main reason for this interest appeared to be the prominence given to the concept of a rapidly changing environment. Some investigators felt that better methods of map instruction were needed if pupils were to develop the flexible knowledge of the relationships among places (7,23). The world appeared to be shrinking in terms of the time required for transportation and communication, and geographic horizons for individuals were becoming much broader. Educators began to feel strongly that maps and globes were the media by which many of the basic concepts of the social sciences were transmitted.

The consideration of maps and graphs as vehicles for communicating knowledge about social sciences has continued to intensify. Recent investigators feel that maps and globes are among the representational forms most important for the transmission of social, scientific, and other forms of knowledge (2,3,11). Their effectiveness for the concise transmission of such knowledge gives them a unique status among communicative modes. Bartz (1) states, "Mapping as a knowing activity is of fundamental value in our culture" (p. 18). Because of these views on the importance of maps in our communications, many curriculum developers are stressing that maps be considered part of the basic reading and study skills, and not be relegated only to geography instruction in the high school (2, 3, 4, 10, 16).

The combined recognition of the importance of mapping skills in our culture and the uniqueness of maps as a means of communication has prompted educators to explore the precise nature of mapping skills and how they may best be taught. According to the literature survey by Otto, Kamm, and Weibel (17), questions have been raised regarding several aspects of mapping. Much discussion, for example, has been given to such specifics as understanding symbols and learning the directional system, and to such general problems as the complexity of map skills and the ultimate goals of map reading skills instruction. The discussion of the symbols and directional system will be included in our discussion of the Representation and Location systems, and we will concentrate on the broader problems in this general overview.

Before mapping skills were under a great deal of scrutiny, educators felt they were inappropriate for young students to study. Research by Towler (22) and by others (8,16,18) on egocentrism in the child's conception of space, however, suggests that instruction oriented to the cognitive development of the child and the conceptual structure of the subject matter can make possible an earlier introduction of mapping skills than was previously thought to be the case. Wide support is generally given to the need for an organizational and developmental framework for map skills instruction (2,4,6,17,18,22). As yet, however, few attempts have been made to link the structure of geography and the conceptual development of the child in order to provide a basic guide to objectives in geographic education.

In the 1960s, public school personnel were beginning to show more interest in including map skills in their curriculum specifications, but while they were able to consult many published lists of map skills, not one was organized into a framework particularly compatible with classroom instruction. The result was that either very few skills were selected—too few to comprise an adequate study skills program—or too many were included, the result being confusion about which ones to teach in what sequence and how to organize instruction.

One of the first attempts to devise an instructional framework, that is, an organization that facilitates classroom instruction and is also based on the research to date, was the *Wisconsin Design for Reading Skill Development,* Study Skills element (5).

In the *Design* map skills are arranged sequentially among several levels of difficulty. The intent is to create a spiraling effect of skill building, that is, students learn the most basic skills early in the sequence, and then gradually build on successive skills as they progress through the grades. At the end of the sequence, students are expected to integrate and use independently all of the skills in the various categories to derive information from graphic representations. This approach in the *Design* Study Skills element has been successful with students and is appealing to teachers (12, 13, 14). We use a similar approach in our selection and development of the skills.

In this book map skills are divided into three strands of skills: representation, location, and measurement. The representation skills concern the use of symbols in depicting information. The location skills refer to the use of grids and directions to describe places of objects, and the measurement skills pertain to the use of a scale to determine distances between places and sizes of areas.

REPRESENTATION

The first aspect of map use to be considered is the representation system. *Representation* refers to the use of symbols to designate objects in the environment. For example, a small drawing of a tree may represent a large, wooded area; a dot may represent a city.

Developmental Perspective

Representation skills, perhaps more than any other group of map skills, have been discussed by educators as to how they should best be taught. One concern has been whether a student needs to initially manipulate concrete objects or to view actual scenes in order to develop a sense of what is being represented by a map. On the one hand, Giffard (8) and Savage and Bacon (20) state that young children (first and second graders) can learn mapping skills on an abstract level. They feel that symbols can be used from the outset in teaching mapping skills, that neither photographs nor pictographic maps need be used as "stepping stones," and that too much emphasis is placed on the manipulation of concrete objects. On the other hand, perhaps most authors would agree with Sabaroff (19) who writes, "Only when a map symbol calls forth a mental image . . . can he [the pupil] use the map 'shorthand' with any significant meaning" (p. 45). Only the familiarity that comes from concrete experience with objects or geographical features can make the interpretation of cartographic symbols fully meaningful to young students. As Otto, Kamm, and Weibel (17) note, "The consensus appears to be that before a child can understand a map, he must be able to envision the reality it represents" (p. 9). In fact, some investigators have recommended introducing problems of cartographic representation by having pupils construct maps of already familiar areas, for example, the classroom, school grounds, or immediate neighborhood (2, 9, 16, 21). Teachers have commented that such a procedure is also very helpful in holding student interest (8).

Taking into account the ideas that have been expressed about the representation skills and in considering our teaching experiences, we recommend that young students who are learning the concept of representation start with concrete examples. Children readily understand that a toy car is not a real car but a scaled-down model of a car. Young children can make a floor map of their neighborhood using toy cars to represent real cars, Monopoly houses or milk cartons to represent houses, a blue ribbon to represent a stream, etc. Once students show they understand these activities, one can create maps on paper using picture symbols, again preferably related to a locally known area such as the immediate neighborhood. A small picture of a house may represent Johnny's house, a small rectangular patch of blue may represent the local swimming pool, and a stick drawing in green may be a tree. Students should study these maps when the maps are lying flat on the floor, as opposed to hanging vertically, so that the students do not forget that a map is a representation of an actual location.

Gradually, the symbols may become more abstract as a child's map use increases in sophistication. Seven- or eight-year-old children can be presented with dots that are used to mark the houses in the neighborhood. The area that is represented can also become more abstract. For example, a dot may represent a whole city rather than just one house. Similarly, various colors can be used to identify the locations where different animals may live on a farm. Thus, both the symbol system and the areas being represented gradually move from the concrete to the abstract as children become more sophisticated in map reading skills.

Quantitative types of information—relating to size or number—can also be introduced by representing familiar locations. Until approximately the ages of seven or eight, children use symbols primarily to locate points or areas. But at this stage they can begin to use symbols to compare amounts and sizes. For example, they can compare sizes of cities by comparing the dots that represent them. The smallest dot may represent a town with a population under 20,000; the largest dot may represent a city with over 1,000,000 people. A middle-sized dot represents a town with a population size that falls between the two extremes.

Line symbols, which also can convey quantitative information, are probably used most frequently on maps to indicate various types of road surfaces and construction. The children learn, for example, that a thin gray line on a state map may indicate an unimproved road, while a thick colored line may signal a turnpike or interstate highway. It is important, however, that children use the map key (or legend) to establish such information. Maps vary greatly in their types and uses of symbols, and the thin gray line indicating an unimproved road on one map may well have a very different meaning on another map. It might, for example, indicate boundaries between counties.

As children grasp the concept of nonpictorial symbols, such as point and line symbols, they can also be introduced to area symbols. One of the easiest area symbols for primary grade children to grasp is the use of colors to represent different types of areas. At first, basic colors are best to use (as opposed to close shades of red, for example), and each color can stand for a separate item on the map. For instance, brown can signify streets; white, buildings; and green, parks. In studing color symbols children should also interpret some maps that show colors with nontraditional associations, such as blue for buildings (instead of water) and brown for water (instead of streets). Reading these maps helps children learn the importance of the key, since they must consult it for correct interpretation. And, they also get needed practice in reading map keys.

After children can successfully use a color key to locate areas, they can be taught that shades of a color may convey quantitative information. For example, various shades of brown may be used to indicate elevations on a map and shades of green may represent different amounts of annual rainfall.

Other area symbols also can indicate quantitative relationships. For example, on a map showing farming areas the symbols for the crops may appear in bunches or in relative isolation, depending on the amount of the crop grown (or harvested). A large group of corn husks may indicate a field yielding several thousand bushels of corn. Two or three wheat stalks might show that only a few hundred bushels of wheat are produced from that area.

Finally, as students reach upper elementary, junior high school, and high school, they can be asked to make inferences from maps. The ultimate goal of map reading ought to be "map thinking"—using information on a map to draw conclusions. Children may be given maps of two or more areas to determine the ways in which these areas are similar and different in using map analysis skills (for example, comparing the crops grown in two or more different areas). Also, students should have the opportunity to use map synthesis skills to compare different types of maps (topographic, demographic, climatic) of the *same* area, in order to draw conclusions about why an area has specific characteristics, such as a large working-class population or tourist industry. In a specific example, students can hypothesize about the occupations of the inhabitants of one state based on maps indicating the rainfall, terrain, and climate. They can also determine why major cities have grown where they are, based on maps of river systems, terrains, and transportation. The skills related to drawing conclusions from map study are extremely important in achieving higher levels of thinking as well as intelligent decision making throughout a lifetime.

The following scheme portrays an effective development of representation skills:

Representation system

Realistic symbols for concrete objects in the environment (three-dimensional representations, picture symbols)	Nonpictorial symbols (points, colors) to identify concrete objects in the environment	Nonpictorial symbols (points, lines, color)* to identify abstract areas and to convey quantitative information; multiple symbols to show quantity	Analysis* and synthesis* of several maps to draw conclusions
5-6 year olds	7-8 year olds	9-10 year olds	11+ year olds

*Skills included in Development Activities section.

In the following section, we have provided development activities to help familiarize teachers with the advanced representation skills. These skills are noted in the above schema. Remember! In order to use the advanced skills, students need a thorough understanding of the preliminary skills.

Development Activities

We have included development activities for the intermediate and advanced representation skills: point, line, and area symbols, analysis, and synthesis. We discussed the beginning representation skills and some ideas for teaching them in our Developmental perspective section, and recommend that the beginning skills be taught in the primary grades so that students in the intermediate grades and above have a firm grasp of them. If these beginning skills have not been taught, however, then developmental instruction in the advanced skills should certainly include a review of these "background" skills and concepts associated with the representation system.

At this point readers should review our earlier discussion about study skills instruction in Part 1, which emphasizes important aspects of skill development, and then work through the following activities to ensure their understanding of the advanced skills. Becoming well acquainted with the skills is not only a great advantage when teaching them, but is important in learning to select and create appropriate follow-up application activities for students to do independently.

When reviewing the activities, we encourage teachers to consider our illustrations and sets of questions as examples of what can be adapted for classroom use. The Remarks following each set of items for a skill are helpful when teachers are actually involved in adapting their materials for skill instruction.

FIGURE 6-1
Population

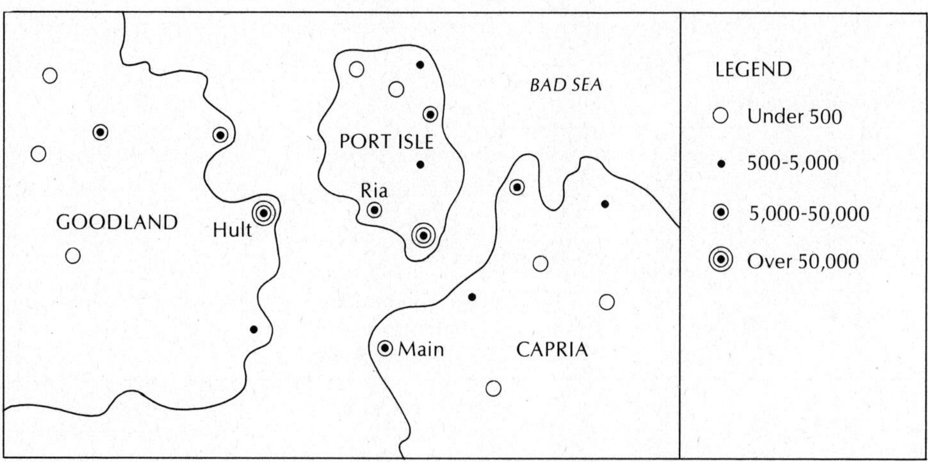

Point symbols

(For questions 1 to 3 see Figure 6-1.)

1. Which of the following would most likely be the population of Main in Capria?
   (a) 450
   (b) 3500
   (c) 5500
   (d) 55,000

2. The most populated area is
   (a) Goodland.
   (b) Port Isle.
   (c) Capria.
3. Most of the people in these areas live
   (a) just inland.
   (b) near the coast.
   (c) in the heart of their country.

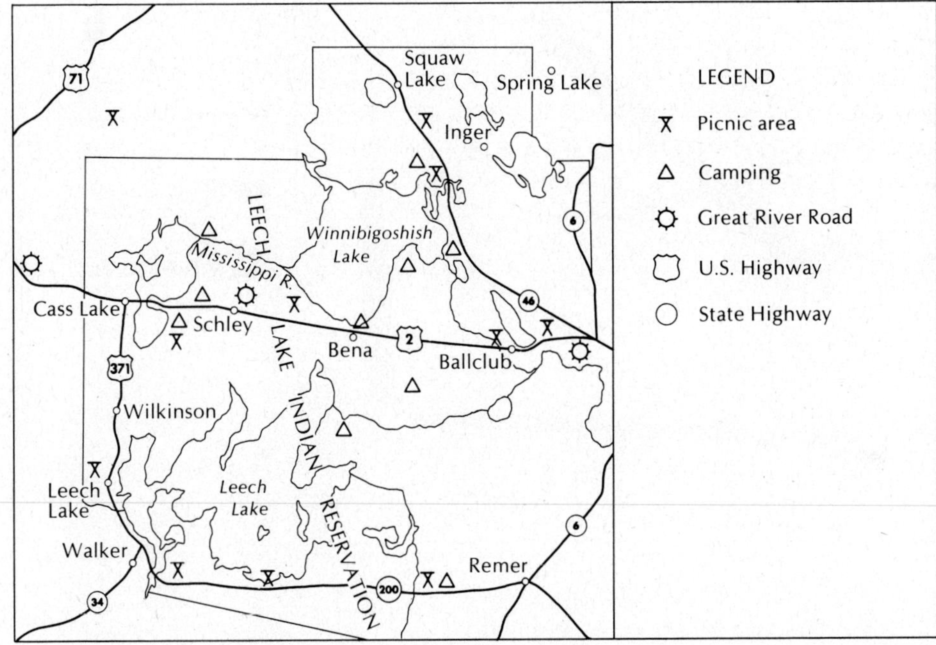

FIGURE 6-2
Road map

(For questions 4 to 6 see Figure 6-2.)

4. How many places to camp are shown along the Great River Road? ________
5. Which cities are shown along Highway #371? ________

____

6. Highway #200 is a
   (a) U.S. Highway.
   (b) State Highway.
   (c) Great River Road.

Remarks on point symbols items

- Two different kinds of point symbols are represented in Figures 6-1 and 6-2.
- Both multiple-choice and open-ended questions are used.
- The first question is designed to get the students "acquainted" with the map, by requiring them to read the legend and find information about *one* place. The other questions require the students to scan the map and make comparisons among areas. (The first question should never be one of the more difficult items.)

FIGURE 6-3
Air ways

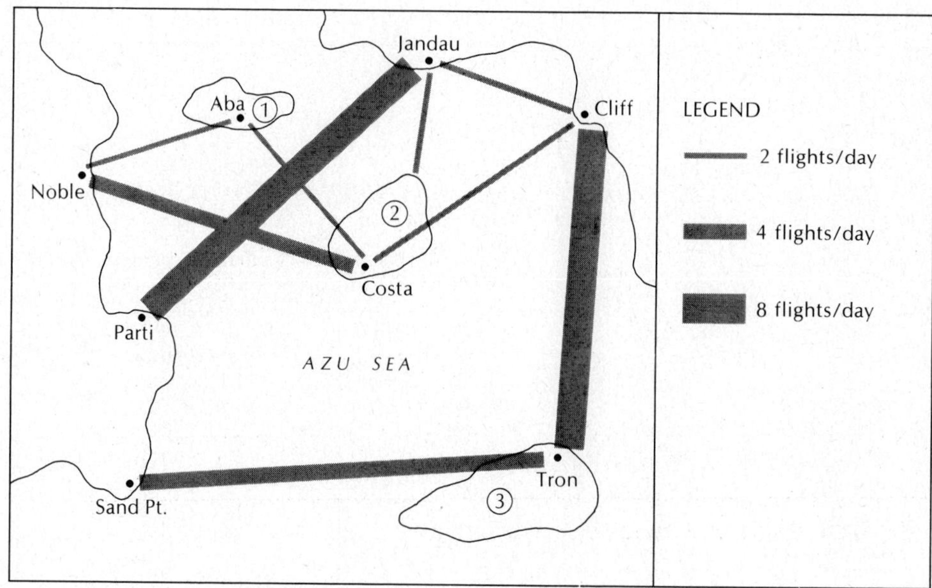

Line symbols

(For questions 7 to 9 see Figure 6-3.)

7. How many flights are there between Noble and Costa each day?
   (a) 2
   (b) 4
   (c) 8
8. About how many flights would there be between Parti and Jandau in one week (Mon.-Fri.)?
   (a) 4
   (b) 8
   (c) 10
   (d) 20
   (e) 40

9. To which island do the most planes fly each day?
   (a) 1
   (b) 2
   (c) 3

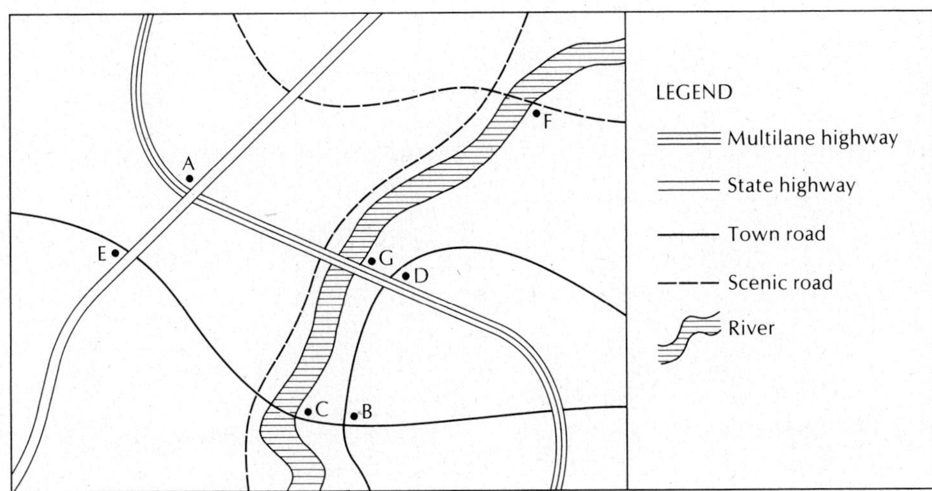

FIGURE 6-4
Highways

(For questions 10 to 12 see Figure 6-4.)

10. What crosses at Point A?________________________
11. At which point does a town road cross the river?________________
12. Where does the scenic road(s) go?________________________

Remarks on line symbols items

- Different kinds of line symbols are represented in Figures 6-3 and 6-4.
- Both multiple-choice and open-ended questions are used.
- The first question is designed to get the students "acquainted" with the map, by requiring them to read the legend and find information about *one* place. The other questions require the students to scan the map and make comparisons among areas. (The first question should never be one of the more difficult items.)

Area symbols

(For questions 13 to 15 see Figure 6-5.)

13. Which area receives some of the heaviest rainfall?
    (a) Nova
    (b) Sauk
    (c) Dane
    (d) Middale

FIGURE 6-5
Rainfall

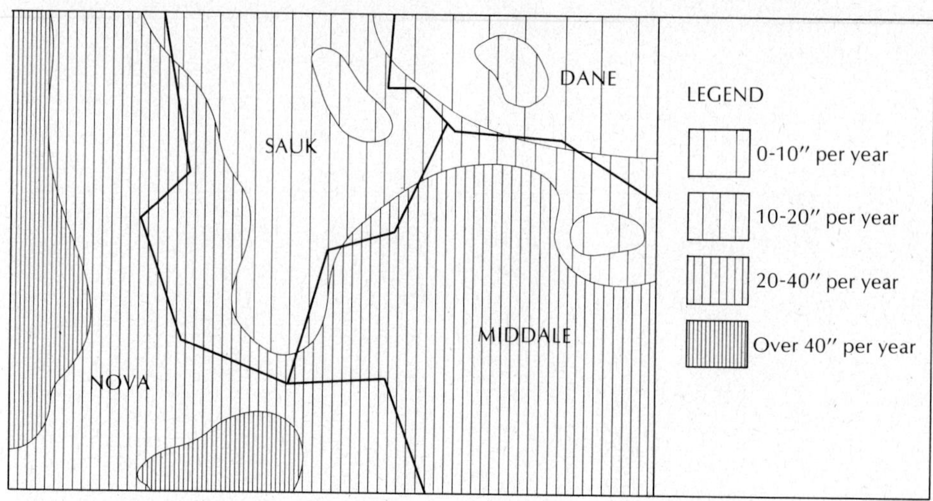

14. The driest area is:
    (a) Nova.
    (b) Sauk.
    (c) Dane.
    (d) Middale.
15. How much rain can be expected in most of Middale each year?
    (a) 0-10 inches
    (b) 10-20 inches
    (c) 20-40 inches
    (d) over 40 inches

(For questions 16 and 17 see Figure 6-6.)

16. Which crop does Mr. Hulter grow the most of?____________________
17. Which crop is not grown along the lake shore?____________________

Remarks on area symbols items

- Two different types of area symbols are presented in Figures 6-5 and 6-6.
- Students are required to read the entire legend and scan the entire map.

In the following activities readers are asked to apply representation symbols in drawing conclusions from maps. Analysis requires one to make comparison among maps of different areas, while synthesis involves comparisons of several different types of maps of the same location. These higher level skills involve thinking as well as reading skills.

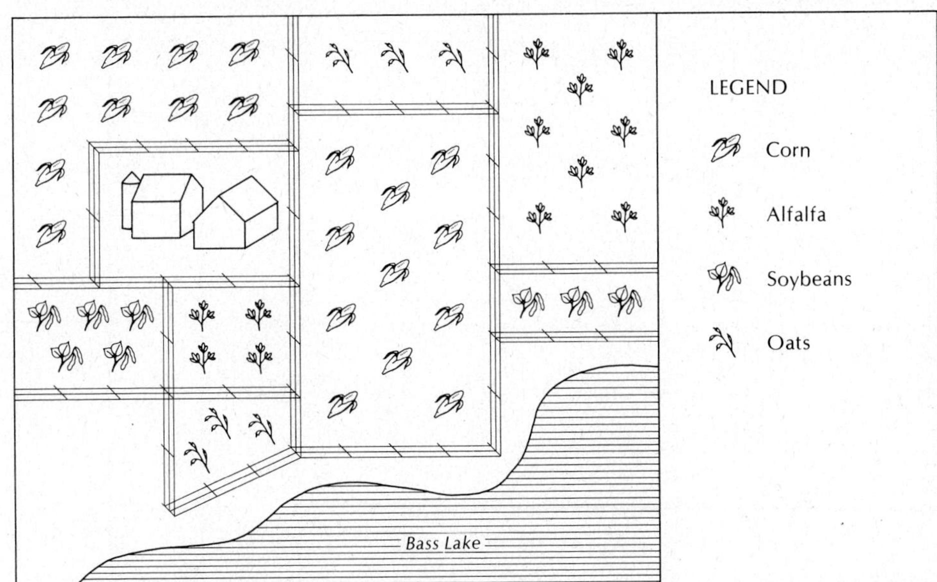

FIGURE 6-6
Hulter farm

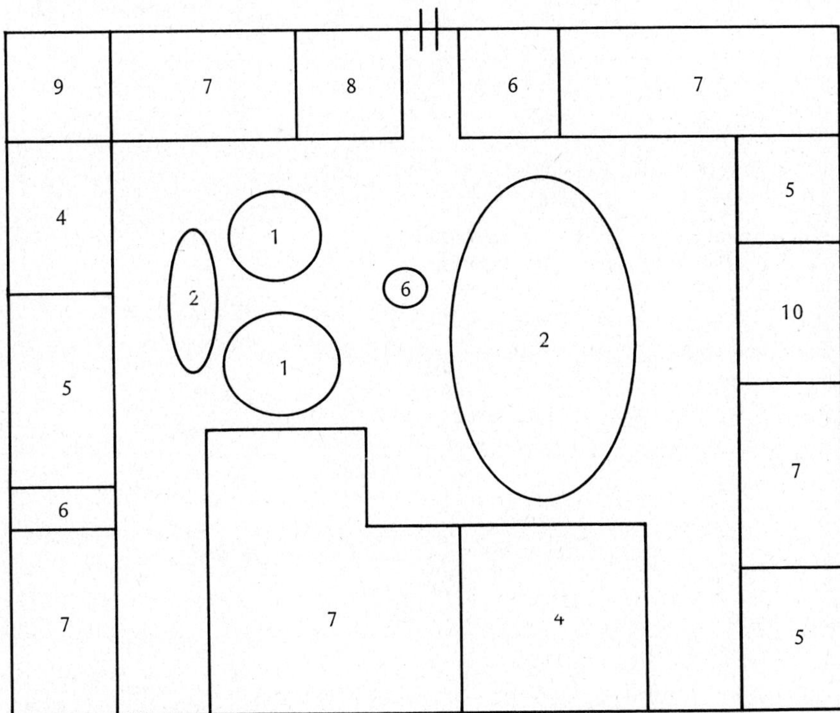

FIGURE 6-7
Mall 1

FIGURE 6-8
Mall 2

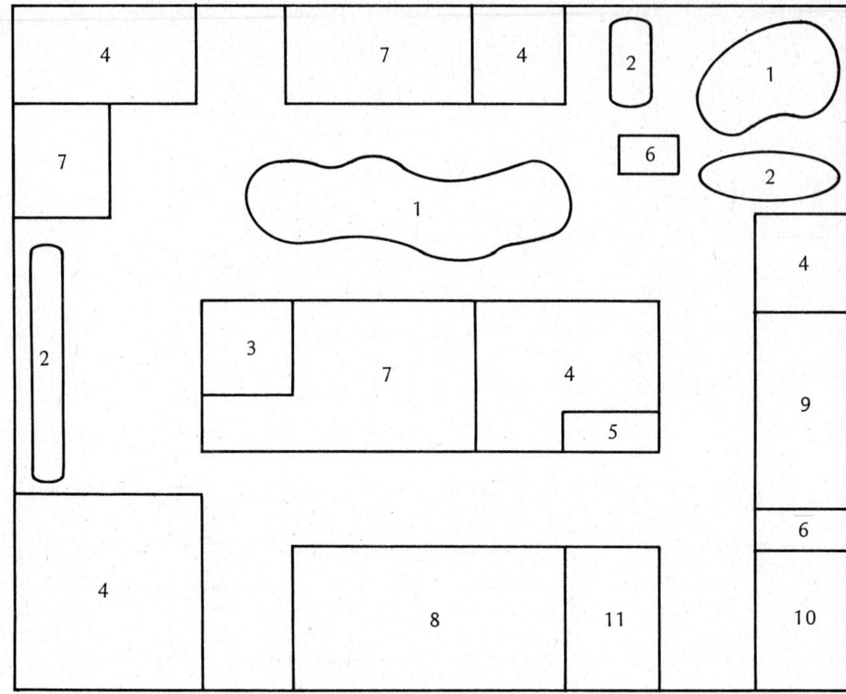

Analysis

(For questions 18 to 21 see Figures 6-7 to 6-9.)

Legend

1. fountains
2. seating area
3. drug store
4. sport store
5. shoe shop
6. eating area
7. clothing store
8. furniture store
9. toy store
10. pet shop
11. paint and drapery store

18. At which mall is each seating area near a fountain?
    (a) Mall 1
    (b) Mall 2
    (c) Mall 3
19. Which mall appears to have the greatest variety of shops?
    (a) Mall 1
    (b) Mall 2
    (c) Mall 3
20. If you were furnishing a new house, which mall would be best to go to?
    (a) Mall 1

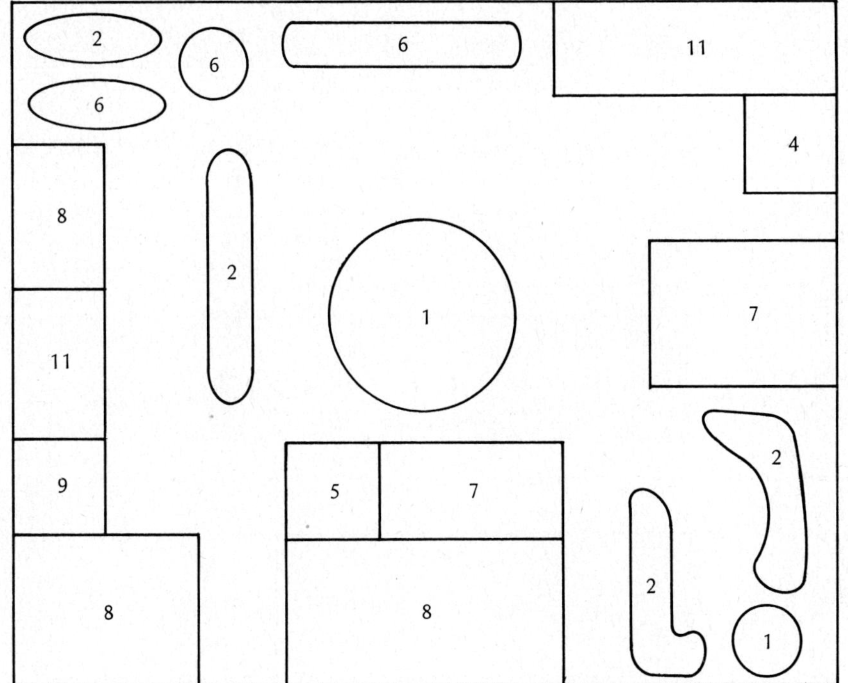

FIGURE 6-9
Mall 3

(b) Mall 2
(c) Mall 3

21. Which mall would be best to go to if several family members needed new outfits to wear?
(a) Mall 1
(b) Mall 2
(c) Mall 3

Remarks on analysis items

- This is a beginning analysis activity.
- Each question requires students to look at all three malls.
- Questions 18-20 ask about several of the designated areas.

Synthesis

(For questions 22 to 24 see Figures 6-10 to 6-12.)

22. Most of the people in Arvada live in a (an):
(a) farming area.
(b) unplanted area.
(c) jungle area.

FIGURE 6-10
Roads

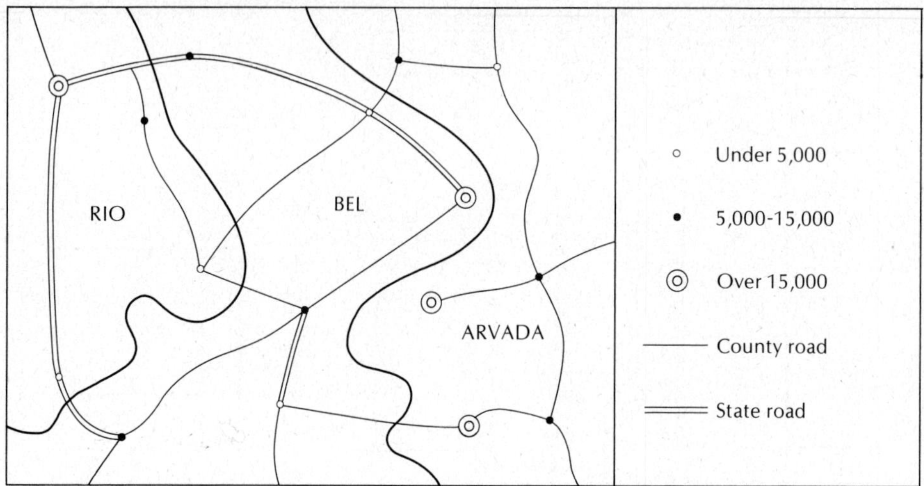

FIGURE 6-11
Crops

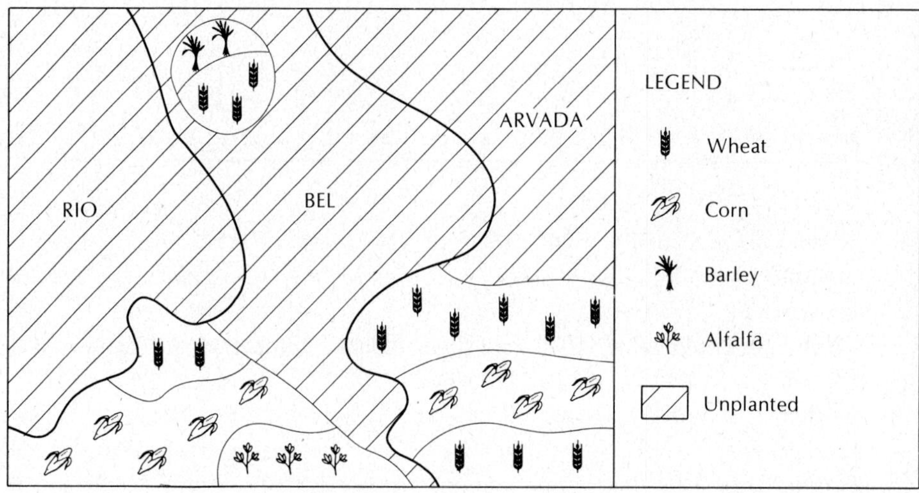

23. How much rain per year do most of the crops in Bel receive?
    (a) 0-10 inches
    (b) 10-20 inches
    (c) 20-30 inches
    (d) over 40 inches
24. In Rio the state highway runs through
    (a) the driest area.
    (b) a semi-moist area.
    (c) good farming region.
    (d) several large cities.

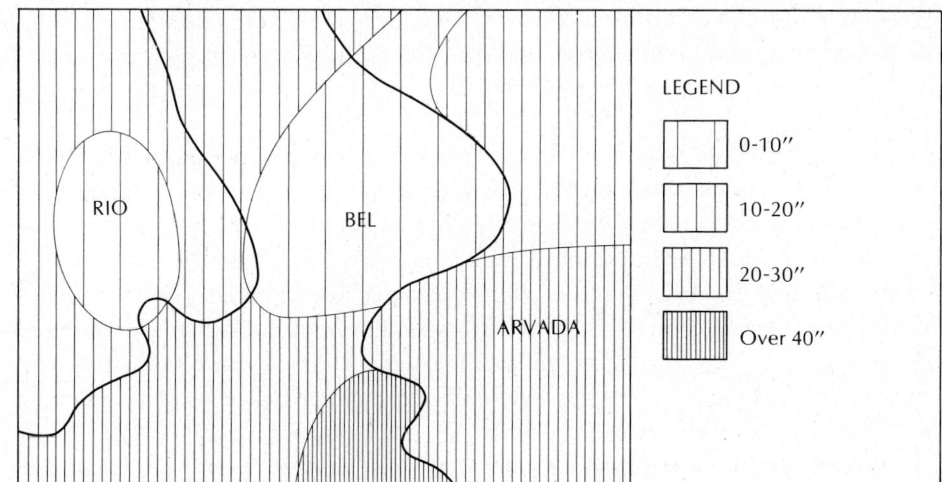

FIGURE 6-12
Annual Rainfall

Remarks on synthesis items

- Each question requires the students to look at more than one map.
- Together, the questions ask about all three maps.

Illustrations

The ideas presented in the following sample activities pertain to the *application* phase of skill instruction. As teachers review the activities, they should think about how they can incorporate the representation skills into their own content study, that is, use the ideas to best suit their own needs.

In order to integrate skills and content effectively, however, teachers must be familiar with the development phase of learning each skill. We recommend that teachers both keep in mind and review our discussion of "Study Skills instruction" in Part 1 and be familiar with the Developmental perspective and activities for Representation skills before proceeding with the illustrations and the follow-up "Practice exercise," which are aimed at helping teachers present the skills in an appropriate context.

Illustration 1

In a sixth grade sociology unit the students were studying urban areas. The teacher introduced some reading material describing model, or utopian, cities and how they may be planned. With the help of the art teacher, she outlined a project in which the students would work in small groups and draw a "rough" plan of a model city. Each map would have a complete legend and include certain features, such as stores, homes, offices, a theatre, and transportation and recreational facilities. To produce such a map, the students had to rely on their knowledge of point, line, and area symbols. At the end of the project the students would present their plan to the other groups and explain the advantages their city offered.

Illustration 2

A high school teacher of anthropology was introducing a section on growth of communities. He set up a project for the students to complete on their own and determined that in order to do so, they would need to use some fundamental map reading skills.

He devoted several class periods to reviewing the representation skills (after learning that the students had worked with them in earlier grades), and then divided the students into groups of five or six. Each group selected a small area of the United States with which none of the members were familiar. The task was to locate a variety of maps depicting this area (for example, topographic, demographic, climatic, political, and road), and then synthesize the information from each map and draw some conclusions about the nature of the area. The students were to surmise the possible economic status of the people in the area, their occupations, typical weather, farming and industrial possibilities, social problems (for example, from over- or underpopulated areas), and transportation opportunities. After making their projections, the students were to write the Chamber of Commerce offices in the area and request as much information as possible regarding their questions.

At the end of the project the teacher and students discussed their findings and, in particular, noted what they could and could not project from their original maps.

FIGURE 6-13
Glaciers

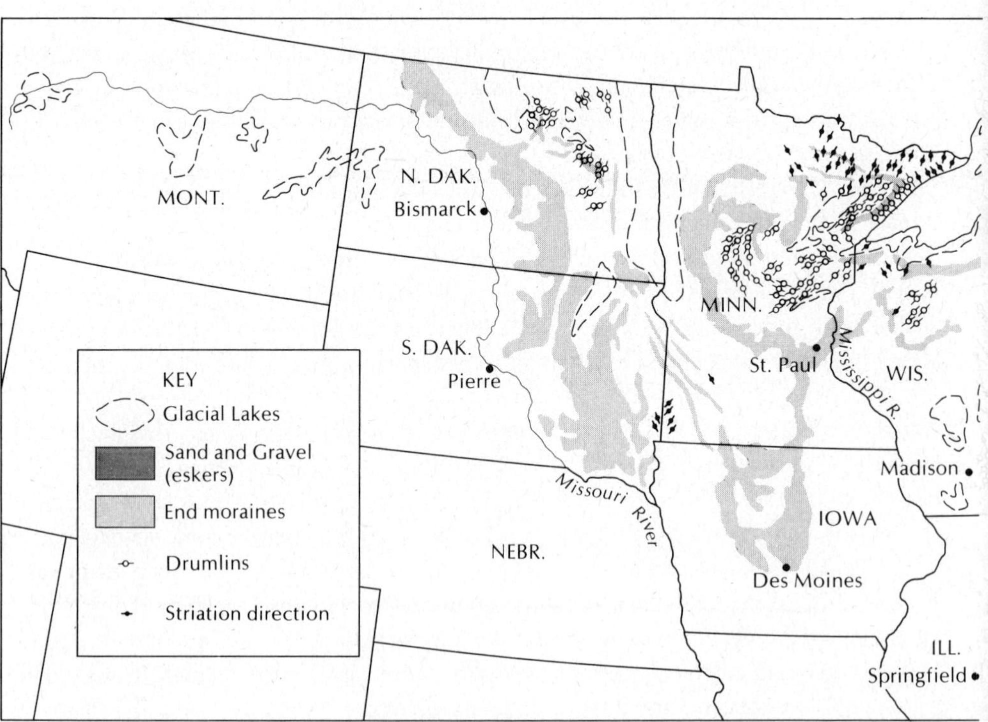

Illustration 3

In a high school home economics class the teacher wanted the students to plan an efficient kitchen. Prior to their planning, the teacher prepared several instructional activities, based on the students' knowledge of synthesis skills. She drew up several different kitchen plans (some good, some bad) and wrote out questions requiring students to compare the plans. For example, the students were to name three inconvenient aspects of the stove location in Plan 1, determine why Plan 2 was poor for family use, and decide what was wrong with the refrigerator in Plan 3.

After the teacher discussed the questions and plans with the students, she divided them into small groups. Each group was to draw three plans: one plan was to be a model kitchen lay-out, and the other two were to include one or two inconvenient features. When the plans were drawn, the teacher had them copied and distributed to each group. Each group was to determine which plan was the model kitchen lay-out and what was wrong with each of the other two plans.

Practice Exercise

Examine the following maps (Figures 6-13 and 6-14) and then decide which representation skills you would teach in conjunction with each one. Write down at least one development and one application activity that students can do to use those representation skills you selected for each map. Figure 6-13 (Lesson A) is part of an earth science lesson and Figure 6-14 (Lesson B) is part of a social studies lesson on world trade and shipping routes.

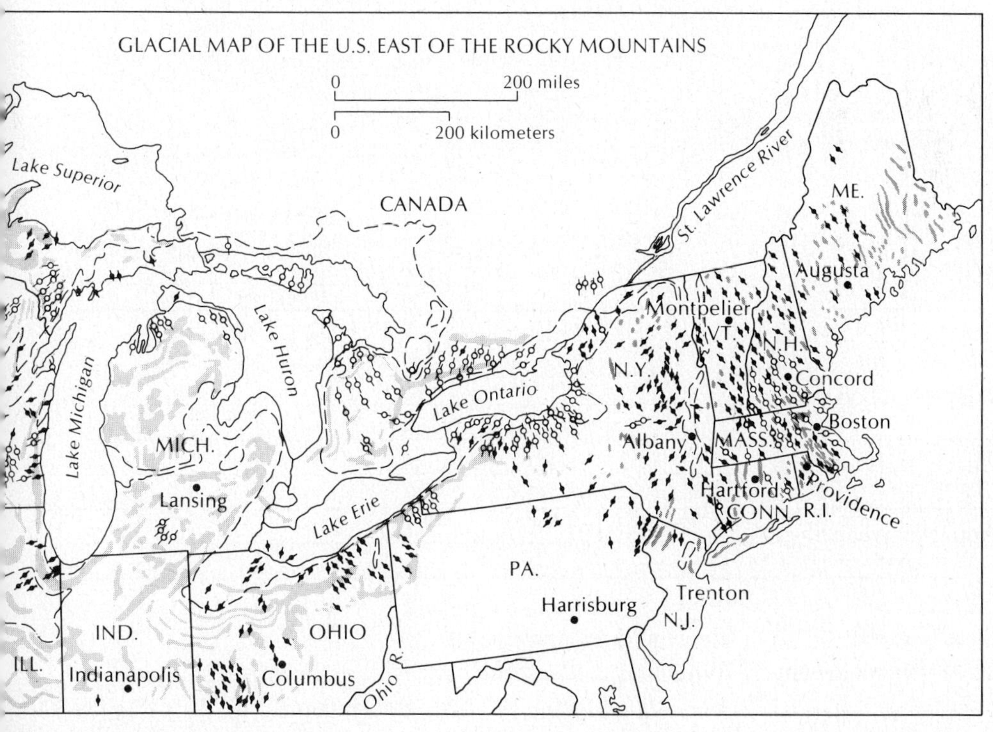

FIGURE 6-14
World

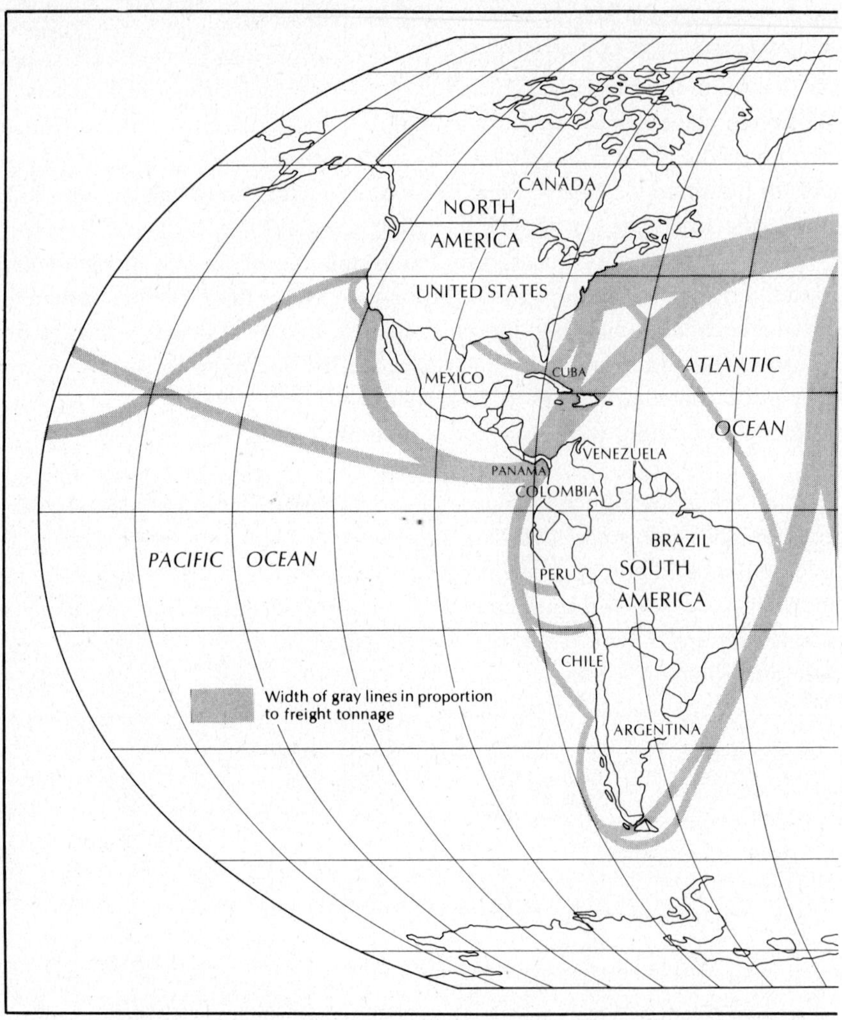

Representation skills____________________

Development activity____________________

Application activity____________________

Example lesson A (see Figure 6-13)

Skills selected: Point and Area symbols

Development activity: What was the land like between Lake Huron and Lake Ontario? (Many drumlins and eskers.)

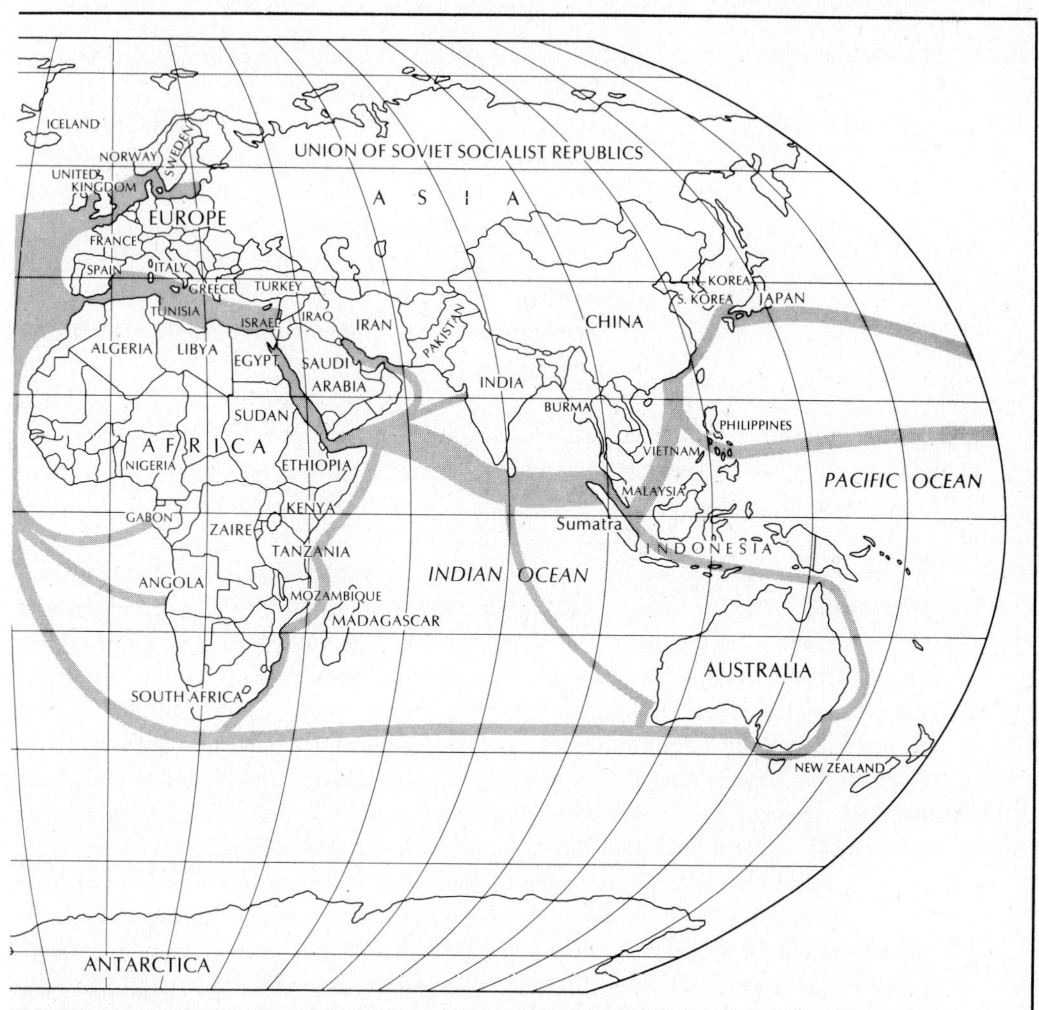

Application activity: Compare and contrast the New England states with the state of Michigan during this glacial age. (New England had many drumlins and striations and less glacial lake area.)

Representation skills____________________________________

Development activity____________________________________

Application activity____________________________________

Example lesson B (see Figure 6–14)

Skills selected: Line symbols

Development activity: In the U.S. where is the greatest amount of freight shipped from? (East coast of U.S.)

Application activity: Decide which shipping routes have the greatest tonnage being shipped and which routes have very little tonnage being shipped. (Identify the routes by naming the countries at either end.) Students should explore reasons *why* the routes vary in popularity. (U.S. and northern Europe, northern Europe and Egypt [through the Mediterranean Sea], and eastern Africa and northern Sumatra)

LOCATION

The second aspect of map use we will consider here is the location system. Location refers to orienting oneself and finding places on maps, globes, and in the environment through use of various grids and the cardinal and intermediate directions.

Developmental Perspective

At a very early age we begin to learn location skills. Small children begin using such terms as up, down, next to, beside, over, etc. to describe the relative positions of themselves and other people and objects. As children mature, they need more sophisticated skills to describe the location of people and objects. For example, an eight-year-old may tell a friend to meet her "at the corner of Pine and Maple Streets." Later, she begins to use directions to describe various locations, such as, "My house is about two miles north of the school." As adults, very specific terms are needed to communicate the location of people and objects, and the use of directions and a grid system are combined to meet this demand. For example, captains at sea or airplane pilots need to be very precise about reporting their location. They describe their position by giving the latitude and longitude dimensions to tell others exactly where the ship or plane is.

The location skills we have identified are outlined in the schema below. They include beginning grid and direction skills, which are separate, and the more advanced skills, which combine the use of grid and direction. The skills parallel the needs of students as they mature, and, therefore, should be taught sequentially. When introducing location skills to older students, especially, teachers should review the lower level skills to help students both gain a perspective on the development of all the skills and to understand the more advanced skills. (See table at top of page 143.)

Grid skills

Grids are networks of horizontal and vertical lines that may be used by students to pinpoint specific places. Long before students are ready to use the very complex grid of meridians and parallels that surround the earth, they can begin to learn about axis and coordinate dimensions by working with a three-dimensional grid on the floor. In this type of grid, like objects are placed in a row across the floor and another set of like

Location skills

Grid	*Direction*
Three-dimensional grids Picture grids Street grids Number-letter grids	Positions of objects Cardinal directions Intermediate directions*
Meridians and Parallels* Latitude and Longitude*	

*Skills included in Development Activities section.

objects is placed in a column down. Then the teacher may direct a student to stand in a certain spot. The other students may describe the one student's location by saying, "She is under the ball and beside the book." Or, the teacher may choose a certain space, such as under the bat and beside the chalk, and then call on a student to go and stand in that space.

After working with three-dimensional grids, two-dimensional grids with pictures designating rows and columns can be introduced and used with similar activities. For example, a group of objects, say, school supplies (books, pencils, erasers), may be used to form the row across the top of the grid, and another group of objects, perhaps types of fruit, may be used to form the column. The teacher can place additional objects within the grid and ask the students to both describe ("under the pen and beside the apple") and find (point to the picture of the dog in response to the given row and column) their locations.

As the students become familiar with the picture grids, street and number-letter grids can be introduced. On simplified town maps students can be asked to describe and find locations of buildings, parks, lakes, etc., given the intersecting streets. At this point students may also be expected to give the location of objects in their environment (for example, their house, if it is on a corner) by designating the cross streets. Number-letter grids associated with maps can be used to show how much easier it is to find places on a map by knowing the approximate area designated by the numbered and lettered row and column. (Playing the game of "Bingo" is a good example use of a number-letter grid also).

Direction skills

The other set of location skills, determining directions, is a skill that needs to be taught explicitly and developmentally. And the instruction can start with young students. One educator (15) has written:

> . . . a sense of direction is not inborn but is learned. . . . The process begins with helping children develop the ability to orient themselves . . . in relation to things in their environment. With guidance very young children can begin to express direction in relative terms. . . . Such expressions as "over there" and "that way" will help beginners develop a feeling for direction and a means of expressing it. (p. 147)

The beginning directions skills we identify help students learn to orient themselves by using "positional prepositions" to relate themselves to objects and objects to objects. A young student may say, for example, that the chair is behind him, the chalkboard in front, the window beside him, the light overhead, etc. On a felt board he may place a variety of objects in relation to a central tree, saying "The duck is next to the tree"; "The dog is under the tree"; etc. All students should have plenty of practice using this skill in the environment, with models (like felt and doll-house representations), and in two dimensions (drawings of objects on paper).

Learning to use cardinal directions (North, South, East, West) follows a couple years after students (five or six years of age) practiced describing positions of objects. As students begin to use directions, they must understand several ideas: the globe is a model of the earth; the North and South Poles are convenient, though arbitrarily established, referent points on the globe; and "going north" means going toward the North Pole, and "going south" means going toward the South Pole.

Initial instructional activities may include having the students trace a line on a globe and identify whether they were moving north or south. The equator and Prime Meridian should be explained as other, arbitrary lines, circling the globe and dividing it into North and South "halves," and passing through the poles and dividing the earth into east and west hemispheres, respectively. East and West directions may be explained on the globe, after students have been introduced to the meridians.

Following the globe activities, determining directions can be practiced in the environment and on maps that have a direction indicator showing where North is. Several maps should show North in an unconventional position (not at the top) so that students realize that North is always determined by locating the North Pole.

The intermediate directions (northeast, northwest, southeast, southwest) can be introduced when students are familiar with the cardinal directions. Again, the skill should be practiced on the globe, in the environment, and on maps. The relationship between the environment and the globe and a map should be greatly emphasized.

Grid and direction skills

In combining the skills of grid and direction, students learn about meridians and parallels. Essentially, they are learning about the earth's grid system and how to use it to locate points. Students who can use the beginning grid and direction skills independently, may be introduced to meridians and parallels through several activities that deal with the following concepts:

(1) An infinite number of lines—called lines of latitude—can be thought of as circling the globe. They are of different circumferences but all parallel to the equator. The ring that is exactly half way between the two poles is called the equator.
(2) In order to describe the location of a given point precisely, lines perpendicular to the lines of latitude must also be specified.
(3) An infinite number of lines—called lines of longitude or meridians—pass through the two poles. They all are of the same circumference, all are Great Circles, and all intersect with the parallels at right angles.
(4) One of the meridians—called the Prime Meridian—was arbitrarily established as a baseline and labeled as zero degrees.
(5) One of the parallels, the equator, was established as a baseline and labeled as zero degrees.
(6) The earth may be depicted in many ways, for example, the North Pole may be shown at the center of a map.
(7) If a point has a particular location on a globe, it will have the same location on any map, although the lines may look different depending on the type of projection. For example, Mexico will fall within the same lines of latitude and longitude on any map although the country will appear to have a slightly different shape and size on a globe, polar projection, Mercator projection, etc.

Students should practice using the earth's grid system on both globes and maps of different projections, say, polar and Mercator (including some with a meridian other than the Prime Meridian at the center).

Using latitude and longitude is the last location skill to be introduced. To understand this skill, students need to have learned the concepts associated with the previous location skills, and take into account the following ones, as well:

(1) Latitude and longitude are measured in degrees. Because there are 360° in a circle, and the earth is a sphere, it is considered to have 360°.
(2) The equator and the Prime Meridian are labeled zero degrees. Meridians to the east and west of the Prime Meridian are labeled in degrees consecutively up to 180°. The latitude, on the other hand, is measure in degrees up to 90° north of the equator (the North Pole) and 90° south of the equator (the South Pole).

To become proficient in using latitude and longitude, students need a great deal of practice—on the globe and on a variety of maps. If students show confusion during instruction and practice, however, often a review of the background concepts and earlier skills is helpful, so that they can see for themselves the basis of their confusion.

Students should always be encouraged to figure out solutions to problems of describing and finding locations, rather than to memorize any aspect of using latitude and longitude.

The activities used to teach latitude and longitude should begin with simple tasks such as finding only the latitude for a number of points and then finding only the longitude for other points. Gradually, the students can be expected to give both the latitude and longitude for each of several points. When students initially describe and find points on a globe or map, the points should be right at an intersection of lines that are clearly labeled, as opposed to somewhere inbetween lines which causes students to have to interpolate. At the beginning, too, students may work mainly with the location of dots (e.g., cities), but ultimately they should describe the location of a country or continent. Providing appropriate context for using latitude and longitude is important for the students, if they are to learn to use this skill independently.

Development Activities

Development activities for the advanced location skills are included in this section. Special attention should be paid to the various types of exercises, because they emphasize both different and particularly difficult aspects of skill use. An example is that of finding directions on a map where North is in an unconventional position or on a polar projection.

Intermediate directions

25. Fill in the directions on the two compass roses.

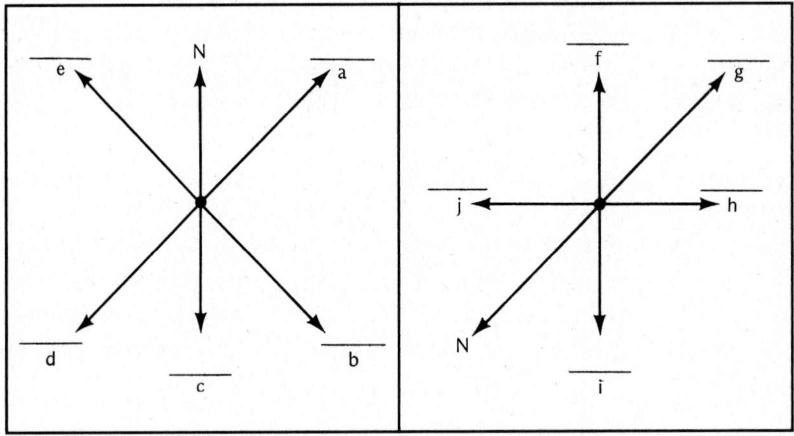

FIGURE 6-15 Compass rose a-e (left)

FIGURE 6-16 Compass rose f-j (right)

26. Write the name of the main direction each arrow is pointing in Figure 6-17.
 (a) Arrow A____________________
 (b) Arrow B____________________

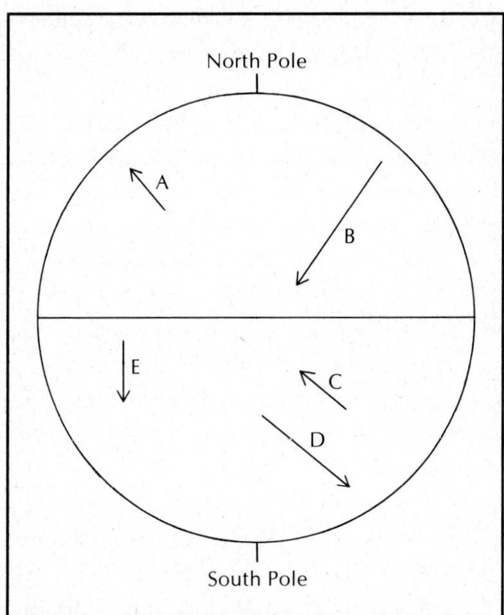

FIGURE 6-17
Arrows

(c) Arrow C____

(d) Arrow D____

(e) Arrow E____

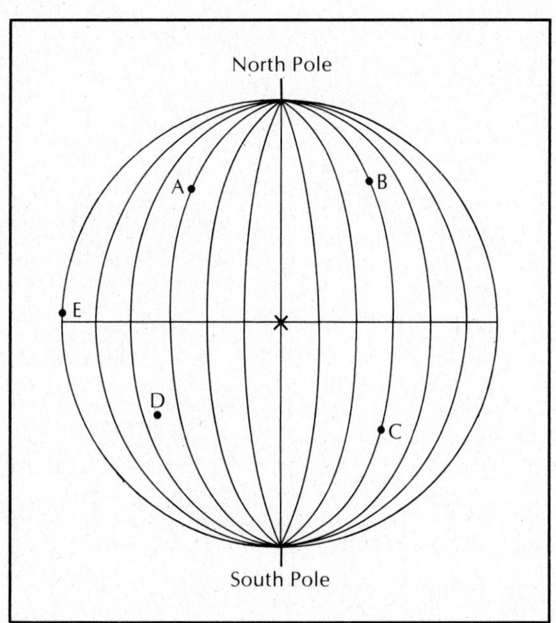

FIGURE 6-18
Meridians

27. (See Figure 6-18) Write the direction you would travel to go between the following points.
    (a) Point X to Point B__________
    (b) Point X to Point C__________
    (c) Point D to Point E__________
    (d) Point C to Point B__________
    (e) Point A to Point X__________

FIGURE 6-19
Dots

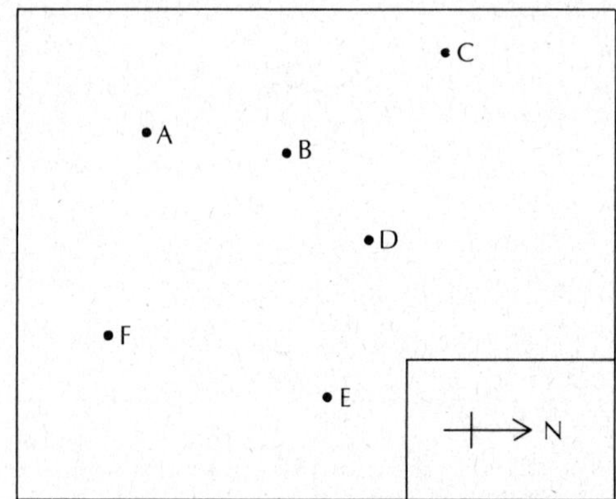

FIGURE 6-20
United States

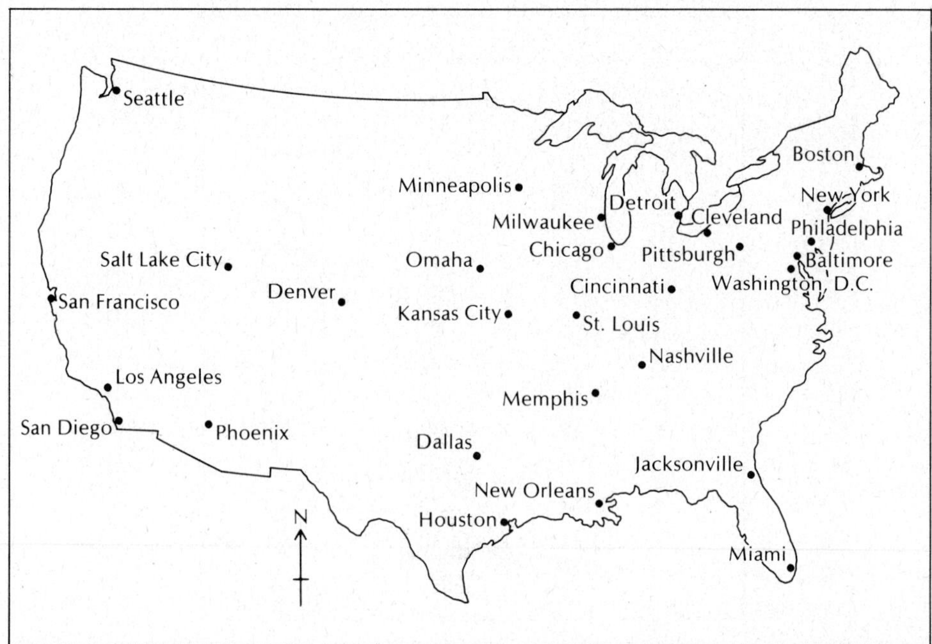

28. (See Figure 6-19) Write the directions you would go between the following points.
    (a) Point A to Point C________________
    (b) Point B to Point D________________
    (c) Point D to Point F________________
    (d) Point B to Point E________________
    (e) Point D to Point A________________

    (For questions 28 to 32 see Figure 6-20.)
29. Write the main direction you would travel between the following cities.
    (a) Houston to Boston________________
    (b) Miami to Dallas________________
    (c) Minneapolis to Phoenix________________
    (d) Minneapolis to Milwaukee________________
    (e) Memphis to St. Louis________________
30. On a globe tell the main direction you would travel between the following cities.
    (a) Cairo to Rome________________
    (b) Munich to Madrid________________
    (c) Buenos Aires to Seattle________________
    (d) Sydney to Cape Town________________
    (e) Los Angeles to Acapulco________________
31. (In a classroom with correctly labeled walls North, South, East and West.) Name the directions you go from, say, the door to the window, your chair to the chalkboard, etc.
32. (Locate a map [that indicates North] of the school grounds.) Take the map with you to a specific point near the school (for example, the tennis court). Locate and mark this point on the map. Then determine the directions between other points on the map. Describe "sets" of directions to certain points. (Ex., "To the library you go 20 yards southeast, 10 yards east, through a door, and take five steps north.")

Remarks on intermediate directions items

- To complete this set of items students must know the cardinal directions and understand background concepts, such as direction is determined by the North and South Poles.
- The first two items are generally easier than the rest of the items.
- Hypothetical maps are used to provide an opportunity for students to respond in a context with very few confounding factors.
- Students must determine directions on a map where North is not in the conventional position. Correct responses indicate students understand directions and have not simply "memorized" conventional direction positions.
- The items include a variety of aspects of using intermediate directions, for example, on maps, on globes and in the environment.

FIGURE 6-21
World

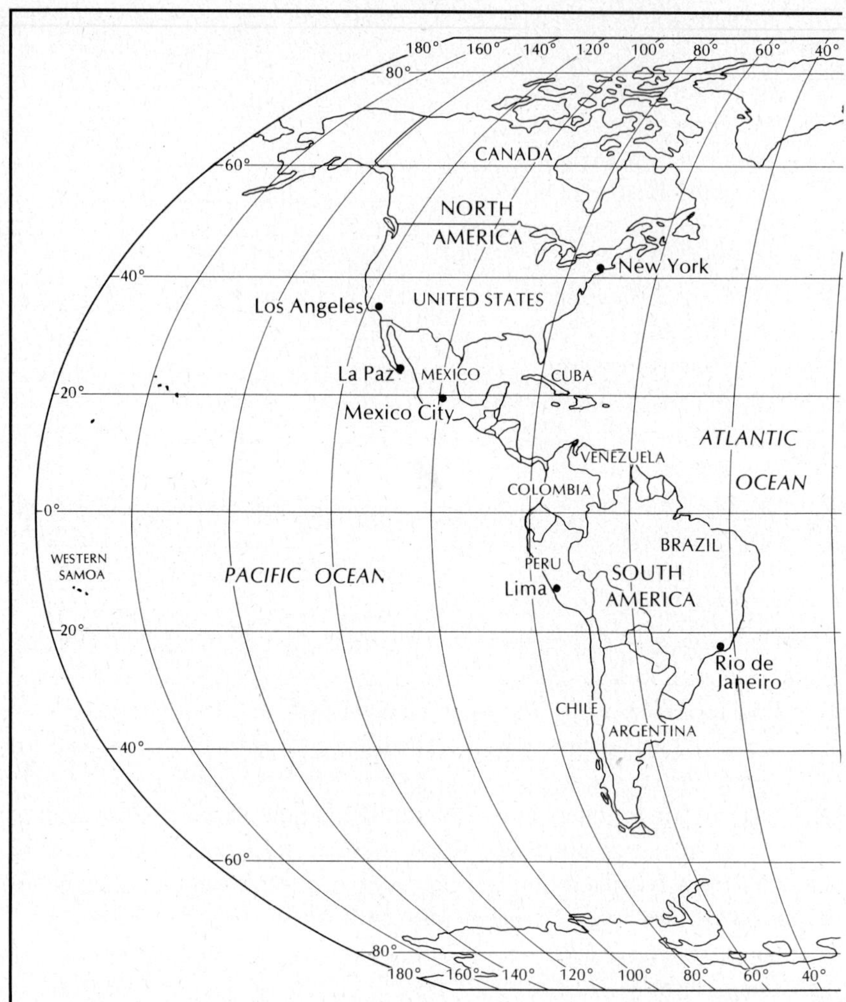

Latitude-longitude

33. On a globe:
    (a) Name one city at 40° north latitude.____________
    (b) Name one city at 100° west longitude.____________
34. On a globe:
    (a) What is located at 60° north latitude and 10° east longitude?____________
    (b) What is located at 30° north latitude and 30° east longitude?____________
    (c) What is located at 0° latitude and 80° west longitude?____________

    (For questions 35 and 36 see Figure 6-21)
35. (a) What is located about 22° north latitude and 112° east longitude?________
    (b) What is located about 13° south latitude and 170° west longitude?________

36. (a) What is located in the area between 15° south latitude and 22° south latitude and 45° east longitude and 50° east longitude?________________

(b) What is located in the area between 30° north latitude and 35° south latitude and 15° west longitude and 50° east longitude?________________

37. (See Figure 6-22)

(a) Where is Los Angeles located?__________latitude and__________ longitude

(b) Where is Godthaab (Greenland) located?__________latitude and __________ longitude

FIGURE 6-22
North America

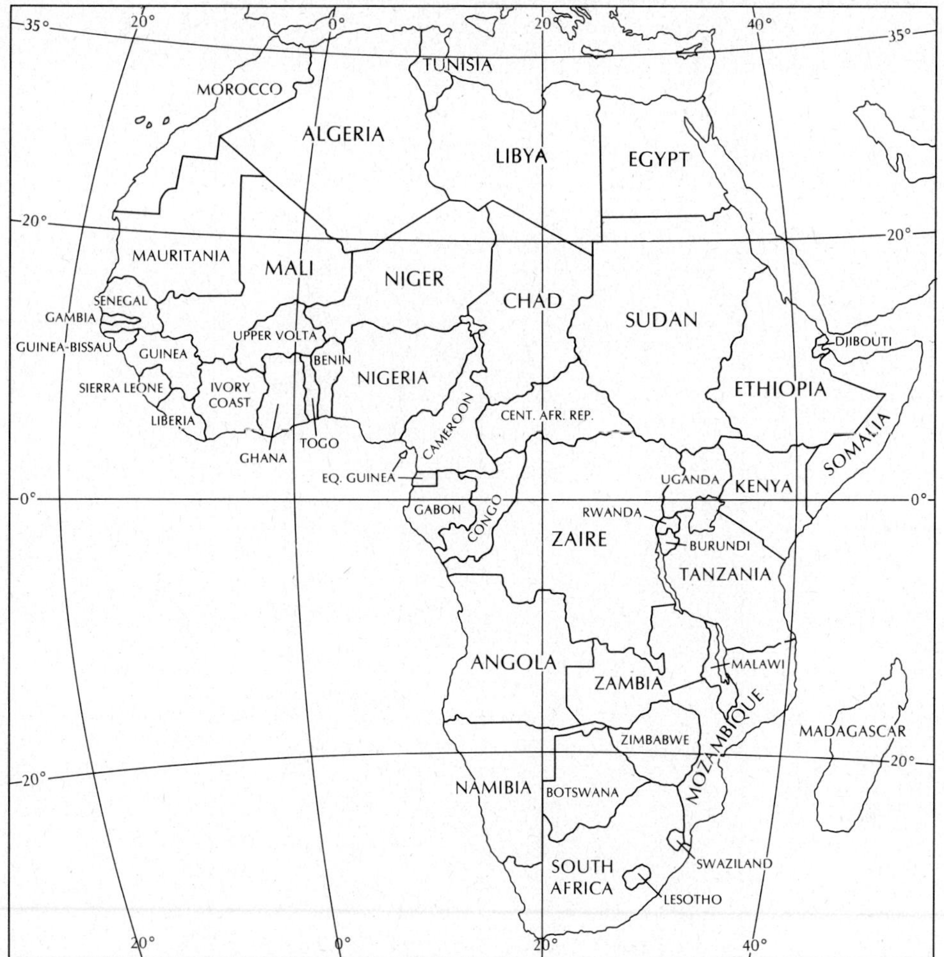

FIGURE 6-23
Africa

38. (See Figure 6-23)
    (a) What is the approximate location of Kenya?______latitude to______latitude and______longitude to______longitude
    (b) What is the approximate location of Algeria?______latitude to______ latitude and______longitude to______longitude
39. In Figure 6-24 draw in two hypothetical countries with the following locations:
    (a) 0° latitude to 35° north latitude and 100° west longitude to 115° west longitude
    (b) 30° north latitude to 75° north latitude and 165° west longitude to 170° east longitude

FIGURE 6–24
North pole

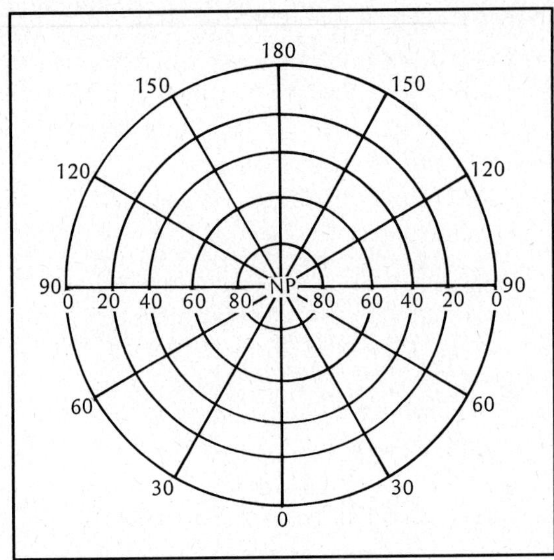

FIGURE 6–25
South pole

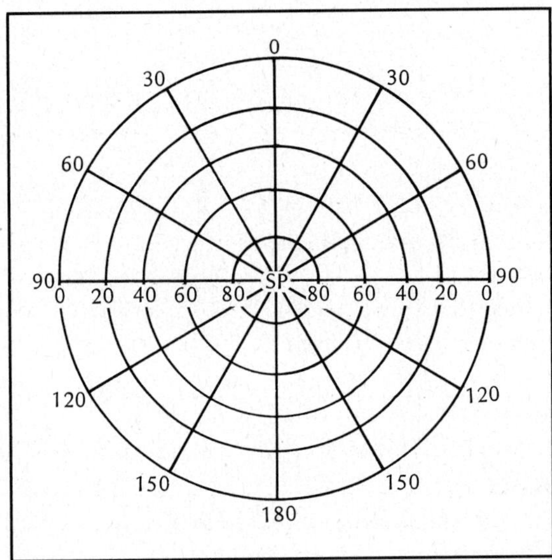

40. In Figure 6–25 draw in three hypothetical countries with the following locations:
    (a) 10° south latitude to 82° south latitude and 65° east longitude to 95° east longitude
    (b) 58° south latitude to 78° south latitude and 165° east longitude to 140° west longitude
    (c) 10° north latitude to 25° north latitude and 30° west longitude to 40° west longitude

Remarks on latitude-longitude items

- Before students begin development activities to learn how to locate points using latitude and longitude, they must understand a number of background concepts thoroughly. Because of the important role these concepts play in learning latitude and longitude, teachers may wish to devise specific activities to reinforce them. We have listed some main concepts below:
  - A type of grid has been "drawn" on the earth to help people communicate about the location of places.
  - The grid consists of an infinite number of lines, and two of them have been arbitrarily labeled the equator and Prime Meridian.
  - One set of lines, lines of latitude, are all parallel to the equator and are of different circumferences.
  - The other set of lines, lines of longitude, all pass through the North and South Poles and are of the same circumference.
  - The latitude and longitude lines are measured in degrees, and the earth has 360° since it is considered a sphere (circle).
  - The Prime Meridian and equator are labeled 0°, and the meridians to the east and west of the Prime Meridian are labeled in degrees consecutively up to 180° and the parallels north and south of the equator are labeled consecutively up to 90°.
- The questions ask the students to both locate certain places (points as well as areas) from given latitude-longitude information and to describe the location of places, using latitude and longitude dimensions.
- The beginning questions are easier than later questions. Some questions require students to "interpolate," or determine the number of degrees between given lines on a map.
- The questions refer to a variety of maps. (Ideally, development activities should include as diverse a sample of maps as possible.)

Meridians and parallels

41. On a globe:
    Find the Prime Meridian. Follow it from the equator to the North Pole. What direction are you going?____________________
    Find the 180° meridian. Follow it from the North Pole to the South Pole. What direction are you going?____________________
42. On a globe:
    (a) Put your finger on Miami. Go north to Baffin Island and stop. What part of the island is your finger on?____________________
    (b) Put your finger on Tokyo. Go south to the southern part of Australia and stop. What city are you closest to?____________________
43. On a globe: Find the intersection of the equator and Prime Meridian.
    (a) Follow along the equator until you find Quito, Ecuador. If you went the shortest way, what direction did you go?____________________

(b) Follow along the equator until you find Nairobi, Kenya. If you went the shortest way, what direction did you go?__________

44. On a globe:

(a) Put your finger on Madrid, Spain. Go west to the 75° west meridian. What city is closest?__________

(b) Put your finger on Juneau, Alaska. Go east to the 10° east meridian. What city is closest?__________

(c) Put your finger on Sydney, Australia. Go west to the 60° west meridian. What big city is closest?__________

FIGURE 6-26
Prime meridian

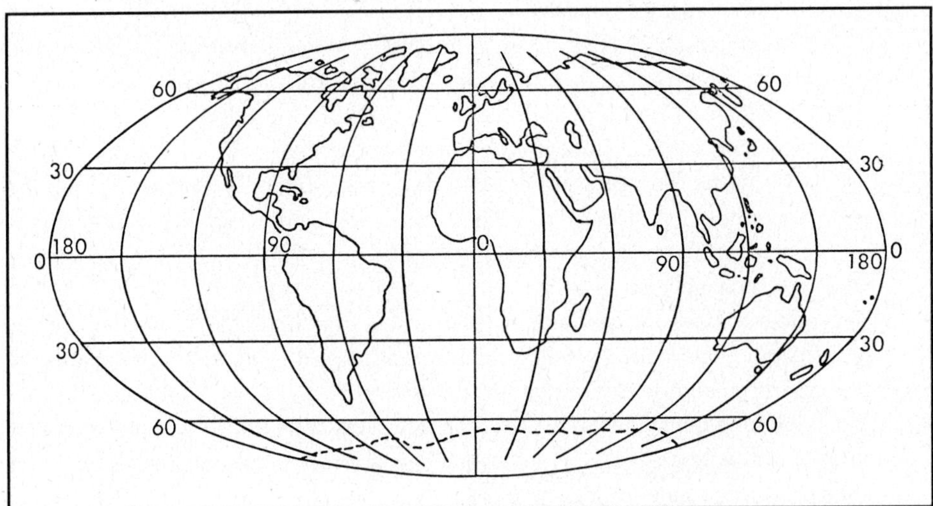

FIGURE 6-27
60° at center

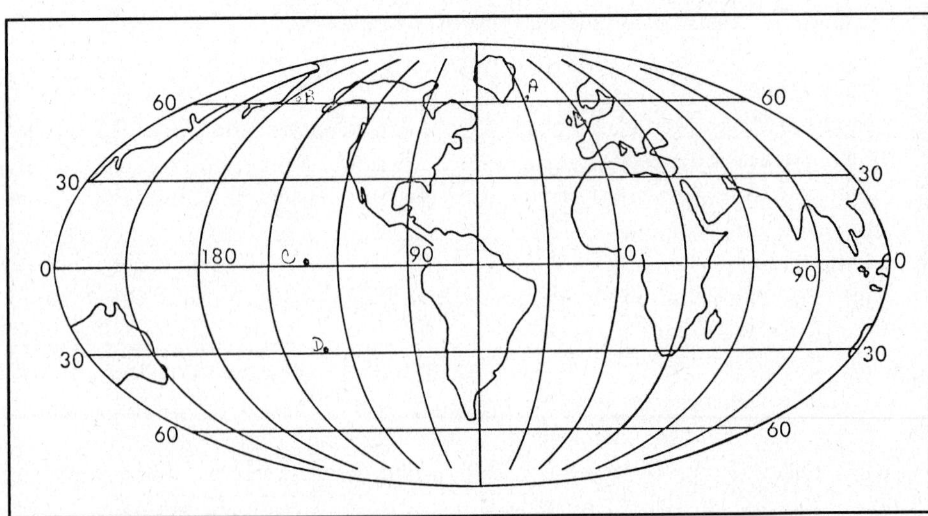

45. On a globe and then in Figure 6-26:
    (a) Put your finger on the intersection of the Prime Meridian and equator. Then go north 30° and west 90°. Where are you?__________
    (b) Put your finger on the intersection of the equator and the 30° east meridian. Go south 30° and east 90°. Where are you?__________
46. (See Figure 6-27)
    (a) Write the directions you go from Points A to B to C and to D.__________
    (b) Start from the intersection of the Prime Meridian and 60° south parallel and go 30° east, 90° north, and 120° west. Where are you?__________
    (c) Start from Point B and go 120° south, 180° west, and 60° north. Where are you?__________

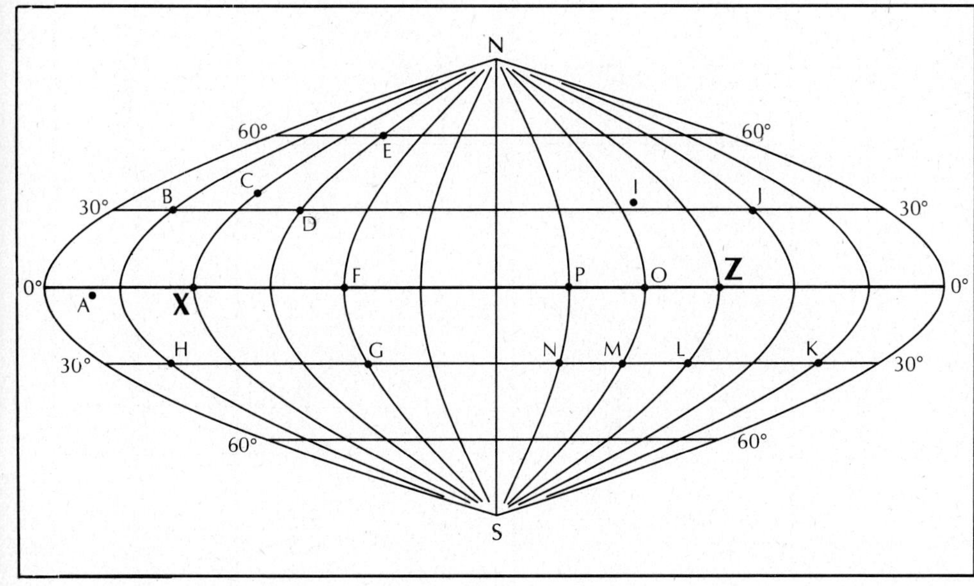

FIGURE 6-28
Ellipse

47. (See Figure 6-28)
    (a) Which point(s) is/are northeast of Point X?__________
    (b) Which point(s) is/are southwest of Point Z?__________
48. (See Figure 6-29)
    (a) Which point(s) is/are southeast of Point X?__________
    (b) Which point(s) is/are northwest of Point X?__________

FIGURE 6-29
North pole

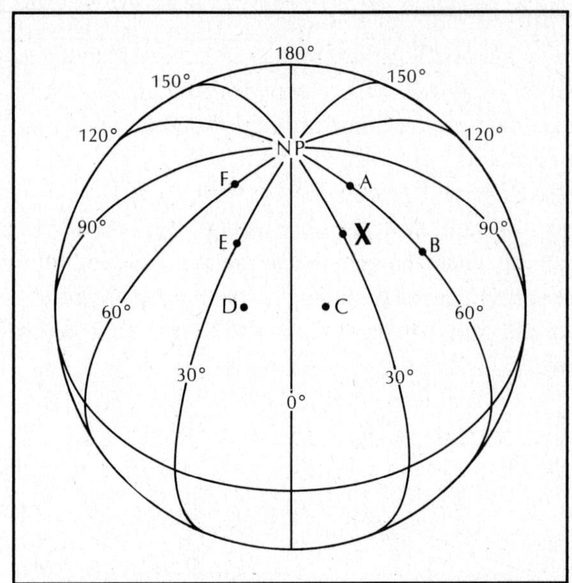

FIGURE 6-30
South pole

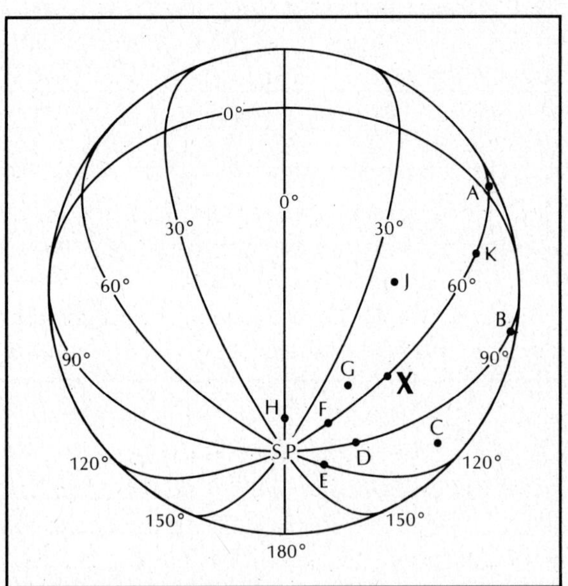

49. (See Figure 6-30)
 (a) Which point(s) is/are north of Point X? ______________________

____

(b) Which point(s) is/are southwest of Point X?______________________

(c) Which point(s) is/are northeast of Point X?______________________

Remarks on meridians and parallels items

- In this set of questions the easier questions are first. The first four questions also ask about the meridians and parallels separately.
- To answer these questions students must know background concepts, such as meridians and parallels are the basis of our directional system, they are labeled in "degrees" and the main references are the Prime Meridian, 180° meridian, and the equator.
- Students are required to respond on both globes and maps.
- Students are required to respond on different map projections, which reinforces their understanding that a map is like a picture and it can be taken from a variety of angles.
- The students must use both cardinal and intermediate directions to answer the questions.

Illustrations

The intent of the illustrations for the Location skills is the same as that for Representation skills. The ideas presented pertain to the *application* phase of skill instruction. As teachers review the activities they should think about how these ideas can be used to incorporate the Location skills into their own content study, that is, they should adapt the suggestions to best suit their own needs.

Illustration 1

A junior high school science teacher was preparing several lessons in which the class would study the moon. He intended that the students learn about the surface of the moon and note where the astronauts landed. He felt that the students could use their directional skills in these lessons, so he obtained a three-dimensional model of the moon and planned for the students to identify a North and South Pole. The students would then describe the locations of the moon's features in terms of the conventional directions used on earth.

The teacher planned later to assign the students to groups and have each group create its own hypothetical "directional" system—or method for describing location of places—which could be used on either the moon or some other planet. The students would have time to work out their ideas, formulate a scheme, and write questions to test whether their classmates understood their new scheme. Following the presentations, the teacher would have the students decide which one of the new schemes was most practical in terms of being an effective communications system.

The teacher hoped his lessons would provide the students with an opportunity to use their map skills as an aid in learning about the moon. He noted that all of the students knew their cardinal directions and most of them were familiar with the intermediate directions.

Illustration 2

A ninth grade history teacher was teaching a unit on the Middle East and decided to integrate the meridians and parallels skill into her planned map work. Since she felt this skill was very closely tied to the latitude-longitude skills and that applications of it were best done in connection with using latitude-longitude, she incorporated mainly developmental work into her lessons on the Middle East. She also involved only those students who were not entirely familiar with the skill.

In the first lesson the students read a very general description of the Middle East that included such topics as location, religion, size of the countries, and recent economic growth. The teacher provided her own simply drawn map with meridians and parallels drawn in and the countries and major cities labeled. The students were to describe the general location of this area in terms of meridians and parallels and to determine the relationship of the major cities to one another in terms of directions determined by the meridians and parallels. The students were also to note the general location on a globe.

In later lessons the teacher would frequently refer the students to a map to pinpoint, using meridians and parallels, where Middle East events were taking place, such as a journey to Mecca, a war, or a meeting between two heads of government.

Illustration 3

In an eleventh grade anthropology course, the students were studying various cultures. One topic of discussion was the effect that geographic location had on particular groups of people. The students were to propose how, for example, climate may have affected living habits over the years. The teacher thought the use of the latitude-longitude skill could be tied in, especially since most of the students knew the skill. Several lessons were planned. In one, the students were to compare two groups of people living about the same time in the same general latitude on different continents. In another, the students were to compare one group living in a northern latitude with one living about the same time in a comparable southern latitude. Throughout the unit of study the teacher planned to encourage the students to draw conclusions about peoples' life-styles and customs based on students' knowledge of the various latitudes and associated climates.

Illustration 4

In a junior high school history class the students were comparing the numbers and locations of hunting and food-gathering peoples in 1981 A.D. and 10,000 B.C. In planning her lessons for the unit the teacher found that in many of her activities the students would need to use the latitude-longitude skill.

At the beginning of the unit she reviewed the skill. Some of the students knew it well and some were only familiar with it. In one of the first lessons the teacher gave the students a world map (with meridians and parallels drawn in) and a list of some major cities to add to it. The students put each city on the map according to the latitude-longitude location given it. In a following activity the students shaded in certain areas of several continents—again, according to latitude-longitude information supplied by the teacher—showing where hunters and gatherers still exist. Other large areas were designated as locations where hunters and gatherers lived long ago.

When the maps were completed, the students drew comparisons and conclusions about the peoples they were studying. Using the latitude-longitude skill was helpful since, given a location, the students could quickly locate a certain area or city on their own map.

Illustration 5

In a sixth grade math class the teacher planned to tie in practice using the latitude-longitude skill with his unit on measurement and time zones. In one activity he gave students a map showing hypothetical shipping routes between several countries and cities. The students placed ships going various directions along the routes according to specific locations given in degrees of latitude and longitude. Later, the students measured the distances between the ships with rulers and converted their figures to kilometers using the scale bar on the map.

As a follow-up activity the teacher formed several groups of students to study the ships, and then devised five word problems for the other groups to solve. One sample word problem went as follows: If Ships A and B are both traveling at 15 knots and Ship A will reach Port City at 10:30 P.M., when will Ship B reach Port City (given the same wind and tide conditions)?

In the unit on time zones one activity required the students to place the capital cities on a map (indicating time zones) of the U.S., according to the latitude-longitude location given for each one. Next, the students responded to several word problems the teacher had worked out. An example is: If it takes 12 hours to drive from St. Paul to Lansing, Michigan, what will be your local arrival time if you leave at 6:30 A.M.?

As an additional follow-up activity, the students placed some other cities on the map, again, using latitude-longitude information to locate them. Then they met in groups and devised some of their own time zone problems for the other groups to solve.

Practice Exercise

Examine the following maps and then decide which orientation skills you would teach in conjunction with each one. Write down at least one development and one application activity students could do for each map. Figure 6-31 (Lesson A) is part of a social studies unit on time zones and Figure 6-32 (Lesson B) is part of an economics class lesson pertaining to world trade and shipping routes.

FIGURE 6–31
Time zones of the world

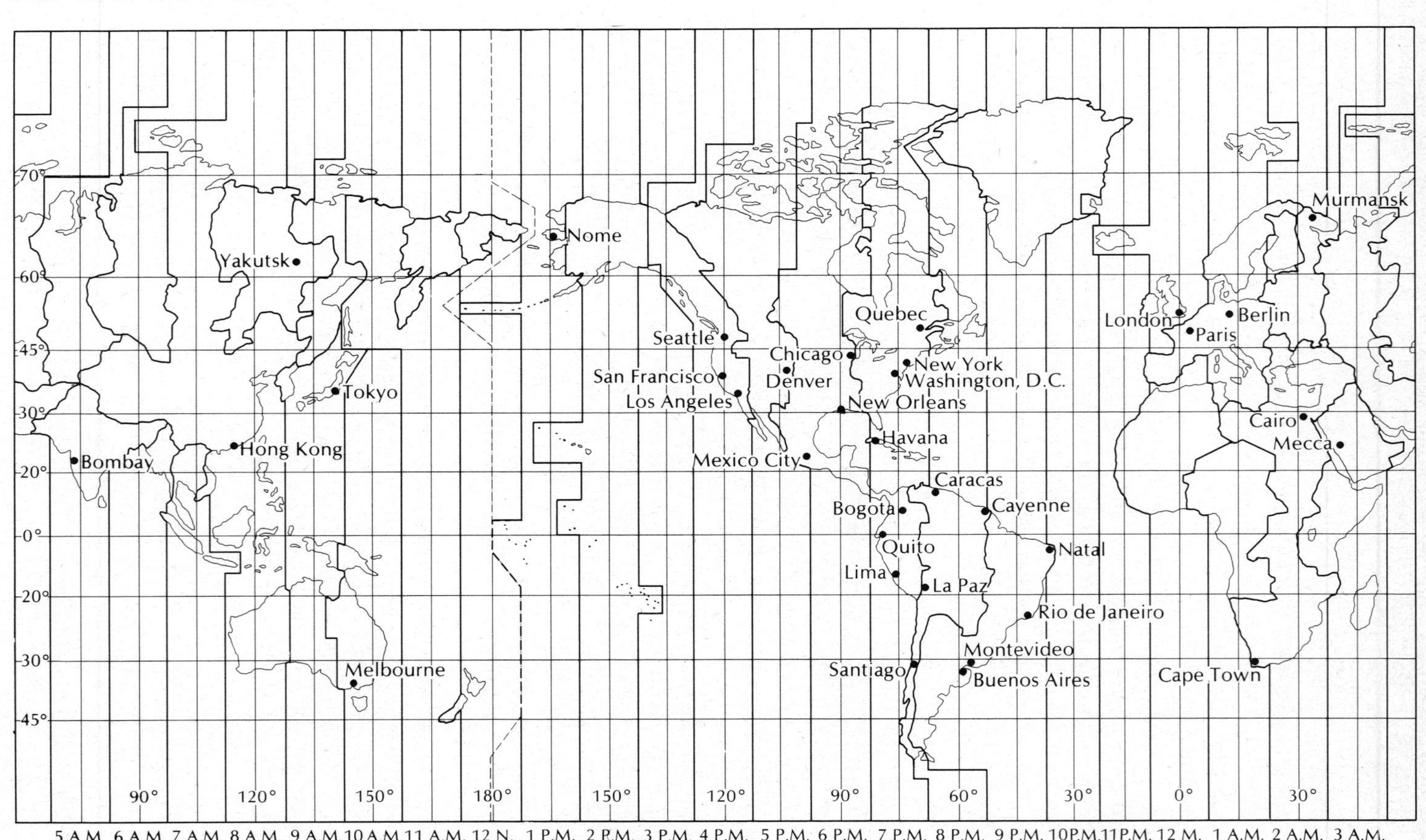

Orientation skills____

____

Development activity______________________________________

____

Application activity______________________________________

____

Example lesson A (see Figure 6–31)

Skill selected: Latitude-longitude (The skill, Meridians and Parallels, would not be pertinent, since the grid lines are not curved and the poles are not indicated on this projection.)

Development activity: Where is Melbourne, Australia, located? (38° south latitude, 145° east longitude)

Application activity: Assign students problems to figure out involving time changes in travel between cities across the continents. Provide students the latitude and longitude location of each city so they may locate it quickly. As a follow-up activity, students can propose their own problems for classmates to figure out. For example, they can designate two locations, not necessarily near a city, by giving the latitude and longitude information for both. Then they may ask the time of day in one place, given the time in the other.

Orientation skills____

____

Development activity______________________________________

____

Application activity______________________________________

____

Example lesson B (see Figure 6–32)

Skills selected: Intermediate directions and Meridians and Parallels

Development activity:

a. Describe the directions of the shipping route that goes from eastern Australia to Sumatra. (North and northwest)
b. Describe the directions of the shipping route from southwestern United States to Panama. (South, southeast, east)

Application activity: Describe several of the shipping routes with the greatest freight tonnage and one or two of the routes with the

FIGURE 6-32
The world

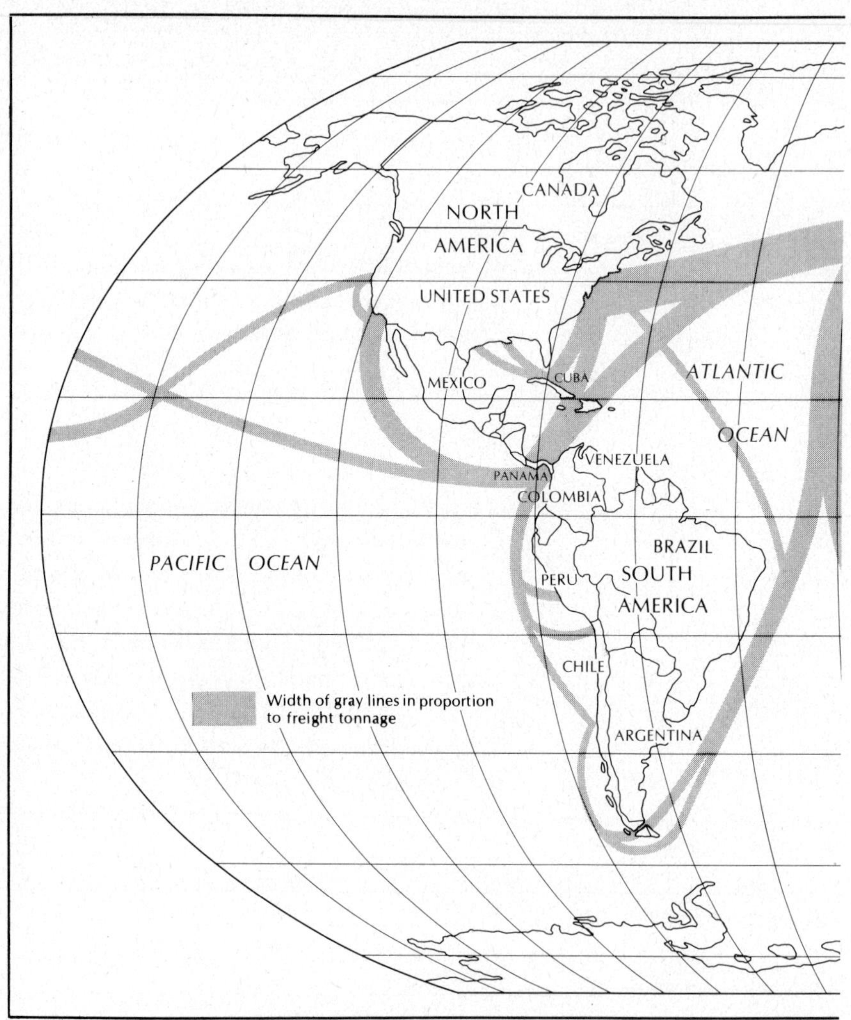

least freight tonnage. Tell in what directions they go and between which countries. (Greatest: U.S. to Northern Europe, Northeast; Northern Europe to Egypt, Southwest and East; Eastern Africa to Northern Sumatra, Southeast and East. Least: Southern Africa to Southern Australia, East; Chile to Panama, Northwest and North)

MEASUREMENT The third aspect of map use to be considered here is the measurement system. Measurement refers to determining distances to using models as representations of larger objects.

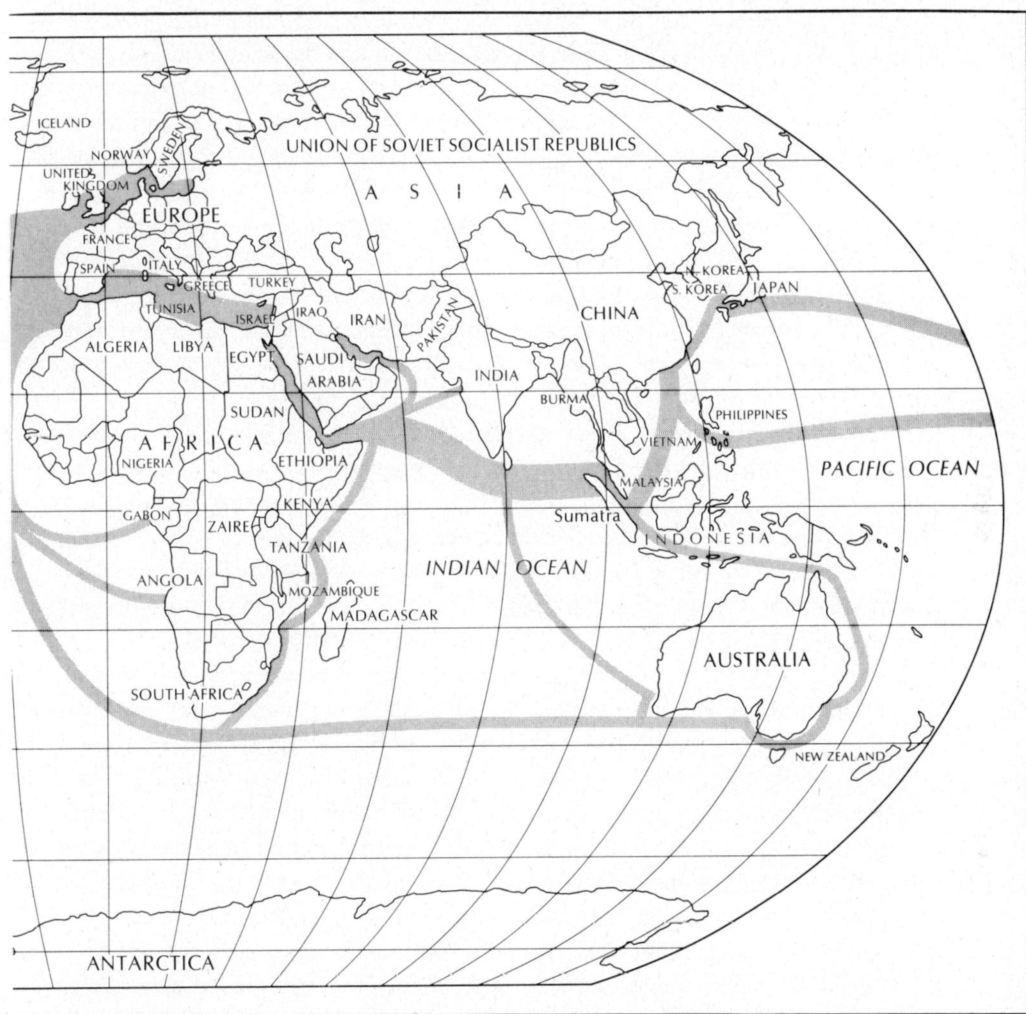

Developmental Perspective

Frequently, when students are asked to either determine the distance between two cities on a map or to draw—in proportion—a map of a certain area, students are unable to do so. One reason may be that students lack practice in these skills, but they may also not have received appropriate developmental instruction. Developmental instruction first exposes students to beginning activities and, later, emphasizes more advanced skills, when the students are well prepared for them. The measurement skills are discussed in terms of "the scale" and to "scale."

The scale

The skills associated with learning how to measure range from using approximations of size and distance to using standard units of measure. Beginning students are learning to measure when they judge the relative size of an object or representation of an object (The apple is bigger than the egg) and the relative distance between two points (It's a long way to town). Both skills, judging relative size and relative distance, should be specifically taught to students, using objects in the environment and representations of objects in models (like a dollhouse) and on two-dimensional maps. As students progress, they may use nonstandard units of measure to describe relative distances like, for example, "The school is three blocks from my house" or "The bank is five stop lights away." This skill should also be practiced in the environment and on maps.

Using standard units of measure may be introduced when students have developed the mathematical skills necessary to using a scale bar (/____/ 0 Miles 2) and/or verbal referent (1″ = 2 miles). Students should understand that while nonstandard units are useful in expressing general distances, more precise measurements are often necessary.

Students should begin using their rulers by measuring in whole units, based on a one-to-one correspondence. For example, initial activities may include taking simple measurements of pieces of paper, desks, or chairs. When students are introduced to the scale bar or verbal referent on a map, it should state a one-to-one equivalent (such as, 1″ = 1 block, 1 cm = 1 yard), and the distances between points should be in whole units (that is, on a map with a scale of 1″ = 1 block, each distance the student measures should be 1 inch, 2 inches, 3 inches, etc., not fractions of inches).

When students are comfortable with taking these measurements and understand the idea that maps, although always smaller than reality, may be drawn to a wide variety of scales, multiple whole units can be introduced. Scales indicating a one to more than one correspondence (1 inch = 5 feet) can be used with different maps —real and hypothetical—to accustom students to the vast changes in area that maps represent. (Again, at this stage measuring in fractional units should still be avoided. The students will find sufficient challenge in determining that several bus stops, for example, although measuring three inches apart, are actually 600 feet apart.) Several activities in teaching multiple whole units may include taking measurements with other than rulers; for example, a teacher can establish that an unsharpened pencil or length of string stands for 10 feet, and have the students determine several distances with these objects.

After students become proficient at determining multiple whole units, they can begin to determine fractional units. The initial activities should be simple, however, and corresponding math skills should be reviewed so students do not bog down in basic arithmetic problems when measuring their distances. One suggestion is to begin with half units. On a scale of 1 inch = 10 miles, for example, the student measures distances that are 1-1/2 inches apart, 3-1/2 inches, and 1/2 inch apart. When quarter units are introduced, numbers should be easy to divide (a scale of 1 inch = 8 blocks is easier to work with than a scale of 1 inch = 10 blocks). Gradually, students should take measurements from commercially prepared maps, say, atlases and road maps, so that they see how to use the skill in situations they may confront on their own.

To scale

The skills associated with "to scale" involve the student's understanding that maps are always smaller than reality and vary in size, but are always drawn in proportion or "to scale." In other words, the objects represented always have the same relation on a map that they do in reality. We identify two skills that require students to apply their understanding of proportion. The first skill is Different scales. To use this skill, the student may draw two maps of the same area but each one to a different scale. When maps of the same area are studied, the difference in the scales can be judged by noting the kind and amount of detail. For example, an airport and its runways may be carefully diagrammed on a large-scale map and yet be only a dot on another, smaller-scale map.

Using inset maps, the second "to scale" skill, also involves using different scales. An inset map is often provided in conjunction with a map specifically showing one area. The inset map is always drawn to a smaller scale than the larger map and shows the relationship of the area depicted in the larger map to the surrounding area, so the reader can get some idea of the relative size. Sometimes, for example, a geographer will present several large maps, say, of individual states, each drawn to a different scale, and then provide one inset map of the whole U.S., so that the reader can compare the relative sizes of the different states. Without the use of inset maps, visualizing the relative sizes of areas depicted is extremely difficult, unless of course they happen to be drawn to the same scale.

Although there is no specific time in the measurement sequence to teach students about proportion, certainly students should be familiar with the notion of "the scale," and have some experience in determining distances by referring to a scale bar or verbal referent before they study "to scale."

In the schema on page 168 below showing the measurement skills, we have identified Fractional units, Different scales, and Inset maps as the advanced skills. We encourage the reader to work through the Development Activities section for these skills, because it provides an opportunity to practice these skills and to see what problems students encounter when learning them.

Development Activities

Teachers should work through the development activities for the advanced measurement skills to ensure their understanding of each skill, before proceeding to the application phase of instruction. We recommend the beginning measurement skills be taught in the primary grades so that students in the intermediate grades and above are well acquainted with them.

When working through the exercises for Fractional units, Different scales, and Inset maps, try to identify situations in your own classroom in which students need to use these skills. Note that while Fractional units may be a more frequently used skill, knowledge of the other two skills is critical to understanding the real purpose of maps.

Measurement skills

The scale	*To scale*
Relative Size Relative Distance Nonstandard units of measures	
Standard units of measure	
Single whole units Multiple whole units Fractional units*	Different scales* Inset maps*

*Skills included in Development Activities section.

FIGURE 6-33
Meters

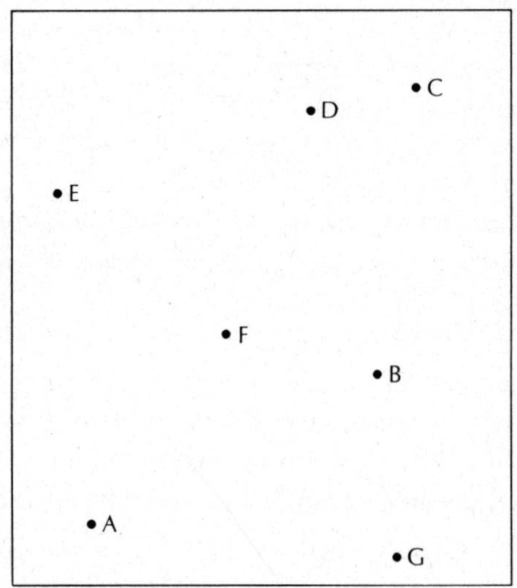

1 inch = 200 meters

Scale:
Fractional Units

50. (See Figure 6-33)
    (a) How many meters are there between Points A and B?________
    (b) How many meters are there between Points A and C?________
    (c) How many meters are there between Points C and D?________
    (d) How many meters are there from Point E to Point C to Point G?________

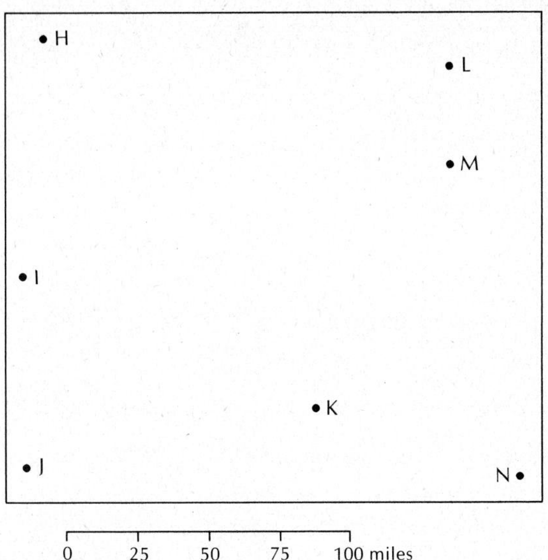

FIGURE 6-34
Miles

51. (See Figure 6-34)
    (a) What is the distance between Points H and N?__________
    (b) What is the distance between Points N and K?__________
    (c) What is the distance from Point I to Point L to Point M?__________
52. (See Figure 6-35)
    (a) About how many miles is it from Bondo (north) to Kisangani?__________
    (b) About how many miles is it from Brazzaville (west) to Lubumbashi (south)?_
    (c) About how many miles is it from Mbandaka (west) to Kalemie (east)?______
    (d) About how many miles is it from Port Francqui (central) to Luluabourg?____
    (e) About how many miles is it from Kinshasa (west) to Kisangani?__________

Remarks on fractional units items

- The questions are based on background concepts such as the fact that distances in the environment can be described through the use of standard units of measurement; a scale is needed to find out how much smaller the map is than reality, and that once the scale is known, unknown distances in the environment can be calculated; maps differ in how much smaller than reality they are and that the scale can be expressed in different ways (for example, verbal statement and scale bar).
- The questions include different phrasing and the maps include different scales.
- The questions progress in difficulty so that the student first becomes oriented to the task and then must make more difficult computations.

FIGURE 6-35
Zaire

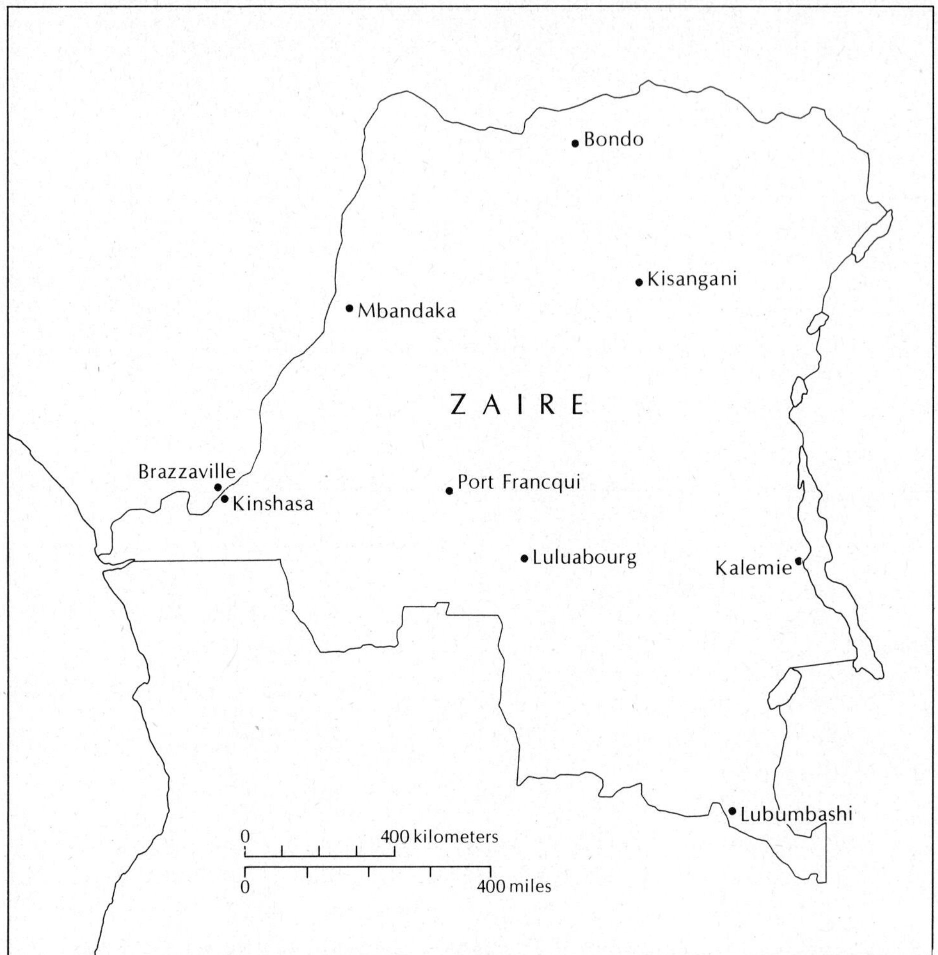

- Hypothetical maps are used to develop the skill initially, since scales on real maps are harder to compute.
- The mathematical computations are simple enough so that they do not interfere with the student taking measurements.

Different scales

53. (See Figures 6-36 to 6-38)
    (a) Which map(s) would you use to locate a certain mountain south of Guadalajara?____________________
    (b) Which map(s) would you use to note the relation of Mexico to the rest of Central America?____________________
    (c) Which map(s) is best to use to measure the distance between several Mexican cities?____________________

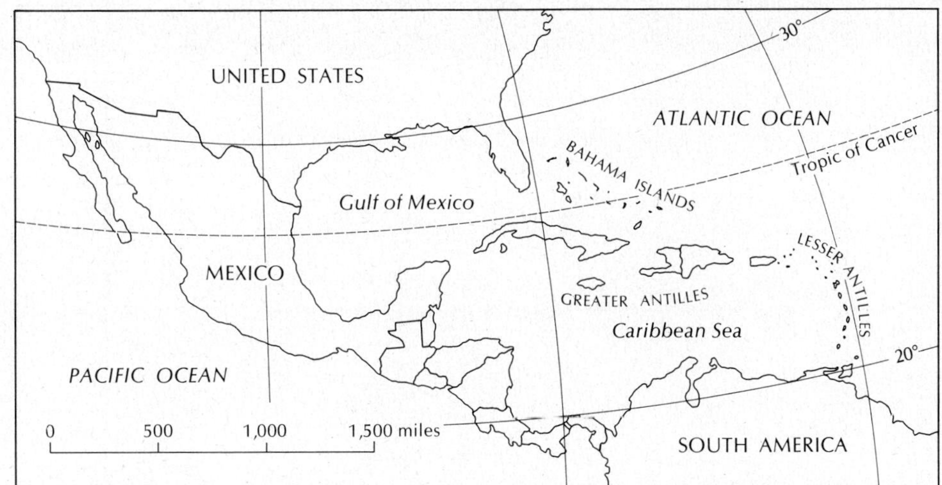

FIGURE 6-36
Small scale

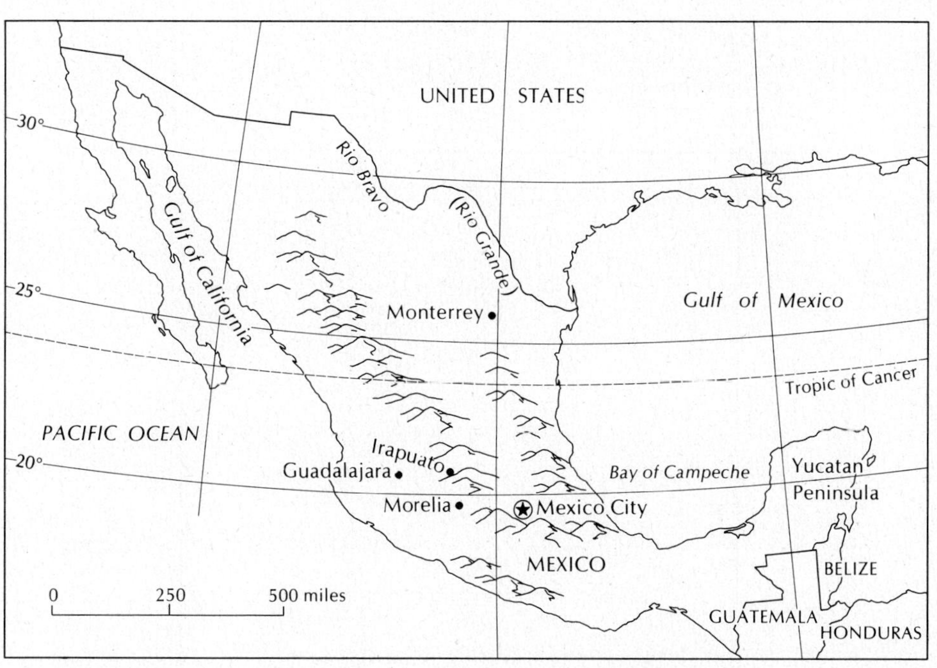

FIGURE 6-37
Mexico

(d) Which map(s) would you use to find the capital of Mexico?__________

(e) Which map(s) would you use to find the capital of Jalisco?__________

(f) Which map(s) would you use to find out at about what latitude Mexico is?___

____

FIGURE 6-38
Jalisco

FIGURE 6-39
Pineville a

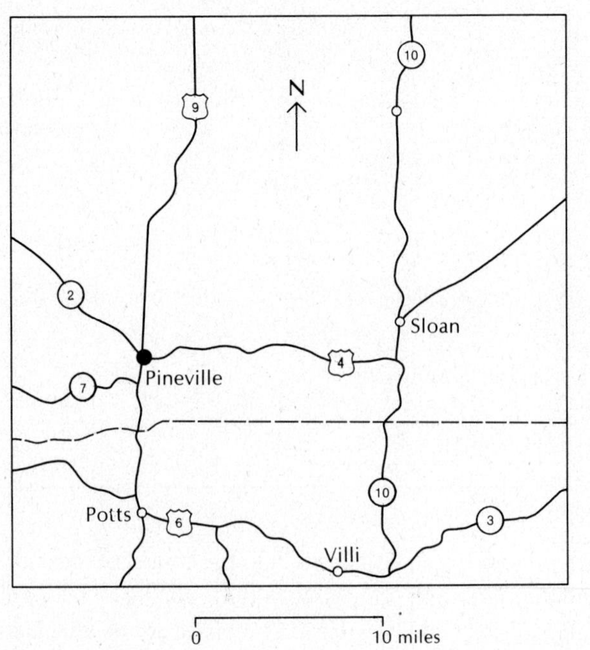

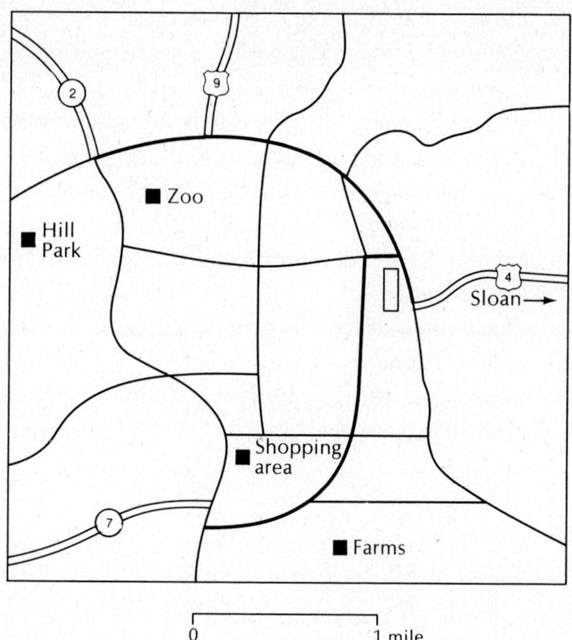

FIGURE 6–40
Pineville b

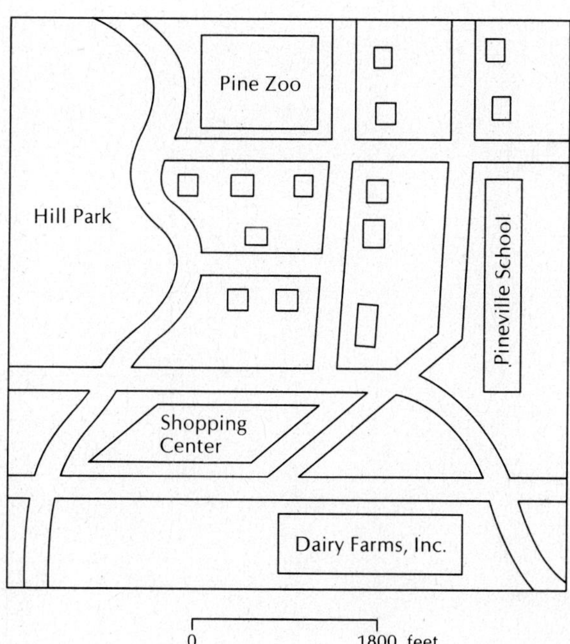

FIGURE 6–41
Pineville c

54. (See Figures 6-39 to 6-41)
   (a) Which map(s) would you use to see how to get from Pineville to Sloan?____
   (b) Which map(s) would you use to see how to get from Hill Park to the Zoo?___
   (c) Which map(s) would you use to see a general layout of the *entire* town of Pineville?____
   (d) Which map(s) would show what roads lead into Pineville?____

Remarks on different scales items

- Real maps are included in this developmental activity so that students practice the skill in a realistic situation.
- The questions require students to determine whether only one or two (or three) maps can be used to respond.
- Three maps of one area are included to provide students perspective on how the amount of detail changes from a small-scale to large-scale map.

Inset maps

55. (See Figures 6-42 and 6-43)
   (a) Which island is bigger?____
   (b) How much bigger is this island (the one you chose in #55a) than the other one?

FIGURE 6-42
Fish Island

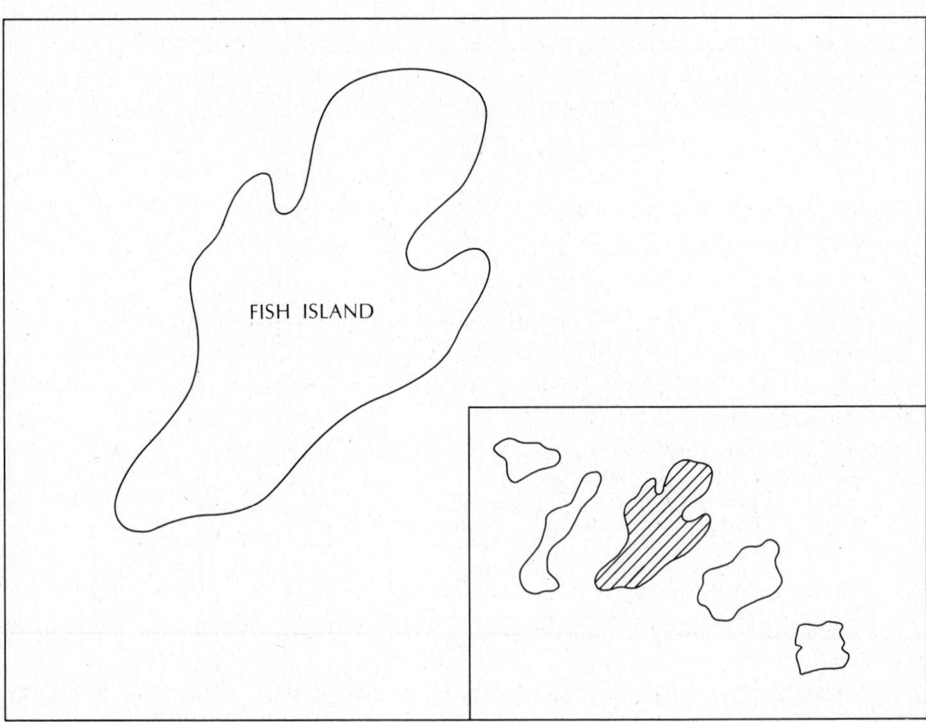

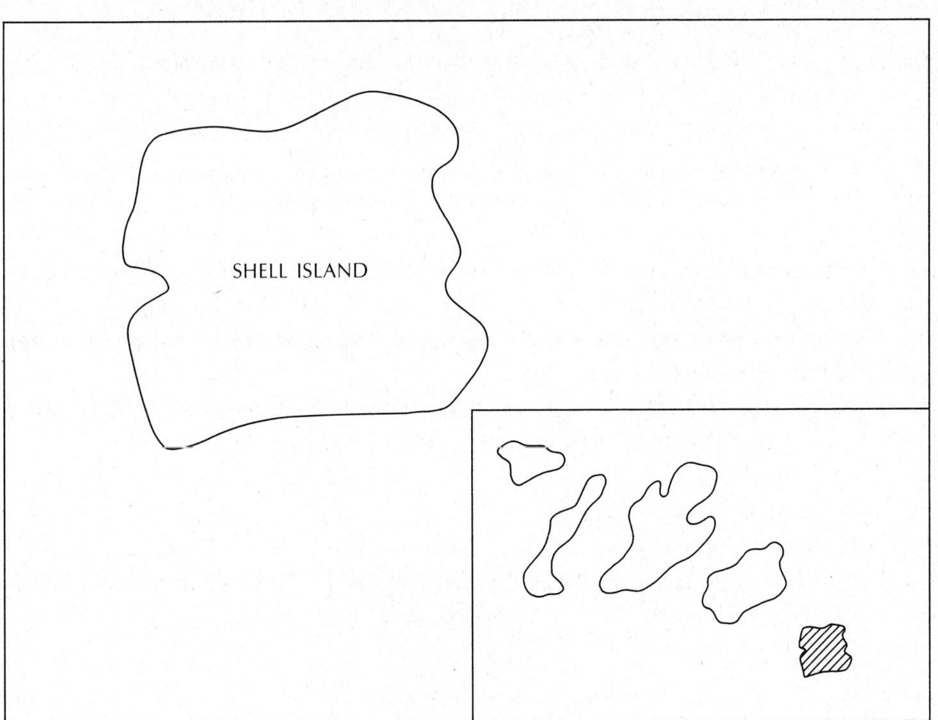

FIGURE 6-43
Shell Island

Circle the correct answer: Slightly
About 3 times bigger
About 10 times bigger

(c) What other information about Fish and Shell islands can you tell from these maps?__________

56. (See Figures 6-44 to 6-49)
    (a) Which state is longest from north to south?__________
    (b) Which state is smallest?__________
    (c) Which state is the widest from west to east?__________
57. (See Figures 6-50 to 6-55)
    (a) Which county is largest?__________
    (b) Which county is smallest?__________
    (c) In which two counties is about the same amount of corn grown?__________

Remarks on inset maps items

- Hypothetical maps are used to provide appropriate practice for students developing the skill. Real maps are used to help students use the skill in a realistic situation.
- To answer the questions correctly, students must consult the *inset* maps; not just the larger, separate maps.

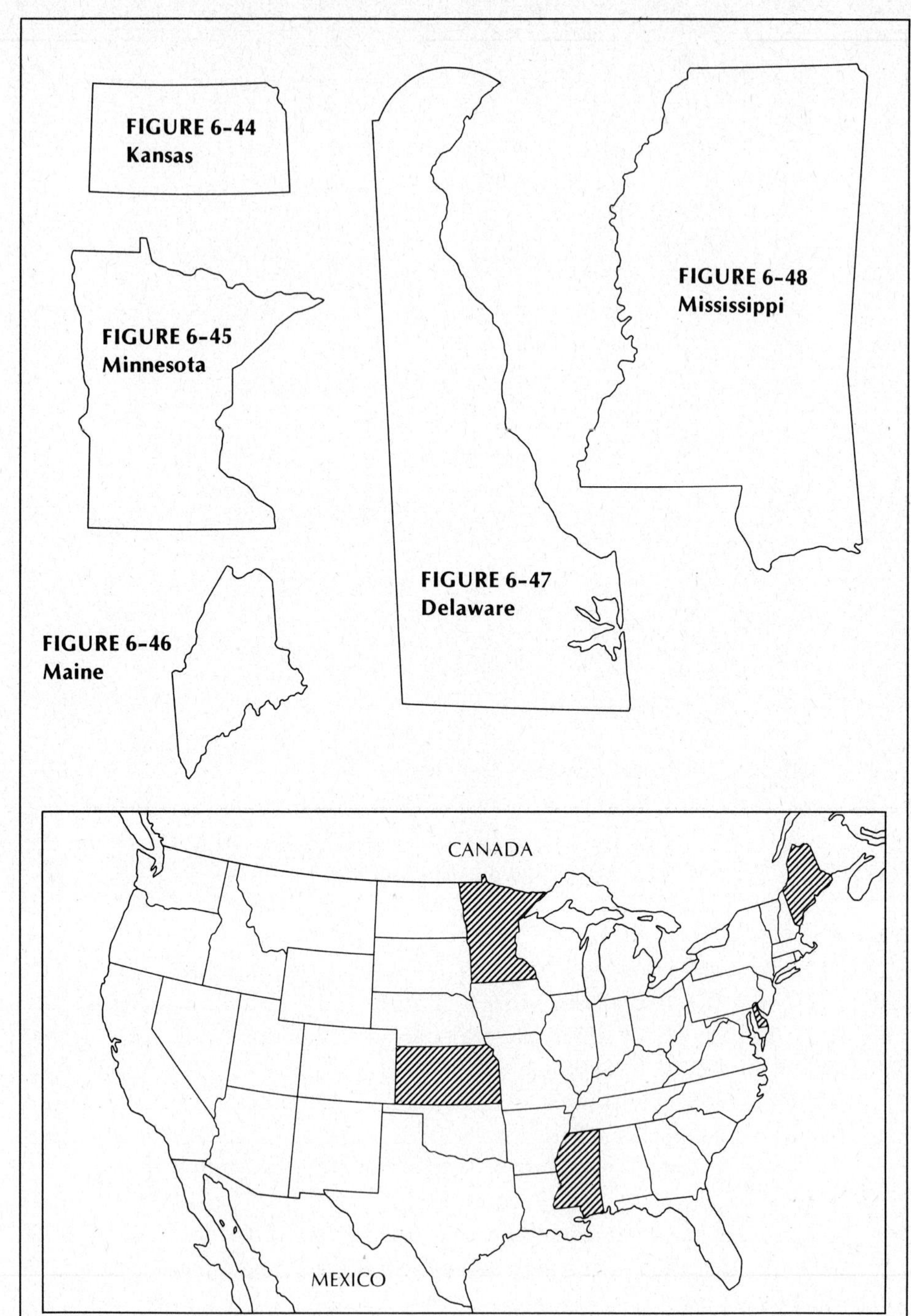

FIGURE 6-49
The United States

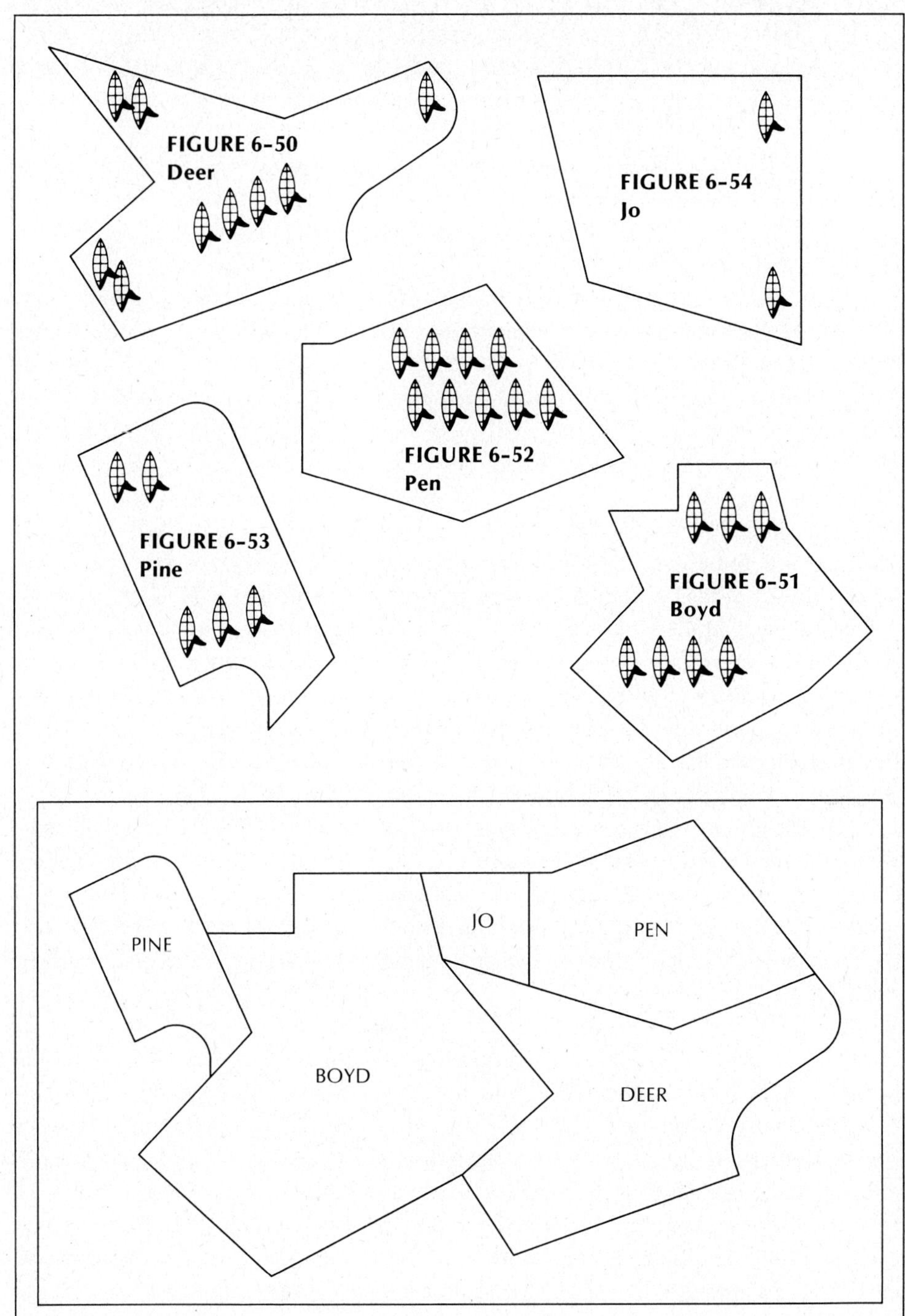

FIGURE 6-50
Deer

FIGURE 6-54
Jo

FIGURE 6-52
Pen

FIGURE 6-53
Pine

FIGURE 6-51
Boyd

FIGURE 6-55
All counties

Illustrations

The intent of the illustrations for the Measurement skills is the same as that for the Representation and Location skills. The ideas should be used as a basis for incorporating the *application* phase of using measurement skills into teachers' own content subjects.

Illustration 1

One teacher of a sociology class was beginning a unit of study on large urban areas. She had prepared several lessons on examining recreation facilities among these urban sites. One lesson planned for students to compare the amounts of space allotted for public parks.

The teacher intended that students look at the information they gathered about the parks in more than one way. She assigned one group of students to construct a bar graph showing each city and the corresponding number of square miles of park space. Another group of students was to locate (with the teacher's help) one map (drawn to a small scale) showing all the cities and park areas and then locate separate maps (drawn to various, but larger scales) of each city, again showing the separate park areas.

The students were to study the larger, more detailed city maps and then draw conclusions about the different amounts of park space by referring to the "inset" map which showed *all* the parks drawn to the *same* scale. The teacher planned to point out to the students that the inset map not only provides perspective—by showing the relationship of several locations to each other—but it allows the student to make comparisons among sizes of areas (which cannot be done by comparing individual maps, unless they happen to be drawn to the same scale). The teacher also planned to have students compare the amount and type of information available from the bar graphs with that available from the individual inset maps.

As a follow-up activity to using the inset map, the teacher planned to ask the students to compare the size of the state of California with Viet Nam, without consulting a chart telling the respective numbers of square miles. She felt this assignment would demonstrate the difficulty of making comparisons of size without having an inset map. (Note: Inset maps of the world—showing individual countries and states—can be difficult to find.)

Illustration 2

In a middle school shop class the teacher helped the students build some model houses. He divided his class of 25 students into five groups and assigned each group to think about a house they would like to build (he specified a maximum number of square feet) and to list some of the features the house must have. Next, the teacher told the students to draw a plan of their house according to the scale, 1/4 inch = 1 foot. After the teacher met with each group and approved its plans, the students proceeded, using the assigned scale and standard notations for stairs, doors, windows, etc. When the students' blueprints were complete, each group redrew its house to the scale, 1/2 inch = 1 foot, on sturdy cardboard. When the second, larger blueprint was finished, the teacher directed the students in actually building the houses: cutting thin pieces of wood shavings to glue on the blueprint as walls, stairs, and removable roofs; cutting out windows and pieces of cellophane; and designing lawns and driveways.

As the houses were being built, the teacher discussed the various procedures they were using. He pointed out that planning a house according to a specific scale ensures, for example, that all the rooms in the house will turn out in correct proportion to the total length and width, and that doors and hallways will be in the right place—not too narrow or too short.

Illustration 3

The students in one high school band were invited to tour and play in several European cities during the summer. While the students were busy raising money for their trip in the winter and spring, they planned their tour. The band teacher suggested they determine the length of the train rides between the cities and the amount of time in each city they wanted to spend. He consulted with a social studies teacher about reading maps and schedules and then reviewed several skills with the students.

The students proceeded by locating several maps and train schedules and figuring out how many hours and miles there were between the cities they would visit. They also located city maps and found the hotels where they would be staying and some of the sites they wanted to see. They then determined how long it would take them to walk and/or ride from site to site.

When the "research" work was done, the students put together a final itinerary and made copies for themselves, their families, and classmates.

Illustration 4

In a sixth grade science class the students were beginning a unit on wild animals that included several discussions about the importance of zoos, their physical arrangements, and the philosophies of their management.

The teacher told the students about several large zoos (such as the ones in San Diego, Chicago, and Washington, D.C.) and then took the students to visit their local zoo. The students were assigned to study one animal in particular. In addition to gathering relevant data on a certain animal, the students were to draw a map of their animal's living quarters at the zoo. The teacher discussed measurement skills before the students took their trip and helped them decide how the maps would best be drawn (that is, what scale would be most appropriate to use).

While at the zoo the teacher obtained copies of a map of the entire zoo area, as well as different sectional maps of the various areas within the zoo (drawn to a larger scale than the whole-area map). When the students returned to the classroom, they completed their own maps (maps drawn to a larger scale than the sectional maps). Then the teacher gave them each an appropriate sectional map and a whole-area map to compare with the map they had made.

The teacher divided the class into working groups of two or three students (putting together mainly those students who had chosen animals in the same section, such as the feline or reptile building) and assigned each group to formulate questions about their maps and animals for the other students to answer. The whole-area map was designated the "A" map, the sectional maps were "B" maps, and the individual maps were labeled "C" maps. One group of students asked the following questions: Which one of our maps is the best one to find out what facilities have been set up for the polar bears? (Ans.: John's C map of the polar bear). Which map is the best one to find out where the peacocks are in relation to the flamingos and egrets? (Ans.: The B map showing the outdoor and indoor bird cages). Which is the best map to find out where the birds are in relation to the tigers? (Ans.: The A map of the whole zoo).

After the students had had a chance to use their three maps (drawn to the three different scales), the teacher held a summary discussion about the physical arrangements and management of their local zoo. Some of the students wanted to follow this activity by comparing their zoo with some of the larger, well-known zoos.

Practice Exercise

Examine the following maps (Figures 6-56 to 6-58) and then decide which measurement skills you would teach in conjunction with them. Write down at least one development and one application activity students could do. The three maps are part of a U.S. history lesson concerning the present-day transportation system.

FIGURE 6-56 Map a—U.S. roads

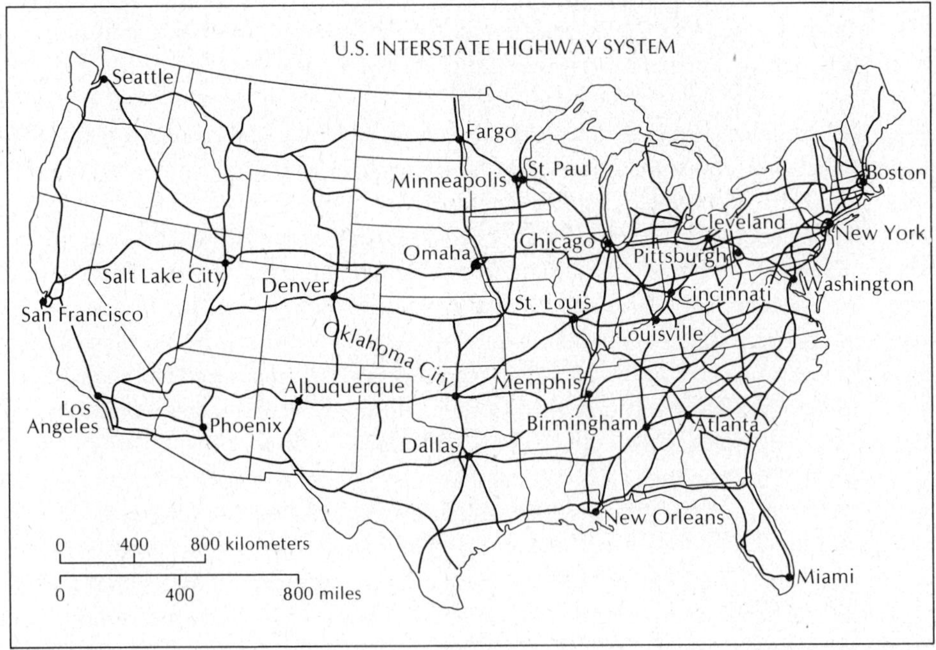

Measurement skills ______________________________

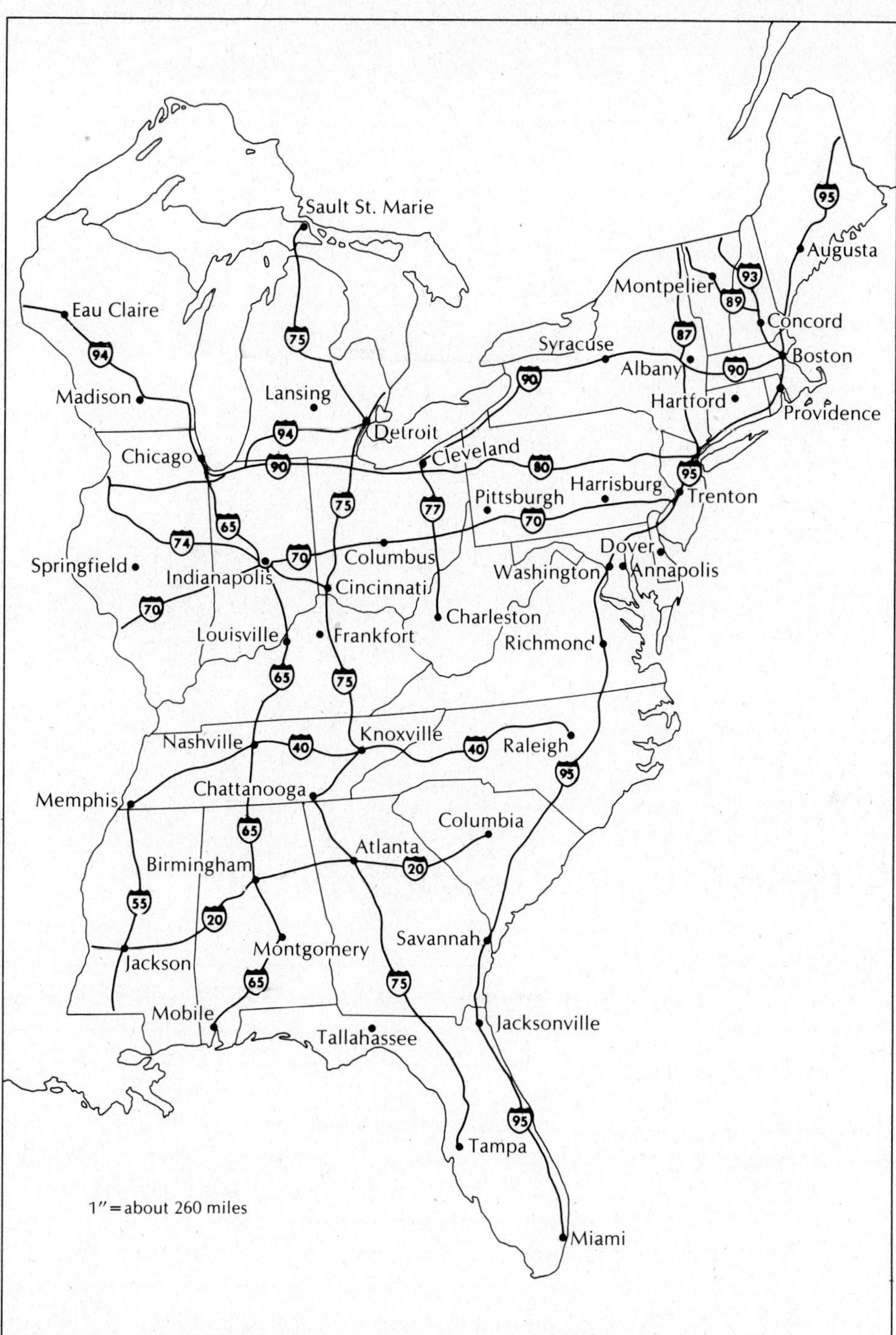

FIGURE 6-57
Map b — The east

FIGURE 6-58
Map c—Georgia

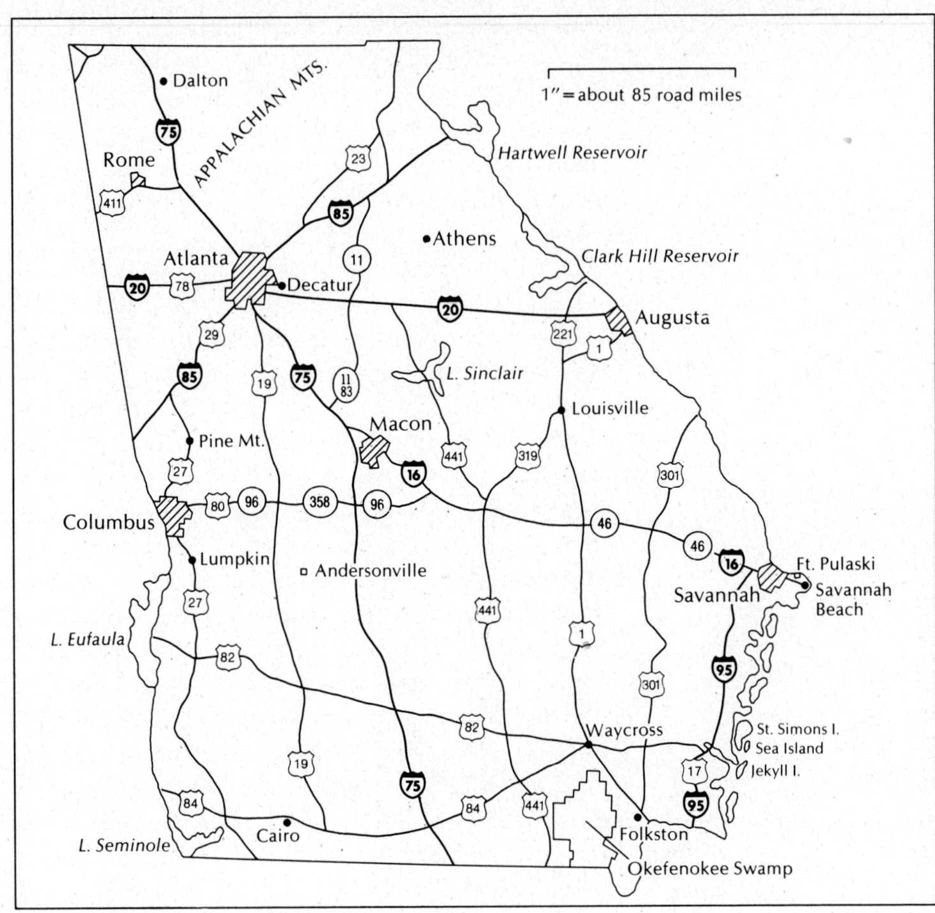

Development activity ______________________________

Application activity ______________________________

Example lesson (see Figures 6-57 and 6-58)

Skills selected: Fractional scale, Different scales

Development activity:

a. Which map(s) would be best to use to find out how far it is from Atlanta to Chicago? (Maps A and B)
b. Which map would be best to use to figure out a direct route from northern to southern Georgia? (Map C)
c. Which map would be best to use to compare the eastern and western U.S. interstate highway system? (Map A only)

d. Which map would be best to use to find out which cities Interstate #75 goes between? (Map B only)

Application activity: Divide students into groups of two or three. Tell them to plan three tours to different cities using only one of the three maps for each tour. The first tour would be based on Map A, the second one on Map B, and the third on Map C.

Through planning the tours, the students become aware of the importance of different kinds or amounts of information on the maps. For example, the description of the first tour, based on Map A, may be only sketchy. Students might list major cities nationwide that a bus or plane may go to, and/or they may present a reasonable sequence of cities to visit (for example, Seattle to Albuquerque via Salt Lake (not, say, St. Louis), and/or give distances in air miles.

The tour description based on Map B may contain suggested highways to take between more than two cities in one state. The tour description based on Map C would be the most complete. Small places, such as towns, islands, and historic sites, can be listed as stopping-off places when traveling by bus or car. The distances between these places can also be more accurately measured when using the larger scale bar. The students should compare their amounts and kinds of information when discussing their three tours.

TEACHING MAP SKILLS IN THE CONTENT AREAS

In each of the previous sections dealing with Representation, Location, and Measurement skills, teachers had the opportunity to first acquaint themselves with the particular skills—through the development activities—and then, by reviewing the illustrations, think about how a set of skills can be integrated with content study. As teachers become increasingly familiar with the map skills, they should ensure that all of the skills are incorporated into classroom material—for both development and application work. Two illustrations are presented below that suggest how a variety of skills can be reinforced in a unit of study. We strongly encourage teachers to adapt these strategies for use with other skills and with their own materials.

Illustrations

Illustration 1

An eighth grade social studies teacher whose students were studying the westward movement in the United States determined that there were several specific map skills—line symbols, intermediate directions, and scale—that could be used with the content material she would soon be introducing. She noted that the students in her first hour class had developed these skills (see our comments on diagnosis in Part 2), so she was confident they were ready to apply them.

In the students' textbook were several maps showing westward routes, each labeled with the names of the men who led the expeditions along them. The maps each contained a compass rose, scale bar, and a key explaining topographical symbols. The teacher wrote out the following questions for one of her lessons:

a. Which trail was most heavily traveled? (It is indicated by the heaviest black line.)
b. Why do you think more people took this one trail than any of the others? (The trail is shown to pass through a valley between two mountains and rivers cross it at several points.)
c. What were some obvious disadvantages of using this trail? (It is longer than the others—as determined by use of the scale bar—and shown to be farthest north, thus colder in the winter.)
d. What directions does the most southern trail go in? (It is quite winding and goes in many directions so that the compass rose must be used to determine which ones.)

The teacher discussed the questions with the class and then directed them to form groups to examine a second map (which was part of a current homework assignment) in their text. From the second map each group was to make several conclusions about the information depicted. Later, the groups would share their findings.

Illustration 2

The art teacher in an elementary school selected a group of students to set up a display for parents' night. Part of the display included a map of the school. The art teacher consulted the social studies teacher who was responsible for including map skills instruction as part of his content study. Together, they determined which skills the students needed to complete the school map. The social studies teacher pointed out those skills that almost all the students knew, as well as the skills that most of the students needed to practice. They agreed mainly the project would provide skill reinforcement for some students and initial skill practice for other students, but the experience would give all students a chance to see the practical value of learning map skills.

In carrying out the project the art teacher encouraged the students to (a) draw their building to scale and include the scale bar referent on their map; (b) use a bright color scheme to show the location of the kindergarten area and two classes each of grades 1-6; (c) indicate north; and (d) use semipictorial symbols to show the location and size of the primary and intermediate playgrounds and eating areas. At the end of the project the students developed questions about their school that could be answered from the information on the map. The questions included references to the representation, location, and measurement systems, and would be responded to by classmates before the map was used as part of the display.

Practice Exercise

Locate a road map of your home state and decide which map skills would be appropriate to teach in conjunction with using the map. Write down at least one development and one application activity that would help students familiarize themselves with the information presented and to see how that information can be used in their daily lives.

Map skills ______________________________

____

Development activity ______________________________

____

Application activity ______________________________

____

Example lesson (see Figures 6–57 and 6–58)

Skills selected: Point, line, area symbols, Intermediate directions, and Fractional scale

Development activity:

a. Which overnight camping spot is closest to <u>(name of town)</u>? (Student must check legend for point symbols and scale of miles, if distances aren't obviously different.)

b. Which lake (park, city, Indian reservation) is largest in <u>(name)</u> County? (Student compares sizes of areas, perhaps using a "rough" scale of miles.)

c. About how many miles is it from the ski area just northeast (southwest, northwest) of <u>(city)</u> to the airport just southeast of <u>(city)</u>? (Student uses directions, point symbols, and computes distance.)

d. About how far is it to travel from ____________ to ____________, if you drive only on federal highways (state roads)? (Student uses point and line symbols in determining distance.)

Application activity: Assign students, perhaps in groups, to plan a driving trip to visit certain historical sites around the state. They should determine their basic transportation costs by figuring how many miles their trip includes and how much per mile their car (bus or van) costs to operate. Side trips along the way (such as taking a longer, but more scenic route, seeing a particular tourist attraction) might be scheduled. If camping out is another part of the plan, then appropriate areas along the route should be selected. The students may also be challenged to figure out from the map additional highlights they want to include on their trip, such as traveling over a certain bridge or through a tunnel; taking a ferry; or going over a mountain, through a forest, or along a beach area. A contest could be established among the groups to see which one could plan the cheapest, but most exciting excursion!

REFERENCES

1. Bartz, B. "Maps in the classroom." *The Journal of Geography,* 1970, *69,* 18-24.
2. Boardman, D. "Graphicacy in the curriculum." *Educational Review,* 1976, *28,* 118-125.
3. Bosowski, E. F. *Cartography as language: An argument and a functional application.* Unpublished master's thesis, Clark University, 1974. (ERIC Document Reproduction Service No. ED 109 000)
4. Catling, S. "The child's spatial conception and geographic education." *Journal of Geography,* 1978, *77,* 24-28.
5. Chester, R. D., Askov, E., & Otto, W. *Wisconsin design for reading skill development: Teacher's planning guide—Study skills.* Minneapolis: National Computer Systems, 1973.
6. Cobb, R. L., & Stoltman, J. P. *Perspective ability and map conceptualization in elementary school children.* Paper presented at the annual meeting of the National Council for Geographic Education, Washington, D.C., 1973. (ERIC Document Reproduction Service No. ED 086 615)
7. Collier, E. R., & Vodicka, E. M. "The place of maps in the primary grades." *School Activities,* 1960, *31,* 212-213.
8. Giffard, E. O. *Cartographic symbolism and very young children.* Unpublished manuscript, 1972. (ERIC Document Reproduction Service No. ED 062 238)
9. Hawkins, M. L. *Skill development—Maps and globes. Social studies for the elementary school. Proficiency Module 8.* University of Georgia, Department of Social Science Education, 1972. (ERIC Document Reproduction Service No. ED 073 984)
10. Jarolimek, J. "The psychology of skill development." In *Skill Development in the Social Studies, 33rd Yearbook of the National Council for the Social Studies,* ed. H. M. Carpenter, pp. 17-33. Washington, D.C.: NCSS, 1963.
11. Job, K., & Weiser, L. *Study lessons in map reading.* Chicago: Follett, 1965.
12. Kamm, K. *The Wisconsin design study skills element: A one year case study.* Working Paper No. 203. Madison, Wisconsin: Wisconsin Research and Development Center for Cognitive Learning, 1977.
13. Kamm, K., & White, S. *A description of the procedures used in implementing an objective-based reading program in four schools.* Working Paper No. 503. Madison, Wisconsin: Wisconsin Research and Development Center for Individualized Schooling, 1979.
14. Kamm, K. *Strategies for implementing skill-based reading instruction.* Technical Report No. 533. Madison, Wisconsin: Wisconsin Research and Development Center for Individualized Schooling, 1980.
15. Kohn, C. F. "Interpreting maps and globes." In *Skills in Social Studies, 24th Yearbook of the National Council for the Social Studies,* pp. 146-177. Washington, D.C.: NCSS, 1953.

16. McCollum, D. "An elementary understanding of maps." *Clearinghouse,* 1976, *49,* 332-334.
17. Otto, W., Kamm, K., & Weibel, E. *Wisconsin design for reading skill development: Rationale and objectives for the study skills element.* Working Paper No. 84. Madison, Wisconsin: The Wisconsin Research and Development Center for Cognitive Learning, 1972.
18. Rushdoony, H. A. "The geographer, the teacher, and a child's perception of maps and mapping." *The Journal of Geography,* 1971, *70,* 429-433.
19. Sabaroff, R. "Maps and mapping in the first grade." *Journal of Geography,* 1959, *58,* 445-451.
20. Savage, T. V., Jr., & Bacon, P. "Teaching symbolic map skills with primary grade children." *Journal of Geography,* 1969, *68,* 491-496.
21. Sunal, C. S., & Sundal, D. W. "Mapping the child's world." *Social Education,* 1978, *42,* 381-383.
22. Towler, J. "Egocentrism: A key to map-reading ability?" *Social Education,* 1971, *35,* 893-898.
23. Whipple, G., & James, P. E. "Instructing pupils in map reading." *Social Education,* 1947, *11,* 205-208.

7 Getting Started with Study Skills

Now that we have reviewed the basic study skills and provided practice activities and classroom illustrations, we hope that our readers have been able to "fill in the gaps" in their knowledge of study skills. The fundamental assumption of this book has been that teacher mastery of study skills is absolutely essential to providing effective instruction to students. Until teachers feel comfortable with the skills, they will either not teach study skills or teach them poorly.

A recurring theme of this book has been the necessity of teaching study skills in content area classrooms. By now we hope that the reader is convinced students will be more likely to apply skills in the content subjects if instruction in those skills occurs while students are learning the concepts and knowledge associated with particular content areas. The developmental reading teacher who teaches reading/study skills apart from content subject matter with workbooks and drill sheets cannot help students apply those skills in actual content study. The reading teacher can teach only the development aspect of skill acquisition. The application phase, in which the skill is truly learned through independent application by the students, can occur only in content area classes in which the student must apply the skill to gain information necessary for the content study.

In Part 2 we applied the diagnostic-prescriptive model to teaching study skills and suggested various strategies for incorporating skill instruction in the content areas. We now want to review some important concepts pertaining to study skill instruction and content area reading.

- Teachers of the same content area at various school levels—social studies teachers in the intermediate grades, junior high or middle school, and high school—

should do curriculum planning together. Not only should the important concepts and knowledge of the content area be identified with the appropriate levels designated, but the study skills essential for learning the content also should be considered. The skills presented in this book can form the basis from which to choose skills related to the content subject.

The importance of introducing study skills early, and reteaching them at successively higher levels with more difficult materials and concepts, cannot be overemphasized. For example, if young children have experience in using a chart on which they must determine the intersecting point of a row and column, then using lines of longitude and latitude to locate points on a map should not be difficult later. The necessary ingredient is content teachers planning together to decide at what levels the skills should be first introduced and then retaught with more complex materials. We have tried in this book to emphasize the developmental nature of study skills and suggest appropriate skill exercises at the various levels.

• Teachers of the different content areas at the same level must also work together. If each content area curriculum has designated skills necessary to learning the subject matter as suggested above, then teachers of various content areas at a given level can work together to coordinate instructional efforts.

To use an example situation, if outlining is a skill identified as important in all content areas, then the teachers of one content area—say, the English teachers—may agree to teach it in their classes. Teachers of the other content areas would provide application activities in their subject materials, but the development activities would occur in the English classes. Social studies teachers, for example, could agree to teach map reading skills, science teachers teach table and graph skills, and so on, with application occurring in all content areas in which the study skill is appropriate. Since most study skills overlap in the various content areas, cooperative planning by the teachers at each level makes sense to prevent duplication of effort. Teaching a common format where appropriate, as in notetaking and outlining, prevents confusion in applying the skill in different content areas.

• Teachers must try to view things as their students do. Throughout the course of a day students are asked to "switch gears" in their reading strategies. Imagine reading Shakespeare at 9 A.M., followed by the paragraph shown in Figure 7-1 at 10 A.M.

And so it goes all day—students must learn to rapidly change their style of reading and thinking. Often we, the teachers, are not helpful because we have been thinking and talking in the language of our subject matter all day, in fact usually for years. We have to learn how to help students make the transition to our subject matter, not only in language and thought but also in skill application. Outlining, for example, while still the same basic skill, may appear different to students in a different context. Teachers need to remind students of the basic skill development process before an application can be made in a different content.

Obviously, we are not even going to attempt to construct such a READ and a PRINT statement to accomplish this. Not only is it awkward and tedious, it is impossible! To see why, recall that we may use any of the following as a variable name.

1. A letter. There are 26 possible variable names using letters only.
2. A combination of a letter followed by any one of the digits 0, 1, 2, 3, . . . , 9, for example, A0 or C2 or Z8. There are 26 × 10 = 260 possible variable names consisting of letter-number combinations.

In other words, using our present system of entering, storing, and printing numbers, there are 26 + 260 = 286 possible variable names permitted in any one program. This then is the second weakness referred to above; we are limited to no more than 286 variable names.

FIGURE 7-1 Passage from a computer programming textbook
(From Z. Jacobs, F. G. French, W. J. Moulds, and J. G. Schuchman, Computer Programming in the BASIC Language. *Boston: Allyn and Bacon, 1978, p. 229.)*

Skill instruction materials—or any reading in the content areas—should not be assigned without background provided. Unfamiliar vocabulary and concepts should be introduced *before* materials are assigned. Students should also be told how to read the material, for example, to get only the main ideas or to learn the factual details. If students are given the purpose for their reading—or if they are guided in setting their own purposes for reading—their reading and study will be appropriate. Again, this guidance can help students "switch gears" as they tackle their various assignments.

In Part 2 we suggested various ways of incorporating skill development activities into a content area classroom. Now we will discuss the hallmarks of an effective skill instruction lesson:

1. Students are told what skill they will be learning and why it is important for studying the content area. This information may also be elicited from the students inductively through discussion.
2. If students have been taught the skill in another content area they should be reminded that they have already learned the skill elsewhere. If the basic skill development is to occur at this point, earlier experiences with the skill in simpler forms should be reviewed.
3. As students work through the skill development or application activities they should be asked to explain what skill they are using and why it is important in learning the content. If students still do not understand the rationale for learning the skill—even if the teacher has explained it—retention of learning is doubtful.
4. An abundance of practice materials related to the content area should be provided. A single exposure to a skill cannot produce permanent learning. Repeated exposures will emphasize the importance of the skill in studying the content area.
5. A check on skill mastery is necessary after instruction and practice. A partially

learned skill will not be retained and applied in new contexts. Additional instructional materials should be provided to those who need further work.

6. After the skill development phase, skills can be combined and applied together. For example, students may be assigned a research project involving library skills, book skills, and reading for information skills. They may also need to read maps or graphic materials, depending on the content. The more "real life" type of integration and application of skills, the better chance that the students will retain the skills for independent use later.

We hope that the reader's knowledge and understanding of study skills have expanded through this book. We also hope that the reader can devise instructional activities for teaching the skills as well as test items for assessing mastery of the skills. Most importantly, we hope that the reader has a positive attitude toward study skills, recognizing their importance in an ever changing world. The more students apply study skills independently in content studies, the more they will do so independently after the more structured learning experiences in the elementary and the secondary schools have been completed. Until students learn to learn independently, they will be dependent on others in seeking answers to real-life questions. Beginning early in the elementary grades and increasing throughout the formal schooling experience, the student's responsibility for his or her own learning is essential.

Readers can reflect on the changes made in the storage, retrieval, and use of information within their lifetimes. Most of us were taught to use the Dewey Decimal system of categorizing books in a library. Now many elementary, secondary, and public libraries have changed to the more versatile and sophisticated Library of Congress system. We must know not only how to use a card catalog to locate a book but also a microfiche reader in more modern libraries where the card catalog is now obsolete. With modern technology it is difficult to predict the skills to be needed by our students in the future. It is clear, however, that students will have greater needs in the future to become more responsibile for their own learning and be able to apply those skills that enable them to function independently throughout their lives.

With the mainstreaming of students of all abilities into the regular classroom, it becomes even more important than ever to move students as quickly as possible to independent learning. *All* students need to learn to function as independently as their abilities permit. They all need to learn some study skills in order to survive in our society. Some students will learn more complex skills and learn them more quickly, while other students may be able to master only rudimentary skills. Nevertheless *all* must be taught the skills to enable them to continue learning when formal schooling has stopped. Study skills are those tools that make this life-long learning process possible.

Answers

PART 3: LOCATION OF INFORMATION IN BOOKS AND IN THE LIBRARY

1. *Managing Your Money*
2. Harold A. Wolf
3. Allyn and Bacon, Inc.
4. Boston
5. copyright date
6. front; the order in which topics are presented
7. back; alphabetical order
8. glossary; back, alphabetical order
9. title page
10. title page
11. preface; before
12. appendix
13. bibliography
14. italics, boldface print
15. main topics and subtopics
16. table of contents
17. index
18. index
19. table of contents
20. index
21. yes
22. yes
23. no
24. yes
25. no

26. 315 and 323
27. 303-307
28. 315-317
29. 177-178
30. 204 and 207
31. 433-434
32. 353; pages listed under "Bonds, corporate"
33. charming, chic, classy, coy Cynthia
34. redheaded, ridiculous, rural, rustic Rusty
35. mad, masked, mastermind, Mickey Mouse
36. page 706
37. page 703
38. page 705
39. page 702
40. page 704
41. drawer 3
42. drawer 2
43. drawer 5
44. drawer 5
45. drawer 4
46. drawer 1
47. He looked in the title/author section of the card catalog instead of the subject section.
48. card 1
49. card 2
50. card 3
51. card 2
52. card 3
53. card 2
54. card 3
55. cards 1 and 2
56. Reading—handbooks, manuals, etc.
57. Reading (Secondary Education)
58. illustrations (ill.); indexes
59. upper left-hand corner
60. International Standard Book Number
61. 500
62. B (biography) under the letter *L*
63. 800
64. 200

65. F (fiction) under the letter *S* (Charles Schultz is author)
66. 900
67. 400
68. 600
69. F (fiction) under the letter *W*
70. 300
71. R (reference)
72. 500
73. B (biography) under the letter *A*
74. 300
75. 700

76.	589	589	589.2	590	590.74
	C	K	M	F	A
77.	947	947	947.07	947.08	947.084
	M	S	P	H	S
78.	332	332.6	332.6	332.678	333.7
	B	E	S	B	E
79.	428	428.2	428.246	428.4	428.43
	S	M	R	L	J
80.	745.013	745.0973	745.0977	745.1	745.2
	E	C	D	D	B

81. 3
82. *Time; Antiques*
83. See Madog Ab Owain Gwynedd
84. 2
85. “Getting Down to Beauty Basics”
86. See Carnival (pre-Lenten festival)
87. P. O’Toole
88. “Frontier of illusion: the Welsh and the Atlantic revolution”
89. maps
90. *Workbench*, volume 36, page 69, January/February, 1980
91. Watched pots never boil.
92. An apple a day keeps the doctor away.
93. A stitch in time saves nine.
94. Wet birds never fly at night.
95. One seldom finds an empty Tabasco bottle.
96. queue
97. phosphatize
98. sluice
99. syneresis

100. esoteric
101. Check the words in the dictionary to be sure that the definitions are self-explanatory; present the words in context (in sentences) so that students have to select the appropriate meaning.
102. a braid of hair usually worn hanging at the back of the head
103. to treat with phosphoric acid or a phosphate
104. a channel to drain or carry off surplus water
105. the union into one syllable of two vowels ordinarily separated in pronunciation
106. limited to a small circle
107. *Webster's New Collegiate Dictionary* (1981, G. & C. Merriam Co., Springfield, Mass.) contains the following information at the back of the dictionary:
    Foreign Words and Phrases
    Biographical Names
    Geographical Names
    Colleges and Universities
    Signs and Symbols
    A Handbook of Style
    Index
108. Look in the encyclopedia index under *president of the United States.*
109. Look in the encyclopedia index under *Audubon, John James.*
110. No; encyclopedia information cannot stay current (*Readers' Guide* would be a better source).
111. atlas
112. almanac
113. vertical file
114. thesaurus
115. *Junior Book of Authors*
116. dictionary
117. vertical file
118. newspaper
119. almanac
120. encyclopedia

PART 4: READING FOR INFORMATION IN THE CONTENT AREA

1. (a) What are three tips given to guide you in notetaking?
   (b) Why should you use more than one source?
2. (a) Why is it important for change to occur very rapidly in Central America?
   (b) What are the problems that may cause the standard of living to fall?
   (c) What are the factors contributing to progress?
3. Change must occur rapidly in Central America to prevent the standard of living from falling. Factors against this change are high population growth, unemploy-

ment, inflation, and wealth belonging to a few. Factors favoring better living standards are a growing middle class, government plans to attract foreign investment, roads, and new farming methods.

4. Forests were valuable to colonists

    Lumber
    Fuel
    Hunting

    Colonists cut down forests for farm land

5. Procedures for making sandstone:
    1. 2 small cans—1″ of sand in each
    2. Add 2T of calcium hydroxide (hydrated lime) to 1 can
        (a) Stir
        (b) Moisten
        (c) Heat solution to evaporate water
    3. Add 1T of sodium silicate to other can
        (a) Mix
        (b) Teacher adds 2t. of hydrochloric acid
        (c) Heat until dry
    4. Let cans cool
    5. Hit them to break sandstone apart.
    6. Compare to natural sandstone with magnifying glass.
    7. Why does sandstone stay together?

6. Single proprietorship = 1 owner

    Most common – 80% of businesses
    Farmers, professionals, retailers, wholesalers
    Easiest and quickest business to enter
    Business can't grow large

7. Diabetes—sugar diabetes

    Cells can't use glucose → weight loss
    → weakness
    → poor circulation
    → slow blood clotting → gangrene
    → minor infections → serious illness
    → upset fat respiration
    Fats →poisonous acetone and acids →lower blood pH

8. English victory → Britain got Canada, territory east of Mississippi, and Florida
    → destroyed French empire → rise of British empire
    → heightened colonists' morale
    → westward expansion → Indian attacks
    → Pontiac defeated

New issues: (1) Does England have to defend western settlers?
(2) Conflict of interests between east and west
→ Britain recognized colonists' value → closer management
→ English war debt → greater taxation for colonies (?)

9. | *Metric system* | *English system* |
|---|---|
| 3 units of measurement (length, volume, weight) | S |
| Units related to each other | D |

10. | *Birds* | *Reptiles* |
|---|---|
| Scales on legs | S |
| Turtle-like beaks | S |
| Adaptations to flight | D |
| Feathers | |
| Large breatbone and breast muscles | |
| Efficient lungs | |
| *Birds* | *Man* |
| Constant elimination | D |
| Good eyesight, hearing and balance | D (?) |
| High metabolism and temperature | D |
| Fast heart beat | D (S:4-chambered heart) |
| Warm blooded | |

11. I. Temperature scales
    A. Celsius (formerly centigrade)
        1. 100 divisions (degrees)
        2. Freezing = 0°; boiling = 100°
    B. Fahrenheit
        1. 180 degrees
        2. Freezing = 32°; boiling = 212°
    C. Kelvin
        1. 1 degree Celsius = 1 degree Kelvin
        2. Kelvin scale = 273 more than the Celsius scale
12. (See figure on p. 199)
13. Federal Consumer Protection Agencies
14. federal agencies
15. work with various groups, not directly with consumers

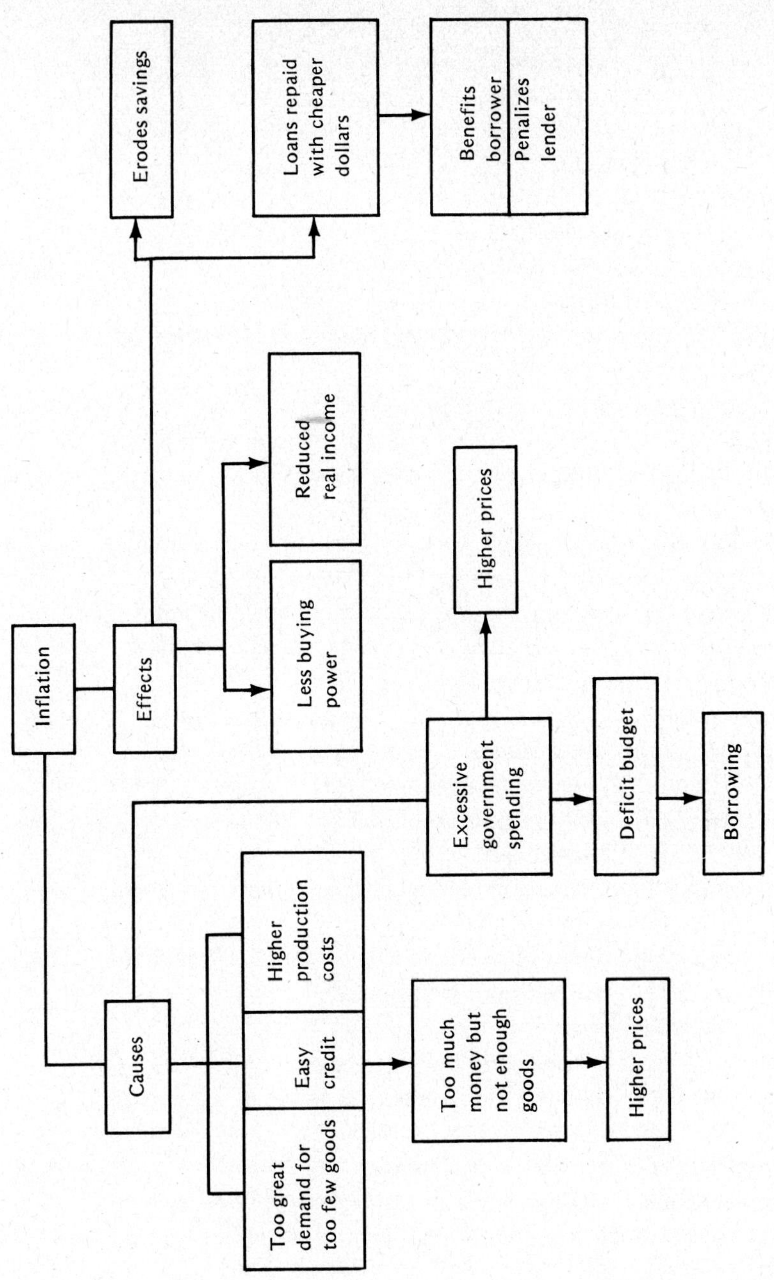
Inflation
Causes
Too great demand for too few goods
Easy credit
Higher production costs
Too much money but not enough goods
Higher prices
Excessive government spending
Higher prices
Deficit budget
Borrowing
Effects
Less buying power
Reduced real income
Erodes savings
Loans repaid with cheaper dollars
Benefits borrower
Penalizes lender

16. regulate actions of business and professional groups
17. either set prices (utilities and public transportation), or set minimum safety standards, or keep competition among groups
18. air-water-land vehicles
    engine-no engine
    old-modern
19. Eagles and Dogies (explicit)
20. 3 (Jones, Leads, and Rowse) (explicit)
21. Cowboys (inferential)
22. process of wearing down the surface of the earth (inferential)
23. build up and tear down (explicit)
24. gradual processes of change (explicit)
25. What surprised Mexican families in a farming community in 1943?
26. Why do we think that the earth as we know it will look very different a million years from now?
27. The adolescents' reading interests are affected by both reading theory and stages of reading development in the following ways.
28. Identification: cite, define, list, enumerate, give, indicate
    Description: illustrate, describe, outline, sketch, summarize, review, discuss, trace
    Relationship: compare, contrast, distinguish, analyze
    Demonstration: demonstrate, support, justify, prove, show
29. Identification: List examples of geological processes that build up the earth.
    Description: Describe geological changes that have occurred in the Northern Hemisphere.
    Relationship: Contrast geological changes made swiftly with those occurring gradually.
    Demonstration: Support or refute the belief that the ice age may return again to the Northern Hemisphere.
30. b (eliminated because of no verification in article)
    d (eliminated because at least b is not included in article)
    e (eliminated because both a and c are correct)
    a (eliminated although correct because c is the more inclusive answer)
31. a (eliminated because it does not apply to the main idea of the sentence)
    c (eliminated because *never* restricts answer unnecessarily)
    d (eliminated because it is too broad and general for the information given)
32. Choose an example(s) of geological processes that change the earth:
    (a) volcanoes
    (b) erosion
    (c) earthquakes

(d) sediment
(e) all of the above

33. Language, religion, economic life, monetary system, political stability, federal government systems, efficient use of available natural resources.
34. French versus Spanish speaking minorities; queen and more powerful House of Commons in Canada; fewer people in Canada; different positions on world affairs.
35. italic print
36. The people of the United States and Canada are alike in many ways.
    They are similar in their language and religion.
    Economic life is similar throughout Northern North America.
    Both the United States and Canada use a monetary, or money, system based on dollars and cents.
    . . . both the United States and Canada enjoy political stability.
    Both the United States and Canada have developed a high standard of living by making efficient use of available natural resources.
    Differences between the countries and the two people do, of course, exist.
37. Record your time.
38. Record your time.
39. Record your time.
40. Progressive Conservative and Liberal
41. Timber is being consumed more rapidly than it is being replaced.
42. b
43. c
44. a
45. d
46. e
47. c
48. d
49. a
50. e
51. b
52. e

PART 5: GRAPHIC SKILLS: GRAPHS, TABLES, CHARTS

1. (a) 1973
   (b) 1975, 1976, 1977
2. (a) 1960
   (b) 20
3. (a) 1/2%
   (b) 1-¾%

4. (a) 45-64 age group
   (b) Cancer is ten times greater.
5. (a) Twice as many
   (b) Comprehensive
6. (a) About 44 million
   (b) About 1/5 as many trucks were registered.
7. It shows the number of deaths per 100,000 men who smoked varying amounts of cigarettes.
8. As the number of risk factors increases, the percent in heart attack rate goes up in multiple increments.
9. Between the ages of 40 and 50 heavy smokers average about 15% fewer chances of a long life than nonsmokers.
10. It shows the sequence of certain events mainly involving Western Europe and America in modern history (1500-present).
11. An event (the Crusades) can have far reaching results (and vice versa, a result often has many contributing factors).
12. It shows the general structure of the United Nations, i.e., the various departments/councils and how they relate to each other.
13. It illustrates a main point of the passage, i.e., the female was dressing differently than previously.
14. The relationship of the cartoon to the text is not as clear as the relationship of the picture and text in item 13. One purpose may be to stimulate the reader to think beyond the information in the text, e.g., what are the far reaching effects of having used the bomb and what is the future for its use in the world?
15. As these "typical" stars become hotter, their color changes from the red and orange hues to blue-white.
16. The electoral vote does not necessarily reflect the popular vote.
17. (a) b
    (b) The population will be growing at a very rapid rate.
18. (a) c
    (b) a and d
19. (a) About the same as it has always been
    (b) Oak Street
    (c) Cedar Street
    (d) Willow Street
20. c
21. (a) 10:25 p.m.
    (b) 5 hours, 55 minutes
    (c) Toronto
    (d) International 155

(e) Maple Leaf 158
(f) John, 2 hours 16 minutes
(g) John, 7/10 mile

22. (a) One at 2:00 p.m.
    (b) 5:52 p.m., no—1 stop, dinner
    (c) Sue, 1:15 p.m.; Joan, 11:10 a.m.
23. (a) 9.7 grams
    (b) Sample selection: 1 serving rice, 1 serving fish, 1 cup whole milk, 1 teaspoon oil, 1 tablespoon mayonnaise, 1 piece pie.
24. Answers should include such information as the forms of nitrogen green plants use, what green plants produce with nitrogen, the forms of nitrogen used by animals, what happens to wastes, and what happens to most of the nitrogen compounds resulting from organic wastes.

PART 6: GRAPHIC SKILLS: MAPS

1. c
2. b
3. b
4. 3
5. Cass Lake, Wilkinson, Leech Lake
6. b
7. b
8. e
9. c
10. Multilane and state highways
11. c
12. Along the river; across the river and a state highway
13. a
14. c
15. c
16. Corn
17. Alfalfa
18. a
19. b
20. c
21. a
22. a
23. c
24. b
25. (a) Northeast
    (b) Southeast

(c) South
(d) Southwest
(e) Northwest
(f) Southeast
(g) South
(h) Southwest
(i) Northwest
(j) Northeast

26. (a) Northwest
(b) Southwest
(c) Northwest
(d) Southeast
(e) South

27. (a) Northeast
(b) Southeast
(c) Northwest
(d) North
(e) Southeast

28. (a) Northwest
(b) Northeast
(c) Southeast
(d) East
(e) Southwest

29. (a) Northeast
(b) Northwest
(c) Southwest
(d) Southeast
(e) North

30. (a) Northeast
(b) Southwest
(c) Northwest
(d) West
(e) Southeast

31. No answer necessary
32. No answer necessary
33. Students should realize a variety of answers are possible since only one coordinate is given.
34. (a) Oslo
(b) Cairo
(c) Quito

35. (a) Hong Kong
    (b) Western Samoa
36. (a) Madagascar
    (b) Africa
37. (a) 35° north latitude and 118° west longitude
    (b) 63° north latitude and 50° west longitude
38. (a) 5° north latitude to 4° south latitude and 32° east longitude to 41° east longitude.
    (b) 35° north latitude to 19° north latitude and 10° west longitude to 10° east longitude.

39. (a)

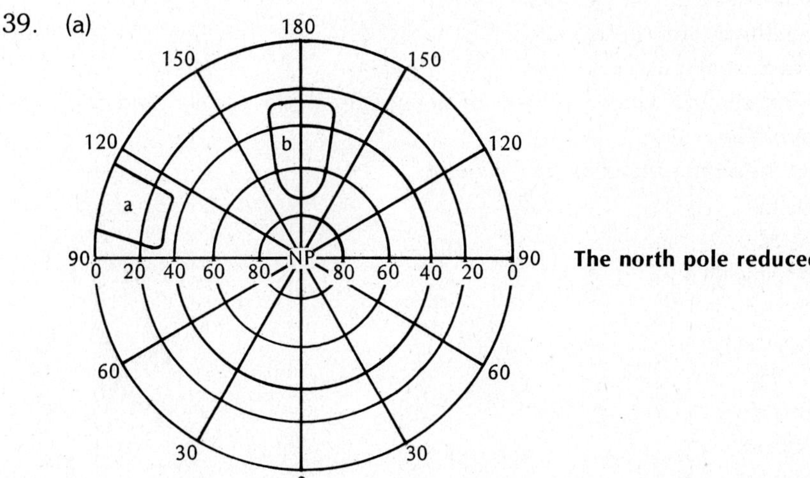

The north pole reduced

40.

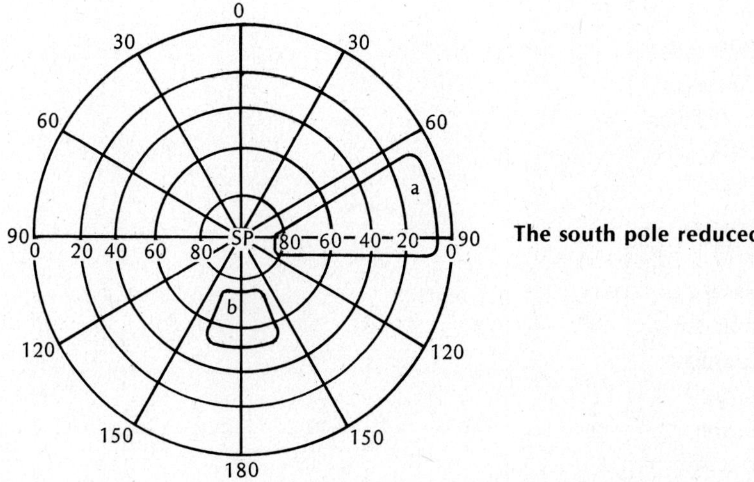

The south pole reduced

(c) This country cannot be shown on this projection.

41. North, South
42. (a) West. (Your finger should have traced on—or very close to—the 80° west meridian.)
    (b) Adelaide (Your finger should have traced the 140° east meridian.)
43. (a) West
    (b) East
44. (a) New York
    (b) Oslo, Norway
    (c) Buenos Aires
45. (a) Southeastern United States
    (b) Southwestern Australia
46. (a) West, southeast, south
    (b) Southeastern United States or at the 30° north parallel and 90° west meridian
    (c) At the Prime Meridian and equator
47. (a) D, E
    (b) N, M
48. (a) B
    (b) F
49. (a) K, A
    (b) G, H
    (c) B
50. (a) 300
    (b) 500
    (c) 100
    (d) 775
51. (a) 225 miles
    (b) 75 miles
    (c) 200 miles
52. (a) 240
    (b) 960
    (c) 840
    (d) 180
    (e) 780
53. (a) b and c
    (b) a only
    (c) b only
    (d) b only
    (e) c only

(f) a and b

54. (a) a only
    (b) c only
    (c) b only
    (d) a and b

55. (a) Fish
    (b) About 3 times bigger
    (c) One answer: that they are part of a chain of islands.

56. (a) Minnesota
    (b) Delaware
    (c) Kansas

57. (a) Boyd
    (b) Jo
    (c) Pen and Deer

Index

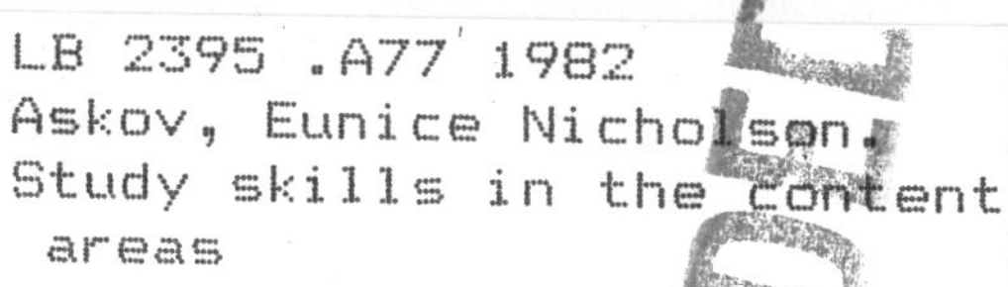

YORK COLLEGE
PENNSYLVANIA
Servire est vivare
DISCARDED